"David, Did You Know?"

by

David Edward Keesey

*God loves you!
To Anya a light that
has come into our lives,
Juanita & David*

David Edward Keesey

Happy Marriage!

DORRANCE
PUBLISHING CO
EST. 1920
PITTSBURGH, PENNSYLVANIA 15238

Dorrance Publishing Co
585 Alpha Drive
Suite 103
Pittsburgh, PA 15238
Visit our website at *www.dorrancebookstore.com*

ISBN: 978-1-4809-2033-0
eISBN: 978-1-4809-2148-1

Preface

These writings have been a long time in the making. The directive has been with me over the years, which has brought me to a closer relationship with my God. What is printed on the following pages has all been said many times over. The differences are in the person experiencing them and the manner in which they are being expressed. It is the prayerful hope that those who choose to take the time to read the words and share the thoughts, expressions, and experiences that have brought me to the action in putting them to paper will receive blessings of the Spirit. I believe you will agree, as you read this epistle, it is not of me. There is a greater power than my human abilities, knowledge, or wisdom spread upon the pages. Credit goes to the one who has directed me to embark upon this undertaking. Living each day with God my creator, Christ my savior, and the power of God, the Holy Spirit, gives me the courage, the confidence, the conviction, strength, and purpose to believe the effort is worth your time to read it.

The introduction of Jesus Christ into my life when received and the in-dwelling of the Holy Spirit has brought about the born-anew transformation in my life when Christ Jesus spoke to Nicodemus. That transformation is continuing today (John 3:1-8).

I recognize the minimal formal education and the absence of credits of academia, which may have been the delay in my responding to this call to this ministry. This has not inhibited the spirit driving the ministry and witness of the will of God. That may sound facetious to some, but to those experienced and having experienced God's will will recognize that all things are possible to believers who call upon the name of our Lord. When I minimize my intelligence, I am reminded of the intellect of God and the intellect and power that are His to work through me. The first disciples were of common background chosen by Jesus. As a believer and follower of Christ, believer and obedient to God's word, I can expect no less of the presence and power in God's Spirit. Evidence of His power and Spirit are daily acknowledgements with others each day of my life.

God has blessed me so much in my life with my wife, Juanita, and my daughters, Cindy, Lynn, Kathryn, and Melanie, who humble me more each day of my life. These five individuals are each creations of God. God has introduced himself to me with great clarity in the life experiences I have had with each of them. They are an integral part of the witness and message God has had for me in my relationship with Him. I believe this to be a successful accomplishment, only and because of what I have already stated, that this is not of me. There are many, many of God's people he has used to touch my life. They contribute to the embodiment and growth that continue to take place in my life. I embrace them in the message of the unfolding of the contents of this endeavor—an endeavor made joyful in the memories of the people and happenings that are composed in this book.

"God's Hand and Spirit"

When did we come into God's being?
Psalm 139 provides us an answer.
For us to gain knowledge and the seeing
Requires our opening HIS BOOK, searching views.
Some biblical writers using scripture,
Give you book, chapter, and verse.
For our growth in GOD'S WORD, find the page
To our worth the more we rehearse.
As we begin to learn of GOD'S HAND'S firmness,
How gentle and loving it can be,
Or the unbending directness,
HIS obedience we cannot flee.
Our blessings continue of HIS SPIRIT,
ITS presence SON JESUS introduces,
In John 14 is where you'll find it,
Some questions we may find reduced.
My prayers and hope is GOD'S presence,
Will ever closer and intricate be
HIS calling to you for the essence
Of your service to the KINGDOM
Will forever bring you glee.

In a small farm community of Ironville, Pennsylvania, northwest of the town of Columbia on the east side of the Susquehanna River, a revival service was held in the small Brethren Church on the second Wednesday of July, 1939.

Ethel Garber invited a twelve-year-old young man to join her and her daughter, Betty Ann, to attend. The pastor preaching was without name owing to the years past since the service. The pastor preaching invited those to come forth to receive Jesus Christ as Savior. A force compelled the young man to go forward in wonder, to learn more of this man, Jesus. He approached the chancel rail, dropped to his knees, and began to weep uncontrollably. Led in prayer, he accepted Jesus as his Savior. He was to learn he was saved, but saved for or from what? Much attention was given to him after the service, creating confusion of mind. He recognized a person had died for him named Jesus. In his young lifetime, neither family nor friends were heard to speak of the action the young man had taken. A mystery remained for years to come. What had happened in the name of this man, Jesus? Unbeknown to David, God had His hand on him from his conception (Psalm 139:13). How had he been invited to this service? Ethel, an outspoken witness for the Lord, had followed the act she was led to perform. Was the invitation made especially for David? Was this the Lord's plan?

Today in writing the account of God's presence, I, David, know it is true. You ask, "Who is this young man?" My first light of day came on January 19, 1927, born to Kathryn Elizabeth Newswanger Keesey and Charles William Keesey in St. Joseph's Hospital in Lancaster, Pennsylvania. The day began when Charles had gone to work at McCrory's Store. Receiving a call shortly after he arrived that Kathryn was in need of a trip to the hospital, Charles hailed a cab, arrived at the apartment, picked up Kathryn, and headed for St. Joseph's Hospital, three blocks away. (The urgency was determined by the fact that the birth may have taken place in the elevator.) The birth did take place at 9:20 A.M., and the child weighed in at nine pounds, three ounces, all fingers and toes accounted for in proper number. He was named David, for his mother's father, David Sylvester Newswanger; Edward, for his father's father, Edward Ferry Keesey, thus named David Edward Keesey in honor of his two grandfathers. I have liked being named for my two grandfathers.

I am not an only child; Kathryn and Charles had been blessed three years and five months earlier with their first son, Charles Robert Keesey. Both of us boys grew in appearance of the different sides of family: Bobby, the Newswanger side of the family; and I, the Keesey side of the family. Dad and Mom had met in the employ of the M. T. Garvin Department Store, owned by Milton Garvin. Milton was Charles' uncle. Charles and Kathryn fell in love and were married. Their lives traveled a new course with the arrival of Charles Robert and the new occupation of Charles, employed by McCrory's 5 & 10

Cent Store in Lancaster, Pennsylvania. He was hired in management training. At the time of Robert's birth, their residence was on Corl Street. With the expected arrival of their second child, a larger apartment was necessary, prompting a move around the corner to a West Orange Street address.

In writing this account, it has been a marvel to learn that God knew me before I was conceived. He knew my name to be, including the future to come, taught and read from the Bible in future years found in scripture. Psalm 22:10 says, "From birth, I was cast upon you, from my mother's womb you have been my God." Early accounts of this young family seen in a picture revealed Bobby sitting on a wall with a leg in a cast, broken in a fall. The picture was taken showing Bobby proudly holding his little brother, me. More than once, Bobby spoke of a scar on my left eyebrow. A suspended bounce seat attached overhead to a bracket with a spring was great fun for Bobby to bounce me up and down, creating giggles and laughter from me. Bobby got carried away, bouncing so hard the spring jumped out of the overhead bracket, striking me on the left eyebrow on the way down, but fortunately not the eye. Several experiences with us boys brought frowns and smiles to Mother and Dad. The first, with son Bobby while enjoying the little creation, admiring him in the raw on their bed, there suddenly sprang forth a stream of water. Baptized, not in that manner. Isn't he cute? Yes, but not under those circumstances.

As Bobby grew, our Cousin Simmy was going to a wrestling match one evening held in the same neighborhood. Kidding, he asked Bobby to save him a parking place. Simmy arrived and found Bobby standing at the curb. The space was empty. Mother enjoyed plants evidenced by the several she cared for on the second-floor balcony. I was found with potted plant soil around my mouth. Cleaning me up produced a crying little boy, the adage of eating a pound of dirt by the age of five. Old wives' tale!

Members of the Newswanger family were many, with grandparents, aunts, uncles, and cousins known by family names such as Weaver, Bradley, Goughenour, and McCoulgh. Just a few were met at times. Members of the Keesey family were Garber, Garvin, Beazley, Simmons, and Bear, not known to Bobby and me for some years to come.

Dad returned home one evening, informing Mother he was to report to the Harrisburg store, as he was transferred as the assistant manager. After six weeks in Harrisburg, a new assignment sent Charles and family to the store in Lebanon to be his first store as manager. Lebanon has few memories for me, young as I was. Pictures of Granddad Keesey, Mother, Dad, and us boys are evidence of being there. Bobby was the chubby round-faced curly head, and I was chubby, at this age with bangs, seated on my kiddy-car in the backyard. One of the first memories of mine was pounding on the wall, hollering for Henni, the next-door neighbor, to play "Danny Boy" on their piano.

These twelve years leading up to my experience of receiving Jesus as my Savior offer stories and accounts of the time and developments of the individuals and family. Living again day by day, year by year represents the challenge of one to recollect in memory those experiences of the immature with more mature mind at this present age, should you consider me mature. Ha-ha, just kidding!

That day, January 19, 1927, my birth, as told by Aunt Pearl, Dad's sister, was clear. The air was warm and light for January. On that little farm near Ironville, Uncle Raymond and Cousin Simmy were replacing the roof on the bank barn on the ten-acre celery farm, important in my future life. As we grow in body, mind, and spirit, we learn of life. The realization comes much later that our lives begin just as our Savior, Christ. We came into this world, certainly not revealed to us at our birth. Our birth, a miracle in the making learned in living by faith in God, enables us to accept His plan for us. We have all been given birth by a woman, our Savior by His Virgin mother, Mary, with and by the power of the Holy Spirit. Your life and mine in the coming together of our mother and father when conceived began our life in our mother's womb in accordance with God's plan.

A great issue is made today as to when our lives actually began. The point to be made, according to scripture, is God has a plan for each of us, His children. At what time in life do we submit to accept that fact? The question is what we believe to be the truth. At birth we know nothing of life, the reason for our lives. As we live, we learn of family and being loved by parents, as Bobby and I have been. It is not always true. Blessed of loving parents and an older brother, my life has proven to be the expected by biblical teachings. The living of life reveals many do not know of such relationships of parental love.

Just before Christmas in 1929, Dad was informed we were to move from Lebanon to Frederick, Maryland. Frederick, a small, quiet farming town, we learned, was little affected by the depression. On a cold full moonlit January night, the Keesey family bundled up in the unheated Model-T Ford and traveled to Frederick. We arrived late, moving into a family rooming house. Memory is Mother, saying as she unwrapped the blankets from me, "This boy is blue from the cold." Frederick proves to be a great place for a young family to grow up together. A rented home at 216 East Second Street was the first home in Frederick. It was three blocks from Dad's work at the store on Market Street. Bobby was in the second grade at Church Street School, across the alley behind our Second Street address. Bobby came home for lunch each day. On his return to school, he discovered the teacher was wearing a black dress with a hood and white collar. He had entered the Catholic school next door. We still hear about it.

Church on Sunday was not the practice of the Keesey family. Once at Easter during our five years in Frederick, there is a memory of us attending a Methodist Church. Bobby and I were dressed in new Easter clothes. Having experienced that Sunday, our parents' faith was never mentioned. At an early age, we were taught this prayer upon going to bed:

Now I lay me down to sleep,
I pray the Lord my soul to keep.
If I should die before I wake
I pray the Lord my soul to take.
God bless everyone Amen

A mystery of mind at this present day of writing, fresh in memory, is learning the bedtime prayer, a wonderment. Our parents saw little reason for our Bible teachings. Recognizing the Church life our parents were heard to have had in their youth attending Sunday School and church raises a question today. We are three years of age, you and I, learning of our limitations at this age. Your memories bring what to mind at this age? Can you recall? Do you have pictures of you and your family at this age? Was your recollection being plump, skinny at this age, having red curly hair, dimples, blond or dark hair? You know, my name is David. Were you a cute little girl or a freckle-faced boy? What was your nickname?

Life in our Second Street home, a two-story duplex home, which had three bedrooms, living room, dining room, kitchen, bath, and vestibule with full basement, brought many learning experiences for our young family, mine in particular, for I am the one writing the account of them. We boys kept coaxing to have a dog. Queenie was a German police dog. Aunt Pearl and Uncle Raymond had puppies on the farm. When we boys learned of this, the pressure was on until Mom and Dad gave into our bringing Sandy home. We about wore the poor dog out loving him. One morning Mother, whom I rarely called Mom, was heard laughing in the kitchen. She called to us to come look at Sandy swinging on the swing strung from the tree limb, his front legs on one side of the seat, his back legs on the other, teetering back and forth. No one went to his aid, and he finally freed himself. Sandy grew in size, prompting the family to return Sandy to Uncle Raymond to find a place in the country for him.

Bobby had an unusual thing happen while playing with a child's golf club. He hit a small wooden ball in the backyard. It hit the slanted cellar door, which deflected the ball off the door right through the kitchen window. The amazing thing was it made a neat round hole the size of the ball, never shattering the pane, which was a miracle.

Have you thought about, in your growing up, things you wanted but couldn't have? Both Bobby and I have to confess we were spoiled. Our Christmases were receiving the gifts most wanted, plus more than what we expected. Thinking about this as we hear people speaking about how difficult things were living in the time of the depression led me to realize today the blessings we received owing to Dad's job.

Halloween was coming, which meant costume time. I had been outfitted in a blue soldier suit with military plumed hat, with visor and brass buttons on the coat. I thought it would be nice to visit Little Bo Peep across the street. Dressed in my blue suit with brass buttons and cork-shooting popgun in hand, I ventured to cross the street. As I stepped out from between the parked cars at the curb, I was met and struck by a passing car. At the age of five, have you ever seen the motor of a car from underneath? The front tire of the car ran over the popgun, giving the driver reason to believe he had run over me with the wheel of the car. The driver froze at the wheel. Hauled out from under the car and placed in my mother's arms, I was carried into the house and placed on the sofa in wait for Dr. Baer. Examined, I was found to be bruised and scraped with nothing broken. I continued to cry, owing to the fact I had wet in my new blue soldier suit. Had I been told not to go in the street, yes, but I had to see Little Bo Peep, which did not happen. "David, did you know?" No, but I was learning.

Our next-door neighbor was the Thomas family. They had a son by the name of Bobby, about the same age as me. At times we would visit one another through the fence. On one of those days, a chow dog came by in the alley. Bobby took one of my mother's clothes poles propped in the corner of the fence at the alley. He began poking it at the chow dog. The dog took him on, grabbing it in his mouth, resting it from Bobby's grasp. We boys argued as to why Bobby did what he had done. Believing the dog had left, I went into the alley to retrieve the pole. I was jumped by the dog, still in the alley. The dog jumped me, knocking me to the ground on my back, the dog on top, going for my throat. Instinctively, I held my hands at my throat. The dog chewed both thumb areas until he was run off. Dr. Baer, to the rescue once more, administered to my needs. At this time, I don't recall if a shot was administered. We learned the dog belonged to the man driving the car I had run in front of and been hit by. The owner paid Dr. Baer's bill.

Writing accounts about these experiences today brings to mind our mother's many problems she faced by the investigation we boys ventured into each day. It can be very informative for us, you and I, of the many involvements we as young people can get caught up in, young as we were.

Today's minds explore the unknown life of Jesus. According to writings, there are no accounts kept. In meditation enjoyed at times, the following thoughts were put to paper.

Thoughts Concerning
the Childhood of Jesus

Often reflecting upon the childhood of Jesus when holding our infant daughters and later our grandchildren, my mind turned to our infant Savior and his childhood days. Realizing the nonexistence of accounts of Jesus' life, the following thoughts and visions came to mind. One of those questions related to the Spirit in Jesus' life at birth. The scripture in Luke 1:41 tells us when Mary visited Elizabeth, the mother of John the Baptist, the baby moved within Elizabeth. Elizabeth was filled with the Holy Spirit, and in that Spirit she spoke to Mary: "You are most blessed of all women and blessed is the child you will bear!" May we begin with Jesus' mother, Mary, confronted by the Angel Gabriel, informing her God had selected her to bear His Son. In the Gospels of Matthew and Luke, the story is told of the birth of Jesus, relating how Mary pondered these things in her heart. In the account found in Luke 2:21-40 of Jesus, Mary, Joseph, Simeon, and Anna, the prophetess, in the temple in Jerusalem, Mary's mind pondered once more as to what was ahead for this child to whom she had given birth. In Matthew 2:13-18, an angel of the Lord appeared to Joseph in a dream. Joseph was directed to take them to Egypt until the death of Herod, then return to Nazareth. The point of inquisitiveness of my mind has to do with Mary knowing of the Holiness of Jesus and the responsibility she and Joseph had in raising this child of God. How did they look upon him in their treatment, discipline, teaching, and human relationship? Was he accepted as the other children of his age and likeness? Was his learning of life and the experiences he had with those he played with natural? Can we envision Jesus drawing in the dirt with the issue of the woman accused of adultery? (John 8:3-11). In his life with his father, was it assumed and accepted by many Jesus worked with Joseph as a carpenter? Once more envisioning the family at meals with his brothers and sisters bantering back and forth as families do, what were the relationships among them all, knowing Jesus was the Son of God? Was Mary brought to the memory of pondering these things in her mind? Luke 2:41-52 shows the first words we learn of Jesus speaking, quoting, "Why were you searching for me? Didn't you know I had to be in my Father's house?" This is the last mention of Joseph, Jesus' father.

I ask you, is this a human- or Spirit-motivated effort on my part to have an understanding of the childhood of Jesus? Have you been brought out of your daily living by unanswered questions about your own life?

Moving along with *David, Did You Know?* Mother was house cleaning with the vacuum cleaner, moving from room to room. The outlets had plate-covered receptacles with hinged covers that were opened, and the plug adapter was screwed into the outlet for the plug to be inserted. Mother had finished in the dining room and was headed for the living room. She removed the plug and left the cover open, telling me to stay away from it. She had no more left the room when she heard me howl. She knew immediately I had not listened to what she had told me. Had I had any curls, the shock certainly straightened them. How many homes had vacuum cleaners at this period of time in the depressed economy of our country? Point made about the depression. Blessed this family of ours was at this time of life.

As often happens, sicknesses are communicated from one child to another in school, then brought home to the younger children, as was the case in the Keesey family. Bobby caught scarlet fever and went to bed immediately, and the quarantine notice went on the front door, which was required for certain communicable sicknesses. Yep, I got scarlet fever and was put to bed for the duration of the quarantine period. Mother could hardly keep Bobby in bed. I went to bed hard with a high fever. I was very sick and listless with delirium. I became so ill, they couldn't get me out of bed. Dr. Baer told the folks they had better find something that would give me reason to want to get out of bed, to give me the will to live, or my life was in jeopardy. I recall lying in bed with the vision of billowing clouds all around me, floating about in them. At a much later time in my life, I questioned if this was an out-of-body experience. I could hear what was being said, but it was as though I were overseeing it all. I would have been five at the time, and yet I can remember that happening so well to this day.

It was the next day, after the doctor's concern, that Dad was moved to go shopping for a gift to get me up. At my age, I knew little of the power of prayer. Today, from the results, they must have been praying, for it worked. Dad came home at lunchtime with a "get-in-and-sit-down peddled airplane." I climbed out of bed to peddle this toy. It did the trick; I was on the way to recovery, not aware of God or his plan for my life at this time. During this time, I remember being brought downstairs, wrapped in a blanket, being held on one of my parents' laps, being rocked in the family rocking chair, listening to that wonderful and entertaining invention, the radio. We listened to programs like Amos and Andy, Jack Benny, Eddy Cantor, Fibber Magee, and Molly and Fred Allen.

Christmas Eve 1932, watching the women students from Hood College walking in the streets of snow with candles, their breath visible due to the cold of the night, singing carols, brought a warm meaning of Christmas. Santa Claus and material gifts, the true reason for Christmas at this time of my life, gave small reason for our Lord Jesus, being focused on Santa. We brothers were not in church, having Mother or Dad sharing the story of Baby Jesus. I pray today I am not unfair to our parents. I believed in Santa at this age. This particular Christmas, I remember having *The Night before Christmas* read to us before being tucked into bed. As I was falling asleep, I was sure I heard the prancing and pawing of each little hoof upon the roof.

Christmas was a wonderful time of the year for our family. The ritual was Dad bringing the tree home after he closed the store. The tree was put in the stand, and there it stood until we were tucked in bed before the decorating was begun. Bobby and I had received a gift we asked for that year. This year of 1932, Bobby wanted a two-wheel bike, and I asked for a red balloon tire scooter. On Christmas morning, they were found by the tree, accompanied by other gifts.

There were other illnesses, including the childhood sicknesses, measles, whooping cough, mumps, colds, and the lot. I developed an infection of the right mastoid gland, which caused a swelling and soreness in my neck in the area of the right ear. A black ointment was prescribed for a day or two without the results the doctor was looking for to heal. The second evening, there was no comforting me, so that prompted a call to Dr. Baer. To the rescue he came once more. When the doctor arrived, upon examining my throat and neck, he asked for a spoon. He placed the spoon inside my mouth in the back of the throat, giving a pressured thrust, which burst the abscess in the mastoid from inside my throat, causing it to open and release the abscess, which brought the beginning of healing.

Where were you at this time of your life? What did you look like? Were you tall, thin, growing like a weed? If a girl, were you wearing your sister's hand-me-down clothes, and likewise, if a boy, were you wearing your brother's castoffs because they were too small for him? All of those great things we didn't think were so great at the time. Of course, Bobby and I went through the Tooth Fairy time in our lives. I had a loose tooth, so my brother, Bobby, "the dentist," was going to be helpful and decided that he would tie the string around the tooth and tie the other end to the kitchen doorknob, then he would open the door, removing the tooth—the idea being that I wouldn't know when he was going to open the door so I wouldn't be anticipating the pain. Guess what? He tied the string to the wrong side of the door. Instead of pulling, he pushed and socked me in the nose. "Ouch!" I cried, calling Bobby "a dumb bunny," which was one of our favorite expressions in those days.

The continuation of this experience followed with Bobby laughing at me, which made me mad, to say the least. I had a very bad temper at this time of my life. I remember taking off my shoe and chasing Bobby out of the kitchen and through the dining room. Bobby ran into the vestibule and closed the door by the time I fired my shoe at him. You guessed what happened: The shoe hit the cut glass window in the door, shattering it into a thousand pieces. I still can see and hear Bobby's taunting words as he looked at me through the broken window: "You're going to get it now! Wait 'til Daddy gets home!" Being the younger of the two of us, you might know Bobby got the blunt of the episode owing to the history of taunting me. I am not sure if this was the first break of my nose.

There are numerous other happenings at the Second Street address. On a day when my search for excitement took over, I decided to see how the world looked from the top of the garage that abutted our backyard fence, which was the means to scale to the top of the garage. I had gained the top of the fence when I lost my grip. In the fall, my two front teeth came in contact with the top of the fence, and those two front teeth broke off halfway to the gums. The teeth in time turned very black and had to be removed. Fortunately, they were baby teeth that were soon replaced by second teeth. Praise the Lord, he provides second teeth after we as children get finished destroying the first. Of course, I was not challenged to accomplish my desire to see what the world looked like from the garage roof after my experience.

I never reached the roof of the garage to get that vision of the world. Dad was a veteran of World War I, serving in the United States Navy, and was honorably discharged in 1919. He joined the American Legion in Frederick and became interested in the Marching Drum and Bugle Corps. He joined as a drummer, practicing at least one evening a week. When competition was coming up, more practice was needed. Bobby and I would get excited because Mother took us to practices. The Corps would be playing and marching to the music, accompanied by us boys marching at a distance, keeping an eye on Mother, who smiled and laughed at her two marching "soldiers." Granddad Keesey visited us taking this all in, enjoying his grandsons marching to the tune and the step. After they had finished practicing, we were walking into town to meet Dad, and we came to a miniature golf course. Bobby decided to get a better view and climbed up on top of the fence. When we were to leave, while trying to get down he caught his pants, tearing a hole in the seat. We had a great laugh watching him trying to walk while holding his pants together. We met Dad at the store, and he took Bobby in and bought him his first long pair of trousers. I was miffed because I didn't get a new pair of long trousers. Granddad told me it wouldn't be too long until I would be big enough for long trousers. Did it help? Not much.

This Drum and Bugle competition had great interest in the early thirties. Competitions were held in many cities and towns. The National Firemen Convention, with parades and judging, was held in Washington, D.C., in 1932. We attended with great excitement for us boys, never having been to a big city before with taxi cabs, big buildings, monuments, and history pointed out by Dad and Mother. There were many competitions in times of celebrations in many places. One in particular was outside of Emmittsburg, Maryland, on the top of a mountain plateau, giving us the excitement of being in that setting. We were seated as all the corps passed by. The group Dad was with won a prize. Another competition was held in the little town of Hanover, Pennsylvania. My memory is sitting on the side of the dirt street, not yet paved. Any envy in tales you've read so far? What a childhood these two boys were privileged to have. There was always one more tale to tell.

Easter arrived in 1932, and we were having family over for dinner. Mother's three brothers came with their wives: Uncle Roy and his wife, Aunt Grace; Uncle Harvey and his wife, Aunt Ina; and Uncle Owen, who was still single. Mother was in the kitchen with Dad assisting with the family around the table. Bobby got his colored Easter egg, walked over to the fireplace, announced to all, "Hard as a rock," and smacked the egg against the marble fireplace. Everyone joined in with laughter. Not to be outdone, I ran into the kitchen, asked for an egg, returned to the fireplace, announced to everyone, "Hard as a rock," and smack! The egg broke the yoke, and egg white ran down my arm. Everyone laughed, but I broke into tears, running to the kitchen to be consoled by Mother. I was very quiet the remainder of the family visit.

I wish we could share moments of yours, those happenings that created memories for you. Had you the presence of God in your life's experiences? Did you know he was present? God was known by name as part of my life in repeating, "Now I lay me down to sleep," the only prayer I knew, the only presence of God. I must tell you this one: It was routine for me to take a nap each afternoon, being accompanied by my friend, Mike, our cat. Believe it or not, there is no memory for me as to when Mike came into our home, into my life. During one particular nap, Mother was at the kitchen sink, working on the coming supper, when she learned how Mike got outside after going to bed with me. The bathroom window was usually open on pleasant days, and Mike jumped out of the window to the top of the fence and then to the ground. There are so many mysteries we have had as family that were not always solved.

It was in 1932 at a Halloween parade or a rally for the election that I first saw the letters "NRA" and heard the name "Franklin Delano Roosevelt" spoken, which meant very little to me at the time. Later, I learned it stood for "National Relief Act," probably the first term of politics for my ears. My memory today was that the NRA posters spoke of the interest in my future of the function of my government. Dad was successful at his work; the store business was producing profits. Mother and Dad's conversations we overheard from time to time mentioned the figure seventy-five dollars a week, plus bonus for increased sales. I had no information as to whether this was the reason for us to move to the outskirts of Frederick. Mother and Dad rented a home at 5 West 13th Street, the last paved street of North Frederick. We moved from Second Street in 1933. What a move—into a neighborhood with families with children the same ages as Bobby and me. We had the Eddy Reineberger family as our neighbors to the east. A young couple by the name Hawk lived to our west with a cute baby daughter named Iris. The Turners lived across the street and had two younger boys. The Palmer family lived across the street and had a son named Homer, and they owned the empty lot between their property and the Turners'. The Grove family was the next home going west with a young lady my age by the name of Betty. The Groves owned the empty lot between the next home, the last one on the south side of 13th Street, owned by the Knight family. The brothers, John and Edwin, became good friends and playmates of ours. The Summers lived west of the Hawks on the north side of the street, and they had a daughter named June. The Staleys were the last house on the north side to the west, and they had a daughter, Alice, and a son, Richard, but we rarely saw them. We had fun playing the games of the day and at times well into the evening until the calls came: "Time for bed!" Cowboys and Indians, Northwest Mounted Police, hide-and-seek, tag, you're it, mother may I, hopscotch, red light, capture the flag, baseball, football, softball—you name it, we played it.

Having moved to Thirteenth Street, we began going to Aunt Pearl and Uncle Raymond's every other weekend. We visited, playing games and having a good time with cousins Anna and Simmy, who lived in Lancaster. Dad and Simmy would challenge Bob and me to pinochle, giving us good lessons on how to play. I was competitive and lost my temper when Bob and I lost. You recognize Bobby is now Bob. It was the same with croquet and other games we played. Today I recognize it helped me learn to control my temper.

Sunday night, before we would leave for home, a dish of ice cream was served, often homemade with Aunt Pearl mixing the ingredients and Uncle Raymond cranking the ice cream maker. At times Anne, Bob, or I would take turns on the crank. There usually were pretzels, peanuts, or crackers. On the road home, a custom was established. We would stop in Gettysburg at a diner. Dad would buy each of us a Texas Hot Wiener, smothered with sauce and chopped onions. I can still smell that aroma. The Sundays we stayed home in the mornings were generally spent on rare occasions romping in Mother and Dad's bed until someone fell out on the floor. We would read the Sunday paper. My specialty was the funnies. After breakfast a trip downtown was made with Dad to check the store, making sure everything was in order. One of those mornings while in the store, I decided to help myself to metal furniture cleats made for the feet of chairs or tables. Why did I want them? I am glad you asked: Returning home and off to the basement, I went to install my cleats (Note: I said, "My cleats"; they weren't paid for by me). While demonstrating the wonderful sound they made on the narrow sidewalk on the side of the house, I heard a window open. It was Dad's voice, asking, "David, what are you doing?" My response: "Oh, nothing." It was followed by, "Come in here." Asked what was making the sound as I walked back and forth, I knew better than to lie. I said, "Metal cleats," followed by, "taken from a counter in the store that morning when I was with you." Dad asked, "Did you pay for them?" Of course I had to answer, "No." The lesson to tell the truth had already been learned. I was then told they didn't belong to me and they would not be mine until they were paid for by me. Yes, I paid for them, one more most important lesson in my life: "It isn't yours until you have paid for it."

Later, I learned this lesson also meant one's actions. When I started school, Mother and Dad decided we should have some money of our own to learn of the handling of spending money. We were given twenty-five cents allowance for about a year, and after our move to 5 West 13th Street, Mother said to Dad, "The boys ought to get a raise to fifty cents." Great news for Bob and me. Every Saturday, Bob and I would go down to Market Street to the deli across the street from the movie and buy a large dill pickle taken out of the pickle barrel and wrapped in wax paper. Then we went over to the movies to see a cowboy movie. Did you have a movie theater where you lived? It was great. There was always a serial movie that was continued to the next week to keep us coming back each week. We learned the names of Tom Mix, Buck Jones, Ken Maynard (our favorite), Hoot Gibson, and Bob Steele, to name a few. When the heroes were shown in the chase, we all cheered, yelled, whistled, and stamped our feet. When it showed the villain, we all booed and hissed and gave them the raspberry—you know, sticking our tongues out and blowing. It was never the same without the dill pickle. After the movie, we were known to go to the drug store for chocolate milkshakes. Bob always finished his before I did, and on occasion he would ask if he could put his straw in my shake. Hey, you think I didn't know what he was going to do? I spoke of Mike, our cat; he was joined by Trixie. Trixie, a fox terrier dog, gave us a lot of fun. She got out and was hit by a car, breaking her leg. The leg was splinted by the vet and wrapped with gauze. It didn't last long until she had it strung through the house. The leg healed, allowing days playing with her. This lasted only a short time. We suspected she followed the mailman on his deliveries, never to be seen again.

Brother Bob was having a birthday, and Mother decided to have a party for him and invited some of his friends. During the course of the party, there was a peanut hunt and the person who found the most peanuts was to get a prize. It was a nice big backyard where hunting peanuts could give a great challenge. You might know I would have to be included in the festivities. Being spoiled as I was, I did not find as many peanuts as I felt I should have and came sulking into the kitchen, followed by Mother. I was crying and angry, that temper mentioned earlier. Upon reaching the door to the hallway, I turned and fired the handful of peanuts at Mother. She was standing in the doorway of the back entrance, and I then ran to my bedroom—an act that I have never forgotten or forgiven myself. I have learned in my walk with God, asking for forgiveness we are to forget. How long do we live to accept this teaching in our lives? For years, and even then not possibly getting a hold on my ill temper.

I sure didn't exhibit love there, did I? What did you say? "A part of growing up." It is wondered if I ever will.

The guys in our 13th Street gang played various games. We were playing football. We chose sides and usually played in the empty lot between the Palmers' and the Turners' property. This particular day, Homer Palmer and I were on opposing teams. Homer was carrying the ball when I made a good tackle on him, which made him angry. He got up, walked over, and kicked me in my groin, which sent me to the ground. After some of the pain subsided, all I could see was Homer and getting even for the pain he caused. It took Brother Bob and John Knight to pull me free of Homer. I experienced some issue of blood for a short time but never shared that information. Years later, we were to learn that I needed surgery to bring the testicle into the scrotum. When Dad discovered I needed surgery, he stated that I was fine at birth. Thus, we deduced the surgery was necessary due to that kick.

Granddad Keesey had surgery in 1933. Dad was told the surgery was a success. The nurse was in the room, heard him gasp, and walked to the bed, discovering he had died. Granddad's death was my first experience of death in the family. This was a very sad funeral for me; it was difficult to understand. Fresh in my mind was me bearing his name, always remembering my middle name was his—Edward—to be honored. When visiting Columbia in passing 845 Walnut Street, the memory of Christmas watching Granddad operate the train on the platform he set up brought out the little kid in him. Our goodbyes when visiting Granddad, his practice was to shake hands, placing a dime in Bob's hand because he was the older, and a nickel in mine. When this first began, Bob was unhappy because his coin was smaller than mine, but he soon learned the difference. Later, it was a quarter for each of us boys. Our return over the years to Bethel Cemetery brought back the fond memories of Granddad, remembering his habit of smoking cigars, accompanied by the odor.

We had many surprises in activities. One Sunday morning, Mother packed lunches for us four, joined with the Turner family, and we traveled to visit the zoo in Washington, D.C. Good weather provided us a wonderful, exciting time, learning much about the animals and birds and their care from their keepers. We picnicked in the park, munching on the lunches and drinking lemonade that had been brought from home. Dad and Mother took Bob and me fishing one day on the Monocacy River near Frederick. We caught some eels, and I can still see Dad cutting his "Honeycut, chawin' tobaccy," which he liked to do when he went fishing. It must have been a carryover from his days on the Susquehanna River, where he was raised as a boy. I learned at a much later time in our lives that Dad would go check the fish lines with his dad and his Uncle Noah on the Susquehanna River. The fish they caught were sold in the Columbia Market House. The mention of the Susquehanna River brings to mind the story Dad told of his boyhood. He spoke of the guys after supper in warm weather who would meet at the river to swim out to the third bridge support, always yelling, "Last one in is a rotten egg!" It was a race this one evening as he got a head start with just one fellow catching up to him. When he got a cramp, he hollered for help and the fellow hollered back, "I'm not falling for that old trick!" As Dad went under the third time, he remembered saying, "God, if you give me another chance, I'll be a better boy." I asked him if he became a better boy. He said, "David, you would have to be the judge of whether I had or not." Some of his other stories I really wouldn't want to relate, not that they were that bad. I just can't remember them as he told them.

You can understand why this was such a wonderful time in our lives. We never realized what the rest of the country was experiencing with the depression. People were out of work, and there were soup lines—a terrible time in our country's history. The experiences we enjoyed gave no indication of these conditions until we grew older. We were sure our parents knew, but whether we were protected from it purposely we didn't know or understand. We lived in the rural community with few affected businesses or manufacturing failures. This subject continues to come up when learned of the lives given up in suicides and the families devastated in the failure of the country economy.

Frederick, I mentioned previously, was a farming community in those days. I'm reminded of the annual fair each summer. Mother put up preserves and baked goods in competition to be judged for ribbons for the best. Mother won more than one ribbon. During one of the summers, the Legion took part in a mock battle of war at night with explosives and rockets being fired with soldiers doing battle, and the sound effects were really scary. You could hear folks saying, "Things aren't the way they used to be." One of those things was the celebration of the Fourth of July. The little boy in Dad would come forth and he would purchase a variety of fireworks, and after dark we had a show for the entire neighborhood. I have no idea the cost of fireworks at that time. They certainly were far less than today. There were no laws against firing them at that time. We had firecrackers of different sizes and kinds. We threw the torpedoes to the ground, seeing them explode. One exploded and a fragment struck me in the shin, which caused a burn. Skyrockets, Roman candles, pinwheels, and flowerpots were set off after dark. Dad built a ramp to fire the skyrockets, and with supervision we were permitted to hold the Roman candles, waving them in a circle as they fired. It was wonderful.

At the Garber farm one year on the Fourth, Jim Garber, Uncle Raymond's nephew, looked into the end of a Roman candle he thought had finished, and a red ball hit him full in the face. Fortunately, he was not burned badly, but his hair and eyebrows were singed without any other injury. In those years, we fortunately were not faced with any serious injuries, except when Bob tried a trick that backfired on him. He had a three-inch firecracker that had not fired. When that happened, we would break them in half and place them under our foot, then putting punk to it, they would spit out fire. We called them hissers. This one that Bob was holding it in his hand, it backfired. He was burnt to the point that he had to go to the doctor for treatment, and his hand was wrapped for some time, preventing the possibility of infection.

Things were going well with the Keesey family. One evening Dad came home with a brand-spanking-new 1933 Buick sedan automobile that replaced the Model-T Ford. It was "the cat's meow," as they say. We were going for a ride the next Sunday evening in the new car when suddenly a thunderstorm with strong winds and heavy rain came up. Dad pulled off to the side of the road to give the storm time to subside. Bob and I were huddled in the back seat, scared to pieces, and suddenly a branch came down on the roof of the car. Did we howl! Finally, after being consoled by our parents, Dad got out and removed the small branch, which had caused little damage to the car.

On Dad's vacation one year, we went to Bethany Beach, Delaware, on the Atlantic Ocean. It was the first time Bob and I had seen the ocean, which produced wide eyes and open mouths. Bob took to the small waves coming in. I was another story; I ran down to the water's edge until the next wave incoming sent me scampering for high ground. The family laughed and laughed until one of the waves dumped me and brought me up, blubbering not to venture close again.

Dad always enjoyed fishing and learned of a group of men going fishing in an open-oared boat that was leaving at about seven in the morning. We gathered on the beach to watch until they could no longer be seen. Then at about four in the afternoon we gathered, scanning the horizon until we saw a small dot that grew larger as they approached the shore. They came home with fish of various kinds: sea trout, black sea bass, porgies, and croakers.

Yes, you can say we were living blessed lives—a vacation, as we would say later in our lives, "one for the memory book." It will never be known where the idea came from other than me that I came to believe the world was made for me. Receiving more than I could possibly want, I believed it was all created for me.

School was starting in September 1933, and Bob and I were introduced to a new member of our family household; her name was Hattie. Hattie was colored—that was how we spoke of black people in the thirties. Hattie was small in build, quiet, warm, and a wonderful cook and housekeeper. Dad felt it to be good for Mother to have help with the housekeeping. What it was that brought Hattie to us, Bob and I were not sure. Had we blocked out what we didn't want to hear? We learned that Mother would be going to Baltimore for cobalt treatments for an illness she had. Today I am not able to put this together in my mind as to when we were told it was cancer.

The school year introduced me to the first grade, meeting my first-grade teacher and all those new faces of my first-grade classmates. My routine: I got up in the morning, got dressed, and ate breakfast, and in bad weather we were driven to school, in good weather we walked. It was about a mile and a half, just a good hike for two healthy boys. In those days, we weren't as advanced as our children and grandchildren are today. I had not learned my ABC's and had a problem with memory subjects. The teacher had me stay after school to help me learn them. When dismissed, I had a problem because getting home later than usual caused questions by my parents as to why their son couldn't learn his ABC's. I dawdled around until almost dark, dreading the consequences awaiting me. The repercussions to be suffered were in my mind, thinking I would be thought lesser by my parents for not being able to learn. I believed I should be liked by everyone. I arrived home as Dad came through the door. My parents impressed on me that the worry was created in me not coming home on time and not my learning problems as the reason for my scolding. One more lesson learned: To face up to the situation, we can make our problem worse in trying to dodge whatever it might be. Yes, I finally learned my ABC's.

One experience I had in first grade was when one morning a girl member of the class became sick. I was moved to help in any manner I could, so I volunteered. But it was impossible without material, so I stood by until the janitor addressed the problem. I learned a trait I had was to respond to the need at hand.

Dad presented the idea for a vacation trip to the shore of the Chesapeake Bay in summer of 1934. Beverly Beach was the place where we were to spend two weeks. I had realized giving Mother a change of scenery and routine was needed. Hattie accompanied us to relieve Mother of the cooking and the cleaning. Mother and Dad invited his sister, our Aunt Pearl, and Uncle Raymond and their daughter, Anne, our cousin, to join us. The location was a quiet setting in groves of trees and sandy roads in a story-and-a-half bungalow. It was restful to see Mother relaxing, enjoying herself. Great times were had in the evenings, playing games and storytelling, and there were plenty of good eats with Hattie joining in on the fun. This was the summer of 1934. Dad, Uncle Raymond, Bob, and I went fishing in a rented rowboat. Bob and I were using hand lines. Things were going well, and we had caught several fish. Bob was not satisfied to drop his line over the side; he had to wing it over his head, tossing it. The problem arose when it whipped back and the hook went into the fleshy part of the large finger of his right hand. We immediately sought medical attention for Bob. Discovering there was nothing within the area, Dad was advised to take Bob to the Naval Academy in Annapolis. There we found a doctor who cut the barb and backed the hook out of Bob's finger. We received royal treatment while being escorted on a tour of the Academy. After that, Brother Bob felt he had to attend the Academy for his schooling. It never happened.

Our two weeks were spent bathing in the fenced-in beach area to keep the crabs out so they wouldn't get our toes. Bob and I experienced crabbing first-hand at Beverly Beach. Food was of great interest to us all. The crabs we caught were not many, but we had them steamed, as well as the roasted oysters we enjoyed at a seafood house. Dad wanted the two of us to try them, for it was a new experience. The oysters were placed on a metal sheet over a fire with wet burlap bags covering the shells until the heat baked them and they opened up. They were good, but not all found them delicious.

Upon our return from vacation, Mother began treatment for her cancer. We drove to Baltimore, always as a family, where she continued receiving cobalt treatments. Fall once more introduced the return to school with the usual routine. Thanksgiving brought family for dinner, with Hattie serving up her delicious recipes. It was Uncle Harvey, Aunt Ina, Uncle Roy, Aunt Grace, Aunt Pearl, Uncle Raymond, and Anne. It was nice to see Mother in the kitchen, helping Hattie. Christmas was a busy time, as we saw little of Dad, even less than usual with the busyness at the store. Bob and I were always trying to put one over on one another. We knew we were getting BB guns. There were three round packs of BB's that fit into a small box, about 3X3X6. The box was placed in three other boxes, each larger than the previous box. Each had a different picture of contents. The largest was a fire engine, next a doll, and the third smaller box was a camera. I really put one over on Bob that time. Don't fret; he always got in his licks. What an expression change with each box he opened.

In early 1935, family and friends were visiting us, supporting Mother in her illness. Mother saw to my every need. I have no memory of her warm, close relationship. A question remains while trying to recall my time spent with her. Don't I want to remember those memories? Have I refused to face the facts? Thinking about this today, at eight years of age at that time I believed Mother favored curly-headed Bobby and Dad was closer with me. Perhaps I might have been the cute little girl Mother hoped I would be.

Well, here we were, January 19, 1935. I was eight, happy with my life, and feeling important with myself, enjoying everything an eight-year-old could want. Was I wrong for feeling so important in myself? Where are you in your family experiences? Are things going along and are you enjoying your growing up? Have our lives knowing of God taken on any change? I can't say that mine had.

The month of March had arrived. We were looking forward to spring and warmer weather, thinking of the outdoor activities. Upon rising in the morning, Hattie informed us Mother had been taken to the hospital in the middle of the night; her condition had worsened. Several days later, Dad took Bob and me to visit Mother in the hospital. I recall being hesitant of going to her bedside. She called me to come closer, asking how I was, then had me hold out my hand. She had something for me, but she placed nothing in my hand. There was nothing in my hand. What was I to say to her if she asked for it back? "Mother, there is nothing in my hand"? I was speechless, near tears, hearing nothing from Dad or Bob, those I looked to for guidance. What did I do? Standing, trying to keep from crying, trying to smile at her, I wondered, where can I run? How can I get out of disappointing her when she wants them returned? She had asked me to hold them, realizing she would ask for them back. Today, I ask myself, what was guiding me to be quietly waiting? To this day, the ache remembered of disappointment felt in my body when she asked me to return them at our time of leaving for there was nothing to give back; my hand was empty. My lasting memory of those final moments are with me to this day. I broke down in tears and was led out of the room. Dad informed me later, knowing how upset I had been, that my mother was not herself due to the medicine necessary to comfort her. She had lost her sight due to the illness.

Today as I relive the last time I saw Mother alive, there are tears in my eyes and in my heart. Mother's brothers and their wives came to visit her and also Aunt Pearl, Uncle Raymond, and Ann. It was Sunday, March 17, St. Patrick's Day, 1935. I suppose I should have realized things were not as they had been. Bob and I remained at home with Hattie. I remember sitting on the cellar step in the basement, where we made sauerkraut and enjoyed many family togetherness times. I was petting and talking to Mike, our cat. I heard the return of Dad and family members upstairs. I remained on the steps. Dad came down and sat beside me, putting his arm around my shoulder, saying Mother had died. What was I going to do without my mother? I don't remember crying at that time. My mind was with the last time I had seen my mother. It was the day before the service for Mother. Dad came to school and picked me up to go the journey to Ironville, Pennsylvania, to his sister's, my Aunt Pearl's, in preparation for the funeral. Services would be held at the Presbyterian Church in Quarryville. Mother was to be buried in the Quarryville Cemetery, where many of the Newswanger family members were interred. I was numb. Things were happening, but I was just going through the motions. People were speaking to me without a response from me. At a later time, I recall Aunt Ina commenting to me how well Dad accepted Mother's death. My dad was not one to show emotion. I remember him clenching his teeth during the service, causing his jaw muscles to tighten. Milton Garvin, Dad's uncle—he was our great-uncle—took us in his grand car that had what they called jump seats for additional passengers to be seated. They were behind the front seats. You sat in them while looking toward the rear of the car. This impressed me. As I remember, it relieved my mind for the moment, but it was still a very sad day for us all.

For many nights after Mother's death, as I lay in my bed, I cried myself to sleep, reciting the nightly prayer taught to me by my mother: "Now I lay me down to sleep." My prayer has now become:

Now I lay myself down to weep,
I lost my Mom how can I sleep?
I close my eyes continue to cry,
Asking God how and asking why.

Brother Bob never heard me or knew of that because I stifled the crying. At least he never asked if I was all right. In this traumatic experience for an eight-year-old, I needed an answer to why. I had no understanding of God in the beginning of all of this, but I couldn't let it go. I knew my mother to be a wonderful person. She did everything for me, though I have no memory of her holding me very often. I suddenly found myself, who previously believed the world revolved around me, to be a person having little anymore.

Yes, over the next several years, the pain of loss lessened but the blame persisted. I felt this God was to blame. God was not a reality. Little did I realize HE was becoming more a reality.

It was a very short time after Mother's death that something came over me. I went into the bathroom after school, lay down on the floor, and fell asleep. Hattie was unable to awaken me, and neither could Dad when he came home. Once again, Dr. Baer was called to the house to check me over. His diagnosis was sleeping sickness possibly brought on by the sorrowing of Mother's death. I was told the doctor laid me face down on my bed and grabbed me in the ribs, and I snapped out of this state. I realized what was happening but could not respond until I was grabbed. Hattie was such a comfort to me. Her soft voice let me know she cared. The expression goes, "We are all the same. It's our experiences that make the difference." You have that experience in your life that needs to be revealed to others. Perhaps this God is new to you. You have not heard yourself speak His name aloud. I assure you, He is there, He is real, and He is available. Why do I speak of an incident such as this? Perhaps you have one back there in your memory that is a likeness to this one. Perhaps you would rather not think of it today. It may be too painful or sad. Remember, God is real and He is there and He cares. "David, did you not know this at this time?" NO! As I relate these things today, I ask the question, where was God then? The answer comes back, the same place He is today: available. Where was God in your life when at that time you needed Him most? Where is He today in your life? A point to be made is the relevance God has always had with His people, all people. Recognizing the awareness of the fact that God is God in all His Glory, the fact that we have not heard His call doesn't mean He isn't calling. The question is, are we listening? Today I thank God for this awakening primarily due to my mother's death.

"David has reason to believe, but does he?" There were so many great things that happened in Bob's and my life while at 5 West 13th Street in Frederick, Maryland. It is the memory of Dad taking the two of us to the bicycle shop on West Patrick Street to purchase a bike for each of us. It is believed it was to help relieve the loss of our mother. Still clear in my mind is my brother selecting the top of the line, a low-built, wide-handlebar, racy-looking bike costing fifty dollars. I was happy with a pretty blue bike, costing twenty-eight dollars. The two of us spent much of our time riding our bikes about the neighborhood. An incident involved the two of us meeting at the corner of a garage that was owned by an undertaker whose paved surface was great for riding our bikes. We ran into one another. I got excited, failing to apply the brakes, which caused us to hit head-on. I crinkled the front fender of my bike but didn't damage Bob's bike. He called me a "dumb bunny." During a return visit together at a later time, we recalled our experiences. It was exciting recognizing things and the changes that had taken place on Thirteenth Street.

The management of McCrory's decided it would be good to transfer Dad to another store because of the memories of the death of Kathryn, his wife. Dad was held in high regard for his work in merchandizing and sales ability. The management transferred Dad to Chester, Pennsylvania, to an A-Class store located on Edgemont Avenue. Chester was a new experience for Bob and me since it was a larger city than Frederick, Maryland. When we arrived, Dad put us up in the Chester Arms Hotel, several blocks down the street from the store. Bob and I felt this was special, having all of our meals served and ordering from a menu. This didn't last long, for Dad got an apartment for us up on 12th Street, near the Pennsylvania Military College, better known as PMC. We lived in the apartment for a short time, the two of us spending time playing tennis as best we could, with Bob winning most of the time and me pouting because I couldn't win very often. Bob didn't take it easy on me, making me work for all I got. Yep, you guessed it; the old temper still had a hand on me.

Many of our days were spent in the movies, there being three to choose from. When we saw the feature in one, we went to the feature in one of the others. This was Dad's means of keeping us busy, knowing where we were. Dad kept us busy until our school year began in September of 1935. Any kids our ages would find this to be great. Yes, we saw all of them through the summer. I need to ask at this point in your reading, are there any similarities in your life at this age? The absence of Mother is very strong in the presence of my mind, causing many moments of searching as to why our lives, my life, was unfolding in this manner. Where are you, God, if you are real? Am I something I shouldn't be to bring this upon us as a family? What would have been your thoughts at this age in your life?

In all this time, I have the memory of us attending Sunday School one Sunday wearing our Easter outfits. Our parents, who were both raised in church, saw no need for Bob and me to attend church. Before Bob and I started school in the fall of 1935, Dad learned of a home where we could take a room with meals. It was with the Greco family at 1129 West Seventh Street. Mrs. Greco's name was Rose. She was a widow, and living with her was her eldest son, Lou. Lou was one of eleven children, nine boys and two girls, all grown and on their own except Lou, who never married. The memory of waking Thursday morning and smelling the aroma of olive oil cooking in the frying pan gave evidence of Mama Greco preparing sauce for the spaghetti that she served for Thursday and Sunday dinners. Usually it would be Mama Greco,

Lou, Joe, and Ernie, the youngest of the children. On occasion, other family members would be with us. It was quite a show to watch Joe and Ernie compete in eating hot peppers. Joe ate the peppers one at a time whole, showing no effects through half the meal, when suddenly he would get flush in the face, breaking into a sweat. Ernie got flush of color. He might not have eaten as many as Joe. Dad, Bob, and I enjoyed the contest—the food most of all. We experienced a bout of sleeping with bedbugs for a short time while living at Grecos'. I mention this only because it happened once in my life, and I'm hopeful you've never lived with it.

Lou's hand at magic invited Bob and me to the corner of the garage after dark. He waved his arms, reached up toward the garage rainspout, and came down with a sparrow in his hand. There was no explanation of how. Behind the residence on the south side of Seventh Street was the athletic field for the Lloyd AC Athletic Club. The baseball diamond and football field were in regular use the year 'round by the athletic club and numerous other groups. Brother Bob played third base for an American Legion-sponsored team. I recall him losing the ball in the sun one day, getting hit square in the nose, but he handled it well. One Sunday afternoon, watching the Lloyd AC team play a scheduled football game, a group of young fellows chose teams and were playing behind the stands. Suddenly, some of the folks started leaving the stands to watch a fight that had broken out in the game going on behind the stands. Later we learned it involved Bob, who was fighting to keep his football. One of the other boys tried to take the ball from him. Bob handled himself very well; he came away with football in hand. I was growing into this eighth year of my life, learning much from Brother Bob. He had taken me under his wing, looking after me in helping with homework of a third grader. I looked up to my older brother with good reason, for Bob was a good student, winning a seventh-grade academic award while attending Franklin Street School in Chester. By the way, my third-grade teacher was quite a good-looking young lady who caught my handsome father's attention, which resulted in a date or two with no future. While at recess, pranks were pulled on one another. One day a prank was played on me on the playground. I was standing talking with a friend when suddenly one of the boys walked up to me and gave me a push that sent me backward over the back of another boy, who was on his hands and knees behind me. I cracked my elbows on the brick surface, which sent my temper through the top of my head. I shinnied up the frame of the laughing boy who had pushed me. That resulted in a fight, sending both of us boys to the principal's office. Fortunately, my teacher had witnessed the episode causing the other boys to be reprimanded for their actions. I liked my teacher. She was my homeroom teacher.

Another experience I recall at Lincoln Elementary School was having my knuckles rapped with a ruler for dropping my pencil and taking liberties in looking upon a young lady's legs. I got caught. The temptations of the mind cause pain to the body at times. What did you say? "You never did anything like that, boy or girl." Come now. Boys will be boys and girls will be girls.

On Friday night, Dad would come home for supper at Grecos' and then return to the store until ten o'clock. One of those Friday nights, Dad invited Lou Greco to ride into town with Bob and me, going to the movies while he went to the store. We were traveling east on West Seventh Street at the intersection of Seventh and Parker Streets when a car traveling south didn't stop at the stop sign. It hit us broadside, causing the car we were in to skid sideways when the right-rear wheel hit the curb and flipped it over into a tree. I remember careening around in the car along with the noise and what apparently was flying glass. When things had settled down, Dad asked if we were okay. I couldn't respond at once until I recovered from the shock. I said, "I think so." I discovered I was sitting on the rear-right-side window with Brother Bob on top of me. They got us out of the car through the left-rear window to check us over. Bob was none the worse for wear. I had two goose eggs, one on the right temple and one on the left temple. A doctor's office was on the corner. His name was Landis. We were taken into the office to have the doctor look for possible injuries. Since the doctor's glasses were being repaired, he could only check limbs and joints. We were declared fine except for bumps and bruises. After riding downtown in the paddy wagon (police van), Bob and I went to the movies. Later, while undressing for bed, we discovered broken glass in our clothing. The accident ended the use of the 1933 Buick, introducing a new 1936 Dodge with many added features.

Our living in the Greco home ended in 1937. We moved across the street, taking up residence with the Kauffmans, an elderly retired couple, at 1124 West 7th Street. Living with the Kauffmans was difficult at times. One of these happened on a Sunday afternoon. Bob and I were playing Cowboys and Indians in the backyard, which was frowned upon by the Kauffmans because of religious beliefs. Dad sent both of us to our bedroom, where Bob got the back of Dad's hand to the mouth, splitting his upper lip for speaking back to Dad. Yours truly got bent over the foot of the bed, having a hairbrush administered to my bottom. We presume the noise the Kauffmans heard had a satisfying effect for our breaking their beliefs. We knew Dad to be fair in his punishment for our wrongdoing; we had it coming to us. It was while living with the Kauff-mans, who listened to Christian programs on the radio, that may have prompted the boys to go to the Trinity Methodist Church. As I ponder this time, there was an Easter drama done by the children, where I was given a part in the story of Jesus. The question in my mind brought thoughts as to who this man Jesus was we sang songs about. Previously in Mother's death, God was my target for the anger and hurt I suffered. Would I ever get over this loss? Would the emptiness, the ache in my chest, be filled? I attended services at Trinity. At times I would go by myself while Bob stayed in bed. I wanted to hear and listen to the words of the pastor, lacking a relationship with God other than still asking why, at the same time blaming him for my loss.

I was now ten years old. Can you recall any of your experiences from age ten? The year was 1937. A new adventure was about to begin in our lives. Your life is unfolding in the relationships you have with those you lived with in ad-dition to the new acquaintances you are making at school and/or in church. What are your thoughts as you learn about God? Is He in your life? I still didn't know. Would I ever? This new adventure I mention has to do with Dad falling in love with Ruth Gill, who was the neighbor girl across the street from the Kauffman home. The two of them had apparently been spending time to-gether, a surprise unnoticed on my part. While we were living at Grecos', Ruth lived three homes away on the same side of the street. "The question" was ap-parently asked by Dad. Ruth answered yes to marriage. Much must go on in the lives of adults that goes unnoticed by a ten-year-old. Ruth was a young lady who just turned nineteen who accepted a proposal of marriage to a gen-tleman twenty years her senior. Ruth was mature beyond her years.

The wedding was held in the rectory of the Catholic Church, but neither Bob nor I were present. As I remember, Dad told us Ruth and he were getting married. Our acceptance of this marriage wasn't discussed. Ah, yes, another move. We now established residence in a new home in Ridley Park, Pennsyl-vania, at 800 Ridley Avenue, five miles from Chester toward Philadelphia. The home was a newly constructed cape-cod-style building, with a living room, dining room, kitchen, two bedrooms, bath, basement, and unattached garage. Visible from our house was Morton Lake, located on Prospect Park boundary. There were two similar houses exactly alike, all built on fill ground, which pro-duced some settling and cracks in the walls in time. Dad and Ruth had the bedroom in the back of the house, giving Bob and me the front bedroom.

A new experience in our lives was the relocation in the change of schools for Bob and me. Bob was now fourteen as of the twenty-second of August and enrolled in ninth grade at Ridley Park High School. I was enrolled in the fifth grade at the Tome Street Elementary School. Marie Holtzapple, my favorite teacher of my formal education days, taught history, geography, math, and English. My best subjects were history and geography. There lingers in my mind a prank I pulled in her class that caused a memory of regret for me. You have read that my dad managed the McCrory's 5 &10 Store, which provided for us boys samples of Chicklet chewing gum packets with two Chicklets in each small box. It was Miss Holtzapple's practice that if she found a student chewing gum, she asked them if they had enough for the entire class. Needless to say, the answer was always no. Being the rascal I was known to be, I set her up when she discovered I was chewing gum noticeably. She asked if there was enough for the entire class. I proudly and loudly answered yes and began passing out the gum. Believe it or not, she joined in and we chewed our gum the rest of that period. I later apologized to her for my insolence. Miss Holtzapple was a teacher who will always be remembered by me.

Ridley Park was a residential change from Chester. The school had different faces and names. An early and lasting friend was Ralph Ashworth because we found common things that brought us together. He was a good student, very bright with varied interests. His crystal radio set was fascinating and took up much of our time together. We had a mutual friend, Nelson Duncan. We all spent good times after school and at times on Saturday. There were girls catching the eye of the boys. Two remembered in particular were Sandra Crossette and Pheobe Lukins, nice looking and easy to make conversation. Sandra and David spent some time together enjoying music and books. A favorite time in the winter was ice skating on the Ridley Park Lake. Winters were cold, providing good ice skating most of the winter months. There were times when a thaw caused the ice to crack, letting water come up on top of the ice. When skating the ice would separate, making it necessary to jump over the cracks. We never saw or heard of anyone going into the lake since the ice was well formed in depth. At night we played tag on the ice, resting around the bonfire, toasting marshmallows and, at times, a hot dog or two and hot chocolate. Much fun!

Brother Bob continued being active in sports, playing on the Ridley Park High football team. During one of those games, Bob took a pretty good shot to the mouth, resulting in a chipped tooth and a split lip. There were some anxious moments standing on the sideline until he got up and came off the field under his own strength. There was quite a ribbing Bob got from me for the crush he had on a pretty redhead he liked named Marion McCadden. We were home by ourselves often, giving us time to get into it with one another. One of those afternoons while teasing him, it went too far. In attempting to get away from him, a break through the dining room didn't work and he floored me with a blow to the top of my right shoulder. The following morning while in the bathroom, Dad asked how I got the bruise on my shoulder. I responded I had fallen off my bike into a pole. End of question. Yes, we did stand up for one another on occasion.

That brings up the subject of the blue bike Dad had bought for me after Mother's death. By now it was getting worn, so I decided to spruce it up with fresh red paint. I can't recall where I got the red paint. This is interesting to me, for I took the bike apart, putting it back together without any help. It is a lesson in my life that sheds light on patience and talent that is beyond me. The upstairs of 800 East Ridley Avenue was unfinished where we had the Lionel train Bob had won in Frederick, Maryland, set up for play. Eddie Gill, Ruth's youngest brother, would come visit, and we would have a great time together. Eddie was several years older than me. Our time together was great. Eddie later was in the Army Air Corp and, during the Pacific fighting, lost his life in a Liberator bomber flight off Honshu, Japan, in the Second World War. His death was seven years later than the account I presently am writing. I liked Eddie; I took his death to heart. The newlyweds in 1938 learned they were to become parents sometime in the first part of 1939, which proved to be correct, and on February 7, 1939, twins were born to Ruth and Charles Keesey. Sadly, only one of them survived the birth. Rita Ann was the surviving twin, being very small and cared for in an incubator for several weeks. Though stillborn, Theresa was given the name for Ruth's youngest sister, who lost her life in a fall down the cellar steps at the family's Seventh Street address.

Lord, I have procrastinated too long in the delay of completing the call you have given me to give witness to your presence in my life. I pray that your Spirit will lead in the further story of the unfolding of my life.

At the time of Sister Rita's birth, Dad was informed of his transfer to manage the McCroy's store in Salisbury, Maryland. I cannot recall whether this was a promotion to a larger operation; however, it was another chapter in the life of the Charles W. Keesey's moving family. Because of the birth of Rita in early 1939 (February 7), Dad, Bob, and I were the advance guards in the move. The new mother, Ruth, remained in Chester so long as Rita was hospitalized until she was able to breathe on her own and was able to take nourishment. The three of us took up residence in a private home on Poplar Hill Avenue. Our home at 155 Williams Street, where we moved when Ruth and Rita were able to join us, was just down the street from Poplar Hill Avenue. The memory of the interim home we lived in was the feather bed on which I slept. I recall sinking down, having the fullness of the mattress folding around the body, a most comforting feel. Bob was enrolled in the Wicomico High School, adapting well to teachers and once again his love for football. We learned quickly to make friends since we had moved so often. David enrolled in the relatively new Park Street Elementary School in the fifth grade, always with the intention of getting better grades. A lasting memory was serving on the safety patrol team, where he monitored the crossing of students at an assigned street intersection. We wore sand-brown belts with a badge, giving the authority to direct and help others cross the street. Big stuff, wouldn't you say? Brother Bob was an excellent student in the upper half of his classes. I was the student with average grades, seldom following through as my grades revealed. No excuses.

The home on Williams Street was a large white-frame house with a garage in the rear. Shortly after we moved in, a stray collie dog adopted us. We fed him each day on the back porch. He was a great pet but was never permitted in the house. On a particular weekend, Dad, Ruth, and Rita made a visit to Chester. Bob and I were alone for the weekend. Bob was now fifteen and I was twelve, old enough to care for ourselves. On Saturday night, our friendly dog woke us with his barking. Bob looked out the upstairs rear bedroom window, discovering a figure walking toward the back of the house, almost to the garage. The dog kept barking, which didn't seem to deter this individual from continuing with what he intended. Bob whispered to me, "Come on, let's see who this is." He picked up a baseball bat and down the steps we went, in our pajamas and bare feet. There were two door entrances off the back porch, one entering to the dining room and the other to the kitchen. When we entered the kitchen, we did not turn on the light. We could see the person's image through the window of the kitchen door. Bob said, "You get to the light switch by the door, wait until I tell you, then turn on the light." When in position, Bob said, "Now." The light came on, which revealed a black face with eyes and a mouth open wide. He spun around and off the porch he ran, with the dog in full pursuit, with Bob and me right behind the dog all the way to the alley. The dog ran down the alley after the man, nipping at his heels until the collie gave up the chase. Bob and I had stopped at the alley, never giving thought to the return to the house on the cinder driveway in our bare feet. We ooched and ouched the whole way back to the house. It brought forth our producing treats for our brave collie.

The summer of 1939 I spent with Aunt Pearl, Uncle Raymond, and Cousin Ann on the celery farm near Columbia, PA, in Lancaster County. What celery Uncle Raymond grew! It was the best celery I ever ate, having found none better in all of my years. The celery I liked the best was named Houser. It was the crunchiest, crispiest, and string-less celery a person ever ate. Oftentimes we put peanut butter or cream cheese if we had it. I can taste it right now.

It was a busy summer going over to Paris Garber's, Uncle Raymond's father, farm to get Calvin, the mule, to furrow the rows or to cultivate between the rows at a later time, keeping out the weeds. We would pull the seedlings from the seedbeds, place a plant about eight to ten inches apart on the mound of the furrow, then run water in the furrows from one end to the other. That done, it was down on your knees, straddling the row, crawling along, placing a plant in the center of the row while using the furrow mounds to place dirt around the root of the plant. It was a simple procedure for a plentiful, productive crop. It was enjoyable work with the results producing the living. Uncle Raymond was inventive and gifted with the development of his business. As the crop grew, it needed to be sprayed to prevent blight and the infestation of beetles and bugs; water also needed to be available to prevent the plants from dying. To provide these needs, Uncle Raymond built a three-sided pool, 20x20, with a depth of four feet at the deep end. He built a tank for mixing the bluestone spray, purchased the pump, and installed it on his own. By the way, it was deep enough for yours truly to learn to swim in the pool. How about that?

There were other chores to be done on the farm. I was more than willing to become a part that summer. A flock of young chickens was kept in a coop behind the springhouse, about fifty of them. The coop had to be cleaned out on a regular basis. The chickens needed watered and fed. Every day in the evening, the coop was opened for the chickens to get some exercise while being offered whole corn. Well, you may have guessed, the chickens saw me and I was inundated with the entire flock of chickens on my head, shoulders, and arms, pecking away at the corn. They were eating out of my hand while I was laughing out loud, talking to the chickens, all the time enjoying the experience. As the celery plants grew, I was assigned to place old newspapers between the rows to defeat the weeds from coming up and choking out the celery plants. An interesting article in the paper would catch the eye, which would find me sitting in the hot sun, reading the paper. More than once, I had to be told by Aunt Pearl to set the paper aside then, when finished, come in under the shade tree and read the paper. I tried it once but continued to read them in the sun.

The schedule that summer was to go on the Grocer's Picnic by train to New York to the World's Fair. The fair was held in Flushing, New York. A young fellow twelve years old would have had to pay full fair, so I was elected to wear short trousers to have me appear younger. It worked. What a trip it was. Several surprises were thrown in as it went. As we debarked from the train and approached the entrance to the fair, we met a neighbor who lived behind us on Williams Street in Salisbury. One more time, what a small world this is! The trademark for the fair was the Trylon and the Perisphere. Interesting enough, the site of the fair later became the Mets' ballpark, called Shea Stadium. At this writing, it is learned the Mets have played their last game in Shea Stadium; it is no longer to be used by the Mets.

One of the most interesting exhibits was the General Motors Motorama, a look into the future for the automobile industry. As remembered by the year 1980, cars were to have the teardrop shape. It is now the year 2014, and they have yet to arrive. You rode in conveyed seats facing to the left, viewing the landscape of communities with high-speed highways much on the order of what we use today. There were many other exhibits that were less impressive but enjoyable to see, and there was much to learn. We enjoyed packed lunches to cut down on expenses. This trip was the treat of a lifetime.

On the way home to Lancaster, we were all a bunch of tired puppies. Many were sleeping, much to some prankster's glee. Upon waking, there was this most unusual smell on the train that created a lot of snickering plus outright laughter. You understood what a foot was when you realized limburger cheese was smeared on your upper lip. It made great fun for all. You, the reader in my mind, have those special experiences in your life. Your reading of another one's experience surely brings to mind those experiences that have brightened your life. It is those experiences that give witness to strengthen believers and nonbelievers in the faith.

We have now arrived at the period of time in my life story in the small Brethren Church in Ironville, where I invited Jesus to come into my life. These many years later, not knowing the questions to ask at that time give evidence and importance to one coming to Christ to have the need of an experienced believer to open the Bible and to nurture one in God's Word. Twelve years of age to begin to learn the character of the individuals called God, Jesus and the Holy Spirit meant little to me for some time to come. That evening in July, I walked out of the church, knowing what he had done was of importance to others but having little importance to me. There was no family acknowledgment, recognition, support, or influence shown like so many of us coming to

God in the Name of Jesus, as we ask, "Is that all there is to accepting Christ as Savior?" David, did you know you have just received life for your eternity?

Today as I write, from my experiences few professed believers have learned or understood the presence or the power of the indwelling of the Holy Spirit or the power of prayer. In Bible study today, believers come forward to speak of the innocence due to the lack of teaching and preaching on the subject of the power God bestows upon us receiving the Holy Spirit. These words are put to paper, owing to the years of study, teaching, and preaching God's Holy Word as I have followed my Savior. Once more, we bring to mind the importance of nurturing I have been advocating these many years. Today, in our retirement community, teaching, studying, and times preaching God's Word, it is evident, folks, believing we are saved has never moved beyond the statement: "That is all you have to do, receive Jesus into your hearts, and you are saved, having been indwelt with the Holy Spirit." The question by most is receiving, "Who and what is this HOLY SPIRIT?" "Born again," "newness of life," what do they mean? Words are read without meaning. For me, at the age of twelve, I went on living as before, not thinking or wondering much about what happened, though I knew something was different. The mind turned to learning this Jesus' Father is the God; I had been accusing of taking my mother from me.

The pain and anguish experienced these four years since Mother's death enabled me to come to a different understanding that I am not the most important person in this whole wide world. There are others experiencing these changes in life just the same as I. I became restless, deciding I was homesick for my dad and family and requested they come pick me up. I was reminded by family of the things I had enjoyed. The summer wasn't over; they could still use my help. Was I ungrateful for those experiences enjoyed to walk away without a thank-you? Didn't matter; I wanted to be with family. Was anyone told of my being converted? Did I seek answers to questions of the experience I had in that little Brethren Church in Ironville? Whom would I ask, never having heard the Word of God expressed in my presence by family members or friends other than the visits I made to churches? On a visit to Chester from Salisbury, my family picked me up at Aunt Pearl's. While in Chester, Bob and I took a walk. Bob spoke of differences he had with Ruth, but he did not speak as to the problem or problems he had. He did not like the way he was treated. I found myself trying to understand how to have Bob realize Ruth was young with a newborn baby and away from her family. She needed patience and understanding considering the additional responsibilities with two boys, one sixteen and the other twelve years of age. He thanked me for listening to him. He said, "I feel better about it, having talked with you."

Moments such as this has awakened a power within me beyond my comprehension. Question: How was I led with such sensitiveness and understanding of this situation at the age of twelve? A warm, satisfying presence was born in me, revealing to me it was the Holy Spirit. "David, did you know?" Not at the time.

I became conscious of a character within me that was shining a different light. Instinctively, a door opened, revealing a presence in my life of perceiving a concern in the matter with Brother Bob, taking into consideration the parties involved with the issues, giving sound advice, and helping Bob recognize the factors in Ruth's life. Surprised, I experienced a presence in my life never observed before. I liked it.

Upon our return to Salisbury, changes began taking place in the Keesey family once more. Previous to the upcoming happening about to take place, we learned Pop Gill, Ruth's dad, and family had been transferred from Chester to Toledo, Ohio. Sun Oil Company transferred him from Marcus Hook. This might help to explain the next change for the Keeseys. Dad, on a bright sunny day, walked to work on a day when the sun decided to go behind clouds, producing a cloudburst. Buckets were falling, leading Dad to go for his umbrella. It was not where he kept it. He proceeded to walk home in the rain, getting drenched. Told his district manager had taken the umbrella angered Dad. Our father was a man with a short fuse. In this experience, the fuse burned up and so did Charlie, as many people referred to him. Upon his return, Charlie informed his boss, a Mr. St. John, what he thought of him. Charlie was immediately informed that he was fired. Charlie responded that he had already quit. Furthermore, Charlie stated he wanted no part of any person with such ill regard for another's wellbeing. End of paychecks from McCrory 5 & 10.

With Dad out of work, he and Ruth decided to move to Toledo, Ohio. It was felt this was Ruth's influence to be near her family. The plan was for Bob and me to be delivered to Aunt Pearl and Uncle Raymond's until the family got settled in Toledo. We two boys were delivered to the celery farm prior to the start of the school year with the understanding that the parents would send for us boys to be sent by train to Toledo. One week led to four months. In that time, Bob and I were not enrolled in school. During this period of time, there was work with the celery, feeding chickens, playing with the two sheep, and attempting to milk Addie, the single cow they had to supply the milk and making of butter for the household. The fall and winter harvest of the celery crop was a learning experience. The process involved digging the individual plants, placing them in trenches in the ground and covering them with black roofing paper and straw, protecting them from the freeze. A wonderful, crisp, mild-flavored celery it produced, which kept until exhausted into January or February. I went along Saturday morning, delivering to customers on the route, then to the stand in the Columbia Market House. There was good snowfall, making it possible to take a flat celery pan to use as a toboggan. A good incline came down from the reservoir, providing a good run across the path to the springhouse, where the clothes washing and some other household chores were done. This created a problem in walking to the springhouse, which made it unsafe for Aunt Pearl. End of toboggan sliding. There was attempted skiing on barrel stays with little success; pictures were taken to commemorate the happenings. It was during small game hunting season, enabling me to hunt rabbits and pheasants (cock birds) with the small .22 rifle Uncle Raymond had. You might say we boys were on an extended vacation. This continued through the Thanksgiving period until Christmas. No thought of church or God.

The time came to place the Christmas tree in the living room. The location was in question between Cousin Ann and Bob, causing some ill feelings and leaving me to wonder why Bob even offered his two cents. As an innocent bystander, I was unable to understand the insistence in Brother Bob being so adamant about the placement of the tree. That straw, I believe, sent Bob and me packing after New Year's.

Christmas and New Year's over, Aunt Pearl and Uncle Raymond agreed after New Year's it was time to send the boys to Toledo. On a given day, we were taken to the Lancaster train station, purchased tickets, and off we went to Toledo. There was great excitement on the part of me, a real train trip all that distance, especially going around horseshoe curve near Altoona. I had never traveled on a train this far on one trip. We arrived in Toledo, smelling like the coal from the steam engine, covered with soot, plus being hoarse of voice, which lasted three days. It was a trip I will never forget.

Our arrival in Toledo was vague in memory at this writing, though it is recalled the two of us were lodged in a home with room and board. Fine food, as memory serves me. Bob was the mentor of my manners and speech, though the suggestions were discreet and in private. Brother Bob was an inspiration in and to my life, even though we found much to disagree on subjects.

Toledo was a different experience for the both of us. The weather was a change in that the cold blast of arctic air off Lake Erie chapped our faces, ears, and legs on the journey to school on a blustery winter morning. The trip home after school was bearable in higher temperature and usually less windy. Shortly after Bob and my arrival, the Keesey family took up residence at 746 Eutaw Street, a few blocks from the Maumee River. Several walking journeys Bob and I made into Center City required us to go over the high-level bridge. Often I heard Bob say, "If you are going to walk with me, stop lagging on behind," responded by me, "Don't walk so darn fast." You agree, there is a note of brotherliness in those exchanges.

During one of our sojourns into Center City, we went into one of the tall buildings, as remembered for nothing more than to look at the sights. Looking west, we suddenly saw the swirling cone of a tornado, producing chills to my scalp. It is a sight long to be remembered, nor do I ever wish to see another, though it was miles away. I never read about damage. The five of us—Dad, Ruth, Rita, Bob, and I—were quite happy with one another. Rita, by this time, was in the stage of learning to walk. During one of these exercises Rita, in going from one person to another, fell backward, striking her head on the floor. Ruth, having lived with the fall and death of her younger sister, Theresa, feared the worst. Rita was scooped up and taken to the hospital, where she was found to be with a mild concussion. Thank the Good Lord it was not more serious. Dad was selling Hoover vacuum cleaners in one of the department stores in Downtown Toledo. Dad, I believe, was cut out to be the manager of a five-and-ten-cent store in any area he was chosen to work. There were other types of jobs he worked at with little success, trying one after another.

Bob was enrolled in Waite High School, where he once more became very active in football. He continued to get excellent grades in all his subjects. I was the same, as mentioned before, the mind could comprehend. It was the lack of interest, guidance, and encouragement to learn that was missing. Was it fair of me to make this evaluation at this time in my life? Basketball was available, providing the first organized and coached sport offered for me to try out. I played center on a mediocre team. I was involved in sandlot football, which again lacked equipment and proper coaching. My estimate was I wasn't bad should I want a personal assessment. The usual scrapes and bruises were a part of it, the wounds of battle. Reflecting on this time in my life, I observed two men enjoying an unusual fondness for one another, something never previously encountered, and it was perhaps another unfair judgment on my part.

Toledo has held the memory of the opportunity of being the first wage-earning experience in this young man's life. It began as a caddy at the Chippawa Golf Course. The course was approximately five miles from Eutaw Street, where the Keeseys lived. Mode of transportation for us two boys was hitchhiking both ways. As a rule, members were polite, understanding of the job we performed, and the tips were good. It was a time in life for relationships with folks we otherwise would not have met. Certain experiences gave evidence of the building of character. A dentist by the name of Dr. Barbor had me as his caddy on this given day, proving to be memorable for both in addition to those in the foursome. On two successive holes, I lost the flight of the ball, irritating the dentist to no end. Several harsh words were directed toward his caddy, provoking the caddy. The third verbal outbreak prompted me to lay the bag of clubs down at the dentist's feet and walk away to the pro shop. Dr. Barbor called for me to come back, to which I did not respond. Dr. Barbor returned to play golf another day, asking for me to caddy for him. I refused the request. Told to speak with the doctor, I received an apology for the doctor's actions in the presence of those who witnessed the earlier exchange in their last outing. I accepted the apology, resulting in my becoming the doctor' regular caddy. The three players in the foursome when the incident occurred got on the doctor's case to the point that he apologized to the people in the pro shop when he finished the round of golf. The lesson learned by me was, keep your eye on the ball and stand up when you are right.

On a Monday morning and on my own, I headed for the golf course. Brother Bob was due to start football practice and was not going along. Standing on the usual corner, a car stopped, offering a ride. Thanking the man for picking me up, I said I was going to the golf course. Having gone a short distance, the man casually placed his hand on my leg, and the hand was pushed away. The driver said, "Don't you like that?" as he once more made a move to try again. At this point, the driver was told to pull to the curb. Informed that the ride was the only thing in which I had interest, the driver said to forget what happened. I responded, "Pull over and stop. If you don't, I will jump out." The man apologized, pulled over, and let me out. A lesson of many learned coming often for future references in my life. Experiences such as this one we can do without. Hopefully you have not had the likeness to remember.

More and more, my life is more focused on the Lord, considering my position of faith. In complete honesty, you must know of a burden I have lived with these past seventy-two years. Fully cognizant of having received Christ that evening in the revival service in Ironville, I must confess an act I was responsible for initiating. It gave reason to ask forgiveness of God. I know believing God is a forgiving God, he heard my prayer for forgiveness. My continued problem has been forgiving myself. It is shameful to the point I will not disclose the act, would it have never been committed. Toledo, Ohio, is never to be forgotten, having had this in my life. Forgiven, but so hard to forget.

In the spring of 1941, Bob graduated from Waite High School with honors, receiving a football scholarship. That fall he enrolled as a freshman in Oberlin College. He was selected to be the councilor of the freshman dorm where he was housed. Proud of my brother? I surely am. I continued to caddy at Chippawa Golf Course to earn spending money as the weather permitted. December 7, 1941, dawned cloudy, cold, and windy. I learned that afternoon an unfamiliar call of "Extra, extra, read all about it!" The attack on Pearl Harbor Naval Base! Hearing a call in such a neighborhood on Eutaw Street was eerie and alarming, like a person crying out, "Help, murder, police!" I turned on the radio for more information. The radio, yes—I turned on the radio, a communication we rarely used, especially me at my age. I came to the reality that this certainly was impossible to be happening. My mind went to the experience Bob and I had lived through when Orson Wells had produced *War of the Worlds* in 1938. As the days progressed and with the time for thought, we learned additional news of having been attacked by the Japanese. How threatened were the ways of our life as we were commonly experiencing? Were they gone forever? To hear the call of the newspaper boy on the street advertising the extra edition of news, telling us of this tragic act, will never be forgotten. We became a nation at war not experienced by my generation. What would it mean to me personally? What was my responsibility as a fourteen-year-old? The answer came: "Pray meaningfully as I knew how," and so I have continued to pray in this manner, having little understanding other than being told, "God hears."

It was early 1942, and Dad applied for a job as driver for munitions transport. He worked for some time until he was disqualified because of age. After this experience, Dad and Ruth understood Dad's future would be better spent working again for McCrory 5 & 10. His inquiry was met, and he was hired as an assistant manager in the store in Youngstown, Ohio. Off to Youngstown, Dad, Ruth, Rita, and I moved but failed to inform Bob of the move because of his being at school in Oberlin. He learned of the move from the neighbors on Eutaw Street. Bob was extremely disappointed in being uninformed of the move. Our new address was 559 Parkwood Avenue, Youngstown, Ohio. It was a corner duplex frame house on the south side of town. I attended James Hillman Jr. High School, which was newly built. My teachers were Miss Double (English), Mr. McPherson (Science), Mr. Metcalf (Math), Ms. Carson (French), Mrs. Taylor (Social Studies), and Mr. Potts (History and Homeroom). My grades were average—B's and C's, depending on the subject—and my interest was to please the teacher more than the knowledge I learned. Mr. Metcalf's math class often led to experiences other than learning algebra.

Rocky, a friend of mine, sat in front of me, creating diversions from learning, so I had to blame it on someone. Sitting in my seat, Rocky Rocco had a straight pin, which he jabbed into my leg. Without a sound, I wrestled it from him without disturbing the class. It didn't end there, for it was payback time. I put the pin into action and jabbed Rocky a good shot in the backside, and he hollered out. Mr. Metcalf asked what was going on. Informed by my friend Rocky that I had stuck him with a pin, Mr. Metcalf became very upset, heading back toward me. Upon his approaching me, I took hold of the bottom of my seat with both hands, and he took hold of my shoulders and began shaking me. I sat still, causing Mr. Metcalf to rock back and forth violently. You guessed it, the class broke out in laughter, inciting Mr. Metcalf all the more.

Youngstown was a great steel-manufacturing town during this period with much work due to the war effort. We were a school of different families—blacks and whites. It was a common practice to have fights on the way home, often continuing on what route led to get them home. A knife was drawn in one of those fights, breaking it up. The fellow threatened took off on the run. It didn't end there. The next day, the one who ran was waiting for the knife wielder in class to retaliate against the one who threatened him with the knife. After a short scuffle, they both were disciplined for their actions.

It was decided there would be a softball tournament between the home-room classes. Our team represented Mr. McPherson, presently our home-room. We were given little chance of winning, for many of us had not played much ball. In memory, while playing third base, a line drive hit my way ended up in my glove. Our centerfielder, circling under a fly, discovered he had caught the ball. Wonder of wonders, we won the tournament.

There were birthday and holiday parties where greater friendships were made. Names remembered are Cloyce Roby, Sonny Davis, Margaret Hicks, Georgina, Rocky Rocco (my math class friend), and others. The neighborhood guys played kick the can on the intersection of our home. There was some contact with other neighborhood kids, developing rivalry and causing some conflict. I found it interesting when those happenings occurred that I was at home. A number of the guys were quartered in the detention home for children several times. Was the Lord looking after yours truly? It never dawned on me at the time.

During the spring of 1942, Bob was home from college, making deliveries for a furniture company. My summer was spent working on a farm near Warren, Ohio. Chores were involved with feeding stock, collecting eggs, making hay, milking cows, and witnessing the breeding of cows and pigs. Quite an education! One day while collecting eggs, I discovered a snake four feet in length in a nesting box. A hoe was administered in doing in the snake. It was a milk snake, hung up to witness the tail movement until dark.

I caddied on a golf course near Canfield, Ohio, outside of Youngstown. There I was initiated, held down while having my private area brushed with shellac. Boys will be boys. One of the caddies picked a fight with me and blooded my nose, ending the fight. Later in private, I gave the perpetrator a lesson not to be forgotten. Retaliation gave little satisfaction affording our becoming the best of friends. Apologies to one another before the gang brought an end to the initiation of new guys on the block.

Bob returned to Toledo to live with the family of one of his Waite High School buddies. In the fall, he resumed studies at college in Oberlin. He worked tables to pay his tuition and board for his education. These years had little to do with learning of God, Christ, or the Holy Spirit. Dad, Ruth, and Rita attended a Catholic church. On special observances, I would go with them. The form of worship in the Catholic services offered little enlightenment to me. Unfamiliar with Latin and the procedures had little to do with scripture answering questions I had in mind.

In May of 1942, Dad got word that he was being transferred to manage McCrory's Store in Dunn, North Carolina. It would be a new part of the country for us. Few streets were paved at this time. Two streets ran north and south, two streets east and west. Trip to Dunn due to gas rationing was a problem. I remember a can of gas was in the trunk of the car for lack of coupons to buy gas on the trip. We arrived in Dunn, taking room and board with the Washburn family until residence was found for rent. Our menu changed, owing to the southern style cooking. We had cereal, eggs, pancakes, and grits with toast each morning. Dinner was a variety of southern fried chicken, okra, and more. We ate there for a week. Dunn was much like a one-horse town at that time. Acquaintances were made with a fellow about my age named Lee Sandlin. We hit it off right away. Lee showed me around, explaining much about the town. His dad and mother owned the laundry and dry cleaning plant in Dunn. Lee worked for the larger of the two grocery stores in town. Lee was quick to tell me to seek a job with Hodge's Grocery Store. I thanked him for the tip, determined to follow up on his suggestion.

The Saturday of that week, I ventured into Mr. Hodge's store, introduced myself to Mr. Hodge, and asked for a job as delivery boy. Mr. Hodge asked if I had seen the three boys out front with their bikes. I acknowledged that I had seen them. He told me he already had two more than he needed. I thanked him and left.

The following Saturday morning, I arrived bright and early, approaching Mr. Hodge for work delivering groceries. Mr. Hodge asked, "Aren't you the same young fellow who was here last Saturday?" I stated that I was. Mr. Hodge directed my attention to the boys out in front of the store as he had done the previous week. I thanked him once more before leaving.

The next Saturday morning, I found myself riding my bike in the rain to Hodge's store. Entering the store, I took note there were no boys with their bikes out front. Once more I approached Mr. Hodge. He asked, "Do you ever give up?" This was the third Saturday in a row I had come for work. I responded to Mr. Hodge's remarks by saying I saw no delivery boys out front. Mr. Hodge asked, "Boy, where are you from? You don't sound like anyone around these parts." I told him I had arrived recently from Ohio. "What are you doing in Dunn?" I explained that my dad was the new manager of the McCrory Store in town. "How would I know where the customers lived in town, and how would I find them?" I countered with, "Try me."

He gave me a basket of groceries to be delivered to the Johnson home. I thanked him for the chance and put the basket on my handlebars with address in hand. I found the house immediately and was met by Mrs. Johnson at the back door. I was invited into the house, and I placed the groceries on the kitchen table.

Mr. Hodge's question was, "Couldn't find it, could you?" I replied, "Sir, I put the groceries on Mrs. Johnson's kitchen table for her, and here I am." Mr. Hodge shook his head and gave me another basket to deliver. I carried it out in the same manner. At this point, I learned Mr. Hodge answered to "Mr. T.," short for Theodore Hodge. Mr. T., as most folks called him, had a fellow worker named Cecil, a light-skinned colored fellow in his forties. Cecil and I worked well together. I was working every day in all areas of the store, including the dressing of chickens on Fridays and the meat counter, in addition to making deliveries. You name it. I enjoyed the work throughout the store. I experienced a delivery I was given while approaching the back door of a house. I was met by the lady of the house, who directed me to place the delivery on the back porch and leave. Upon the return to the store, Mr. T. asked, what took place when you called at the home. I explained that the lady of the house barred my delivering her groceries into the house. I was told the lady had called, informing Mr. T. to not send that "northern boy" to her house again. Mr. T. told her how fine a young man I was and if I couldn't deliver her groceries inside her house, perhaps she should find another grocery store. She continued to buy her groceries from Mr. T., giving a tip each time a delivery was made. Growing, yes, you can say I was learning a great deal about people and situations with people. "David, did you know?" No, but I was learning!

Mr. T. and others in the store got on my case, teasing me one evening at closing. I considered it out of line. I left the store on my bike and went home without another word. The next morning, while reporting for work, Mr. T. said, "I didn't expect to see you this morning." I responded, telling Mr. T. he didn't know me very well.

Dad and I were going to a civil defense meeting at the armory one evening. We were walking down the middle of our unpaved street. Dad pulled out his pack of Lucky Strike cigarettes, offering one to me. I lied, saying I didn't smoke. Dad said, "I saw you riding on one of your deliveries with a cigarette hanging out of your mouth." Dad then embarrassed me more by saying, "You may as well smoke in front of me instead of behind my back." So I took one and lit it up. At the time, I didn't question if this conflicted with the invitation I had given Jesus to come into my life. I hadn't told the truth—I had lied.

Lee and I had a good time together. He had a set of drums he played to records he would put on while I listened and tapped my foot. We visited a couple of gals Lee knew who lived on a farm that had a pond where we would go swimming at times. One Sunday morning, we were out for a bike ride about town; our bike rides were me peddling with Lee perched on the handlebars. Passing a colored folks church, we heard them singing. They sang praises to the Lord. We sat for almost an hour, listening. I recognized the lack of joy in my life now being heard by these folks, singing and shouting for joy for the presence of the Lord in their lives. Had God brought us, Lee and me, to this place on this morning, reaching out to me, beckoning me to draw closer to God's Word? It had been three years in my life since Jesus had been recognized as the way of life, revealing the absence of that Spirit-filled person or persons God had called to lead me in the way God was leading.

Ah, yes, I was now fifteen, starting the tenth grade at Dunn High School. I am not able to give you the names of any of the teachers at this period in my life. A very attractive secretary in the school took my eye, prompting those who knew to tease me about a relationship we had that never existed. Shucks.

Time marched on with my working for Mr. T. after school and on weekends. The store stayed open until ten on Friday and Saturday nights. Usually I was tired and ready for sleep. Dad's understanding for merchandising the 5 & 10 store was evident; he had made contact with a traveling peddler. He would get stock from the store, going out into the country, calling on rural areas of people on his routes who looked for him each week. Every Monday he would come by the store to replenish his car. Dad was a good manager. The company would spend great effort in setting up displays of merchandise, submitting pictures with instructions to follow them to the letter. In each store that I had knowledge of, Dad would set up a team of employees who would go into action the minute word got out that his district manager was in town. He had it down to a science. These folks went into action and had the job done, replacing the present display to match the picture. As soon as the district manager exited the store, it was back to its previous display before the district manager entered the store. Dad's displays apparently were successful.

In late November, Dad received word he was being transferred to Parkersburg, West Virginia, beginning in early January, 1943. Yep, another move was in the works. Can you top this in moves? We were once more packing to make the move northwest from Dunn, NC. Dad informed me later that Mr. T. had come to him, requesting that he consider having me live with him and his mother, assuring him that he would see to my education of high school and college. I was never given any information until after the fact. Dad would not consider the offer. When I learned Mr. T. had gone to my Dad I thanked him for his love and the opportunity of working for him for those six months.

It was another move, another high school, this one Parkersburg Senior High. It was a large school compared to the schools I had attended until now. I tried out for basketball, making the junior varsity team. One experience to note was dribbling down the court at Wheeling High School and being body blocked into the bleachers. Neither of us was injured, save a bruise or two. We lost the game.

I tried out for the track team in the spring, running the 220-yard race. It lasted but a short time, for Dad needed a stock boy. Shortly after I started the janitor and restaurant cleanup, the help quit. In addition to stockroom work, it included the cleanup of floors and the restaurant cleanup every night. My grades were not improving. In the second grading period, I received an F in Geometry. I had few friendships. School and work were my life at this time.

I was at work in the stockroom after school, working until the store closed and often later, completing cleanup and distribution of stock to the counters. Dad came to the stockroom door on one occasion and asked how I was. I answered, "Tired." He asked, "Tired of what?" I said, "Tired of living." He turned and left without another word. I embarrassed him to no end, having done this in the presence of other employees. I never heard another word about that exchange.

It was the spring, Easter. Ruth had bought Rita a pretty dress with a little bonnet. I still can see her coming down the stairs. She paused, asking, "Aren't

I pretty?" She surely was cute and pretty. Parkersburg, located on the banks of the Ohio River, was subject to floods in the spring. Nineteen-forty-three was no exception. The water rose enough to cause flooding in the basement of the store through floor drains. You got it, Dad and I, the cleanup team, did a good job and had to elevate stock. At this time, I was sixteen and in the tenth grade. I had improved the F in Geometry to a D in the final grading period. It was suggested that I attend summer school.

In your sixteenth year, did you attend church? On Easter, I went to church with the family. Conversations with God on occasion gave evidence of my belief in God. My talk with God was different than the ones after Mother's death. I had discovered folks found it easy to like me, filling me with joy from being liked. Reporting to work after school one day, I learned the tragic news that my coworker Naomi Hall had fallen to her death in the elevator shaft in the warehouse building across the alley behind the store. She and Betsy Dunlap had gone to get merchandise for the store. As they were ascending to the four-floor building, Naomi playfully stepped off on the window ledge. Before she could step back, the elevator passed her, causing her to fall to her death. Services were well attended by family, students, and friends.

I had never seen my dad shaken by anything harder in his life. Mother's death did not seem to be harder for him, probably due to Mother's lingering illness. Dad felt a deep responsibility for Naomi's death. I had never considered the aspects of my own death prior to this tragedy.

School had been completed for another year. Dad needed to put this tragedy in the past, if possible. The Gills were back in Chester. Pop Gill was working for Sun Shipbuilding and Dry Dock Company of Chester. Dad approached me with the idea of my leaving school to go to work in the Sun Ship Building and Dry Dock Company. The plan was to pool our money with the prospects of our opening a Ben Franklin 5 & 10 store. The idea was new, challenging, and exciting to a sixteen-year-old. I agreed. Dad resigned his position with McCrory once again.

Back to Chester we moved, most likely supported by Ruth since her family resided in Chester. Brother Bob joined us in Parkersburg, traveling east with us to report for military duty for his basic training in Texas. We lived with the Gills for a short time, finding residence at 1043 Eyre Drive in Eyre Park, located close to the Chester Hospital. The Chester Creek was across the street from our row home. Having gotten settled, I applied for a work permit to leave public education. Thoughts later came to mind, realizing a college education was always a possibility.

In June of 1943, I was hired as a pipe fitter's helper in the North Yard of Sun Shipbuilding and Dry Dock Company, working 4 P.M. to 12 A.M. Dad was hired as an electrician's helper in the South Yard, working 8 A.M. to 4 P.M. There were four separate yards: South Yard had four shipways; Central Yard had eight shipways; North Yard had eight shipways, all building T2 Oil Tankers; and #4 Yard had eight shipways, designed for building freighters. One ship was launched from one of the twenty-eight shipways every two weeks. There were four wet basins and a dry dock between the South and Central Yards. I worked in the pipe crew as a pipe fitter's helper, running for materials, learning the tools of the trade, bending pipe when needed, applying dope, and fitting joints.

Russ Crowley was the foreman, and Phil Barrows was our pipe gang leader. The pipe gang consisted of Jack Hemphill, a senior in age for whom I had a high regard, and he knew his craft. John McCauley, in my second year, was responsible for much of my learning and understanding of the trade, contributing to my rate advancement. As were many employees in the yard department, John was from the coalmine regions of Pennsylvania. I also worked with Turk Anderson, Earl Knotts, Jack Barr, Red Innerst, and Mike Kaminitski. Lou operated the pipe threading machines. Red Innerst was the first fitter with whom I worked. I later discovered he liked the bottle, even partaking in it at work. Later, when I was no longer assigned to him, he failed to ring out. They discovered Red in the bilge of the ship, asleep. Our shift was usually done at twelve unless we had work requiring overtime for a deadline. Being tall for my age, I was served in all of the bars and restaurants but one, which we frequented in the wee hours of the mornings. On our trolley from Eddystone to Chester after work, a friend of Mike Kaminitski, Mike Pollock became my friend. Mike was employed by Baldwin Locomotive Works, just beyond our trolley stop. We became the three bar and restaurant dwellers of Chester. I learned early Mike Kaminitski was quite a ladies' man. His twisted smile must have had something to do with it. Traveling with Mike, he introduced me to some ladies I otherwise would never have met. I believe the expression is "sowing one's wild oats"—I will leave it at that.

Living my worldly life, I had little thought of God. It is said we are known by the company we keep; one finds that to be true. Six months as a helper taught me much of the pipe systems in the T2 tankers being built. At that time, I was made a third-class pipe fitter. Many of the jobs I was given were familiar. I had ideas of reducing the number of fittings in installation assigned. In place of many of the fitting assemblies done previously, my helper and I were bending angles, negating the need for elbows, forty-five fittings, and pipe nipples, reducing cost per job. We saved time and material, producing better bonuses on those jobs. It was much satisfaction on my part, and I was given recognition for jobs well done from those overseeing the work. Advancements to second class and first class followed in the year ahead. Working with John McCauley helped me qualify for all jobs. The yard was turning these boats out on a regular basis, requiring much overtime. Many weeks were twelve hours a day, seven days a week, eighty-four hours. My money was used for the purchase of a bond with fifteen dollars for me, and the rest went to the fund Dad and I started to establish the 5 & 10 store.

On March 27, 1944, the Keesey family increased to six with the birth of Jeanne Marie. There was more learning and loving about sisters and entertaining when babysitting. I would dance about the room, tripping and falling with other antics, enjoying the giggles and screams from Rita and Jeannie as they grew. We once had a scare when Jeannie's bottle of milk was mixed with boric acid water. Thankfully, she was not harmed.

On a Tuesday morning in the spring of 1944, I arose with a stomachache. Ruth drove me to the doctor's office, and I was diagnosed with a virus or an upset digestive system. Lunch was packed. Off I went to work at 3:00 P.M. for the usual 4-to-12 second shift, but I didn't last until lunch because of my upset stomach. On Thursday morning, Ruth called the doctor to report the condition had worsened, prompting the doctor to make a house call. The doctor arrived before noon and directed me to lie down on the sofa to be examined. The probing of my stomach while lying down showed no noticeable change in discomfort. The doctor had me stand up. Upon his touching me in the appendix area, a sharp pain went through my entire body. I had never experienced pain like it in my life. I arranged my clothing and sat down on the sofa with the doctor seated on the chair across the room. The question was, "What does your finding indicate?" The response was appendicitis, with choices of freezing it or surgery. Without hesitation, I heard myself say, "It is giving me trouble. I want to have it out." The doctor left, telling us he would call and give instructions as to when to report to Crozer Hospital. At 1 P.M., we were told to be at the hospital by 3:00 P.M. Dr. Crist was to perform the surgery. On arrival for the preparation for surgery, they informed me of the risks of not coming through surgery successfully. The introduction that the chance of death could occur brought me up short, increasing my need to seek God, if he existed. I prayed God would be with me during this time of need. A meaningful prayer was accompanied by a calmness, a peace never before experienced. I accepting for the first time in my life a surrender to my God, recognizing I was at the mercy of God and the doctor. It was a time in my life that I understood God was the need to provide the successful surgery. At the most, that possibility I would know of God's presence, living or dying.

Ruth was present until it was time for Dad to come home from work. The two of them held vigil until the surgery was completed. They were told later a thirty-minute surgery lasted for two hours due to the rupture of the appendix. The poison needed to be cleaned out of the incision and a drain inserted to assure the healing, preventing infection. My life with God has taken a very meaningful change from this time forth for the rest of my life. Had God not been real to me before, he was now. An experience during my recovery in the ward that first night was explained to me when I asked, "What is that sound I hear?" A patient was nearing death with the death rattle of his throat. It was a very sobering experience that led this young fellow of seventeen to pray for another person. The sound is one I will never forget. A lesson learned from this experience is scriptural, through the calm peace, and nothing separates us believers from the love or presence of our Lord. Recovery was scheduled for the next six weeks.

During hunting season, I invited two buddies, Harry Davidson and Bill Madill, to go hunting. The plan was for the three of us to go to my favorite little farm of my aunt and uncle near Ironville. Requesting permission from the doctor, he gave an okay after a month of healing. I have mentioned earlier the importance this farm has had in my life. It proved to be a good hunt for small game of pheasants and rabbits. I met Harry and Bill playing baseball and football on the Chester Baron Team. Both of the guys liked the area as I always have. Harry was our captain and coach, providing good times for exercise and good fellowship. On my return to work, I was invited to join a game of poker after work at some of the guys' homes, usually Earl Knott's home. We would play into the wee hours. My losses were more than my wins—never more than fifteen dollars, that was my limit. My last night to play, I rode on a motorcycle with a welder at work. Frank was his name. We made a left turn onto another street and hit loose gravel in the intersection, causing a spill. Not seriously hurt, we proceeded to the card game. This night was a night to be remembered, for I could do no wrong. I played mostly every hand and won ninety-six dollars. That ended the invitation to play cards with them again. I was disappointed, for I liked the guys, but I also liked the spirit of the gamble.

Returning from work one morning, June 6, 1944, the news brought word of the D-Day invasion of Europe on the coast of France. Sitting in front of the house in the car, I listened to the radio reporting the course of events. I learned of the terrible loss of life in establishing the beachheads for advancement toward the eventual end of the war in Germany in 1945. The need for prayer came to mind, and I did. It was known that Brother Bob had finished his training in preparation for the war in Europe. A furlough home was given before his assignment. In my mind, I didn't know if I would ever see him again. We learned from him that he was going to be a replacement for troops already in action in France that landed at Marseilles on the Mediterranean Sea. We learned much later of his tour of duty during the war.

In March of 1945, I received my greetings from the President of these United States to report for physical examination in Philadelphia for fitness to serve in the military. After examination, I was classified for limited service, leading me to believe I would be perhaps driving a truck or some other job rather than in battle. I wanted to serve, but when classified by mail I was listed as 4F, not fit for service, due apparently to the kick from Homer Palmer that day playing football. Prior to this exam, I had tried the Merchant Marine service. Fifteen of us were lined up in our birthday suits. As the examining individual went down the line, he directed me to get dressed; they couldn't use me. When asked why, I was told, "You have flat feet." Turned down for flat feet. Working on steel decks eight and twelve hours a day in the shipyard wasn't evidence enough to be accepted.

On the train to Chester from Philadelphia, I fell asleep, awaking in Marcus Hook, about five miles beyond the Chester station. I was given a ticket back to Chester after explaining my plight of missing my stop. To me it seemed quite evident there was little evidence of Christ in my life, for I was not in the Word nor was I attending church. At age eighteen, was God, Christ, and the Holy Spirit a part of your life?

On a night at the end of our shift, we were collected on the top of our stairs and approached the deck of the T2 tankers we were building. The stairs wound around like a fire tower or observation tower you found on historical sites such as those found at the battlefields at Gettysburg, Pennsylvania. We were waiting for the whistle to end our shift of work. Many jokes and stories were exchanged. One of the guys told a very smutty, dirty story that upset me. "The Holy Spirit?" Something in me was challenged to clean up my language. Ever after that, I was conscious of words that were to be spoken in expressing myself. Please understand it didn't end my storytelling completely, just made me selective as to the ones I chose. The abuse of my Lord and my God's name has never been acceptable. A consciousness of God in my life has become personal ever since. Folks choosing to speak in this manner, I can't help but have a lessening of respect for them but not to the degree that I correct them. At times prayers are said for them.

Are you able to relate in your life at age eighteen a pretty young lady with an eye for the boys or a handsome guy the girls had plans to meet? Being the romantic I was, I was looking for that special person. But it was not to be at this time. "David, did you know?" NO! Life continued in the shipyard, working eight to twelve hours a day, seven days a week. After the ship was launched from the way, the hull being completed, it was placed in the wet basin to complete the equipping and functions of the engines and generators, including inboard tests, before the initial trial run down the Delaware River.

History records the death of our President Franklin Delano Roosevelt on April 12, 1945. He died at his retreat in Warm Springs, Georgia. His flag-draped casket was transported to Hyde Park, New York. The route by rail passed the trolley stop adjacent to the railroad tracks in Eddystone, Pennsylvania. The time coincided with the end of our shift at midnight. Those interested collected at the vantage point to observe it passing. It was impressive to see the observation car lit, the representatives of the branches of service at the corners of the flag-draped casket. It was quite a sight, a part of history never to be forgotten. Memories of an earlier day of history came to mind. In 1934, after President Roosevelt acknowledged the memorial service at Gettysburg honoring the Civil War, upon his leaving in an open car, I had the excitement of being lifted to my dad's shoulders to experience the President of the United States of America looking right at me, waving and smiling, making me the most thrilled person in the crowd. Today I recall the history that this president had lived most assuredly the place and influence he had upon his time. The surrender of Germany came to General Ike Eisenhower in Reims on May 7, 1945. Harry Truman became president upon the death of Roosevelt, facing him with the responsibility of the bombings of Hiroshima and Nagasaki in Japan, ending the war with Japan on August 14, 1945. We were at Aunt Pearl's visiting when the first bomb was dropped on Hiroshima. Dad was beside himself with the power and destruction it created. I was devastated. Faced with the multiple loss of life, I came to the revelation it brought an end to the war after the bombing of Nagasaki, an end to the continual killing of people on both sides. We couldn't get enough information about it on the radio.

We continued to work for Sun Ship until January, when Dad and I gave notice to resign. Russ Crowley, my foreman, called me into his office to inform me there was a good future to consider staying with the pipe crew. I thanked him for the opportunity of working with him and the experience I had gained, wishing him and his family the best. I signed up for unemployment. I collected it for two weeks, giving it up, feeling uncomfortable with a "handout," knowing I could have continued working. Brother Bob returned from the war in late spring of 1946. I gave thanks for his safe return unharmed. What a surprise, for I was now looking my big brother right in the eye, for I was now six foot two, discovering there was a difference of one inch, myself the taller. We were both surprised to find I had grown that much since June of 1943. The family was preparing to go out for dinner one evening, leading to our both taking showers. Bob came out of the bathroom with his wet towel, snapping me several times, causing retaliation on my part. Shoving developed into a battle, ending up in closed fists. I went sprawling when hit, knocking me across the bed to the floor. Upon rising, a blow to Brother Bob's lip brought an end to the fisticuffs, never to venture into them again. Pleased, Bob said it was enough, but I would probably have continued. Bob, being with us at Eyre Drive, heard yelling from a little boy across the street on the bank of the creek area. He responded to the cries, discovering a little boy about five years old submerged in the water off the edge of the large rock. Bob rescued him, cleared his lungs of water intake, and successfully revived the boy. The mother came over, learning of the mishap. She clutched her boy and thanked Bob through her tears. She told Bob her husband would want to see him when he returned from his work. The father arrived home from work and came to the house, insisting they reward Bob for his heroism. Bob stated he was thankful he could be of help, stating he needed nothing more than an appreciative thank-you. Eventually he accepted a trip to Murray's Men's Store and was fitted in a new suit, satisfying the parents.

We learn how the Lord works in the lives of people, placing them in needed situations. Bob wanted a car because he was planning a trip to college before the fall. He bought a gray four-door 1940 Dodge sedan. Dad became a salesman for Guardian Service Cookware, preparing meals cooked in private homes, demonstrating waterless cooking that retained vitamins and minerals for healthier meals. The menu was chuck roast, baked potatoes, carrots, and French beans. Desserts varied from time to time. Ruth and I traded off on the cleanup details of washing the cookware and dishes while Dad made his pitch for the sale of the cookware. The Ben Franklin business I had left school for and the purpose of accumulating funds never came up again. Apparently money was not put aside for the venture. Dad reasoned a better market for the cookware was in the area of my favorite farm near Ironville.

We moved into the house where the Garber family had lived. They bought the Kreider farm, adjacent to the ten-acre celery farm where I grew up as a boy and learned much of life. Uncle Raymond was working as security for a company. Bob was still with us in the move. We had a family of Ruth, Dad, Rita, Jeanne, Bob, and me—six of us, until Bob's return to Oberlin College. The trip Bob wanted to take to Oberlin prior to his return in the fall of 1946 included an invite for me to accompany him. I was pleased he would want my company, as well as the experience of travel. An experience I will never forget is joining the buddies of my brother, serenading the young ladies outside the girls' dorm. It was not a panty raid, just great to be with Bob.

The family was seated about the dining room table after lunch one day: Ruth, Rita, Jeannie, and me. Suddenly this car came careening down the road. We observed Bob frantically waving as he went by the house. You must know the condition of the road to appreciate the problem in which he was involved. The road from the Ironville Pike was a one-lane dirt road downhill for about a hundred yards to the wooden bridge across the small stream. There was another fifty yards to the incline, winding up at a thirty- to forty-degree angle, crossing two water divergent gutters that ran across the road about twenty feet apart. Shale rock veins crossed the road above and below the gutters. We had no idea he was in trouble until he came driving up the hill, pulling into the driveway around the house. He entered the house, flopped down on the chair, and related the scare he just had when the brakes failed on the car. His being safe, not sure how sound, we all roared. Oh! That 1940 Dodge.

Dad was required to attend Guardian Cookware meetings in the Philadelphia area every two weeks. I was on a driver's permit and was given the opportunity to drive for experience. On a night returning from the meeting, driving through Downingtown at midnight, we were pulled over by a local police officer. He cited us driving thirty-eight miles an hour in a twenty-five-mile zone. The summons totaled twenty-six dollars, thirteen for exceeding the speed limit, plus thirteen for reckless driving. Being disturbed by the reckless driving charge led me to the local state police barracks in Columbia. Upon entrance, I was confronted by a large officer, a sergeant with stripes on his uniform. The sergeant asked what he could do for me. I related my question might not be appropriate for the sergeant to address. I showed him the summons, and the officer stated, "You never spoke to me. You are responsible for exceeding the speed limit. The reckless charge would not stand up when challenged." I thanked him for his information, ensuring him I had never met the officer.

During our next trip to Philadelphia, while entering the police station in Downingtown, I asked who I could speak to about the summons. I was directed to the garage where the chief was having his car serviced. On the hood of the chief's car, he crossed off the reckless driving charge, and I paid thirteen dollars for speeding and the chief marked the summons paid. I learned much in this experience of speaking up for what is right. I spoke with Dad about going for my driver's license. I went to the Lancaster Motor Vehicle Department. I had the verbal test, and the next was driving. Why are we always inhibited by these huge state trooper officers? He filled up the front seat and then some. He directed me onto the rural two-lane road. Driving down a slight grade and approaching a road to the left, he suddenly directed me to turn left. I should not have made the turn at the speed I was going, for had the officer not pulled the emergency brake available between us, we would have run into the culvert. He gave a grunt as he settled back in his seat. He turned to me, asking if I was able to drive us back to the station. I drove back, failing my driver's test, but I passed the next attempt.

Rita was seven years of age in 1946. Bob invited her and me for a ride in his Dodge. We went down the dirt lane, headed for Columbia, going nowhere in particular. We started across the bridge between Columbia and Wrightsville when Bob said, "Let's throw Rita off the bridge into the river." I couldn't believe Bob had said this; I certainly never believed Rita would take him seriously. Why do such thoughts come into a person's mind? In her adult life, Rita still believes Bob was serious.

At the time of Bob's return to college, he asked me if I wanted to buy his car. He could not afford to keep it on campus. I learned at this time my war bonds provided the funds for me to buy the car. Dad was not happy to have me use the bonds in that way. I bought the car since the bonds were mine from my work in the shipyard.. On a Sunday afternoon in September of 1946, my sisters Rita and Jeannie and I took a ride in my 1940 Dodge. We went to visit with Mother's brother, Uncle Harvey, and Aunt Ina. We had a good visit. During the visit, the question arose as to what I was doing in my line of work. I spoke of helping Dad with Guardian Service, and my pay was my keep and room and board. Uncle Harvey asked what I thought of learning the shoe business. The business needed a person in his Lancaster store. I thanked Uncle Harvey with my intent to discuss it with Dad and get back to him. Dad listened to the possibility of me working for Uncle Harvey with a positive conclusion. The result: I began work in the Newswanger Shoe Store at 144 N. Queen Street in Lancaster, PA, on November 11, 1946. My boss was Norman Shaub, and my coworkers were Tilley Tort and Bertie Dunlap. During the course of learning, Anna Simmons, Cousin Simmy's wife, previously mentioned in the story of the family, came in for a pair of shoes, revealing she was having difficulty with the ball joint of her feet. I recommended metatarsal pads for her to try. When she returned the following week, it was determined the pads were installed backward. Boy, was my face red. I was informed this was how we learned. To help expenses, two young ladies in the Ironville area worked in Lancaster to help pay for gas in transporting them to and from work each day.

Returning to this area and once more attending the Brethren Church, where I received Jesus as my Lord, brought questions. I never received answers, for they were never asked. The acquaintance with Jim Garber, scout master, led to being asked to serve as assistant scout master, sponsored by the church. A group of eight boys complemented the troop, challenging Jim and me to the antics of boys full of pep, vim, and vigor. My question was, what were my qualifications for filling the position? Apparently they felt I filled the bill.

On an overnight at the scout camp in the hills of the Susquehanna River in January, we had a great nature study. We hiked in the snow-covered terrain, tracking the trails of various animals, identifying trees, and enjoying the outdoors. The food was good. The guys responded to the experience with, "When are we going again?" May we say it was cold, cold, cold! On the way home, while rounding a ninety-degree intersection turn, a patch of ice caused the rear of the car to skid slightly. Unfortunately, an officer was seated in his car, viewing the skid. He followed us down the road. Realizing he was after our car, we pulled over, respectfully addressing the officer. He cited me for driving too fast for the conditions. I prayed this was a good example set for the boys. The fine was twenty-five dollars.

While approached by the pastor of the church, he invited me to lead the boys in a Bible study on Sunday morning. I informed the pastor of my lack of Bible knowledge. He countered as he placed a Bible in my hand, informing me there was no time like the present to start learning. I accepted the responsibility because there was the sense of a God-directed message. This was my introduction to the Bible. There is a common general familiarity of our usual godly expressions we hear spoken in our daily walk of life. True, learning to some degree, our study in the months to follow began an inquisitive interest to know more of this Jesus, invited into my life eight years before in this very church. Eight years earlier, it was feeling, emotions, and belief that moved me to the altar, making the decision in Jesus. Today I believe it was the leading of God, Christ, and the Holy Spirit. I was inexperienced with the power of the Spirit, but today the Spirit is recognized as the power. I have never heard a witness of faith of family members or their friends. Why? There have been accounts of Aunt Pearl and Dad singing in churches in their youth, not to mention Sunday School. These last eight years had led to no satisfaction of my inquisitive mind. My thoughts were filled with those years of sorrow, laying the loss of the life of my mother upon God. The beginning of God loving me is evidenced by the suffering and death of this person, Jesus, dying for me. Recognizing the changes made in my speech was prompted by the mental processing in my relationship with God through Jesus Christ. Was I coming on too strong? Perhaps for you. For others, certainly not in my newfound faith.

On a Saturday morning, having picked up my two passengers for work in Lancaster, we had a flat tire in Silver Springs, a little hamlet on the Marietta Pike. We drove into the service station garage, presenting our problem to the owner. I explained I had no money at the moment but would return on our way home from work to pay for the tire and offered my wallet as collateral. I was told the wallet was not necessary as he changed the tire. Returning home, we stopped to pay for the tire, thanking him for trusting my word to pay for the tire. Lesson learned. As the owner looked me in the eye, he was convinced I was as good as my word. Any credit for such an observation is due to the Spirit in me, as unaware of it as I was at the time.

During the time working in Newswanger's Shoe Store in Lancaster, driving the 1940 Dodge, the car required a new front-end suspension, plus it had other smaller problems. I learned I couldn't get it in gear parked with front forward on downgrade. I discovered it was in the linkage of the shifting connections. Calling upon my God-given ability, later learning it was a gift, I corrected the problem. Jim Garber operated a garage, telling me he had a customer interested in my 1940 Dodge. Would I sell it for a 1936 Ford sedan? I was offered a trade for the Ford plus one hundred fifty dollars' credit worth of work. I liked the looks and went for the deal. I went for a ride with some buddies into York County, driving through Windsor, Red Lion, and Dallastown. The Ford was smoking all the way. I entered York and pulled into the Atlantic Station on South Queen Street. I discovered the need of four quarts of oil to fill it to the safe driving mark on the stick. Needless to say, something had to be done to correct the problem of burning oil. Jim came up with the plan to replace the engine with a rebuilt Mercury motor for the one-hundred-fifty-dollar credit. The engine installed was so tight, the starter motor was unable to turn the engine over to fire. Jim put the car in neutral and pushed it out of the garage to the downgrade toward the river to drift it to try to get the motor to fire. No results. He let the clutch out, and it came to a complete stop. Jim suggested we push it with his 34 Ford downhill and pop the clutch to see if it would fire. It fired but would not continue to run. To keep it running once it started, Jim drove behind as we drove the Washington Borough Road along the river until we could engage the clutch, continuing to have the motor run. Once that accomplished, the motor ran on its own, without help. Making sure the coolant and oil were circulating properly, we put time on it until it ran on its own. At every new development, I asked Jim, "Is this going to work?" He assured us we needed to keep forcing the pistons until they were freed in the cylinder walls. Fortunately, he was right. It had to be driven at a moderate speed for braking in purposes of not burning it up. An education was learned about engines. Patience and perseverance was the lesson learned by this twenty-year-old young man. "David, did you know?" No, but it was a learning process. God gets the credit.

Transportation back and forth to work in Lancaster, plus the good mileage per gallon of gas, was a profitable deal. Having had it into the fall and winter convinced me it needed a replacement of the canvas roof. This was borne out when Brother Robert used the car to visit his girlfriend, Eileen Moore, and family in Arlington, VA, at Christmas in 1946. Unfortunately, he came down with a heavy chest cold, putting him in bed over the Christmas season because of the leaking roof. Shortly thereafter, the roof was replaced like new. At this date, I can't recall the miles it had on it, but I had much satisfaction having made the decision.

The shoe business was a challenge, having to learn from the ground up. I had to learn the various parts of the feet and the appliances to give greater comfort, providing better fit. At times I was fitting unhappy babies and children, in addition to women, shoes of varies styles. The greatest accomplishment was in discovering an individual in discomfort and producing relief when learning later of the newfound comfort. I gained much satisfaction in running stock and learning the trimming of windows and displays from Charlie Adams. Consider the various jobs held to this time in my life: paperboy, caddying golf, child sitting, celery, plus farm work, grocery business, stock boy, janitor, pipe fitter first class, kitchen cleanup engineer of dinners, and shoe clerk all around in education in the shoe business. "David, did you know?" I had no idea.

You ask how the Bible teaching was going with the boys. I was learning as the boys learned, hopefully. The need to take stock of these experiences, plus the involvement in the raising of celery and caring of chickens, was a broadening of my abilities. Please don't misunderstand; my purpose is not to brag but to get greater esteem for whom I have become. I have given our Lord His presence in it all. Look at yourself in retrospect as to who you were at twenty years of age. Did you hear God's call, calling your name to follow His direction? Not sure? There is an understanding of our relationship. God has gotten my attention, control, and direction? I'm not sure. I'm very sincere, asking you to evaluate your relationship with God.

During this time, living on this farm, memories of hunting small game—rabbits, pheasants, squirrels, and foxes—were exciting. I went to Roots Auction, a well-known country market in Lancaster County. I bought a 12-gauge single shot shotgun for eight dollars at auction. I learned the choke on the barrel was so tight, it was blowing holes so big in the rabbits that there was nothing left to eat. I cut an inch and a half off the barrel with a hacksaw, making it more affective, which was another learning experience. It worked.

Uncle Raymond's brother, Elmer, had a litter of beagle puppies for sale. They were fifteen dollars each. I purchased the male pup and named him Bosser (an assist from Uncle Raymond, his play on names). From the sound of the name, I believe Uncle Raymond had a hand in naming him. He was a wonderful rabbit dog with instincts beyond my imagination. At two months, he kicked up the rabbit, trailing it. He circled and brought the rabbit back to the original haunt. Staid, the rabbit came about, providing a shot, which proved successful.

During a morning in the bathroom, while I was preparing for work and looking out the window, I spied a cock bird in the celery patch. I grabbed the 22-rifle, went out, and propped my elbow on the hood of the car. I pulled the trigger, causing the cock bird to flop all around. Realizing the bird was hit, I went to retrieve it but could not locate it at once. One of the greatest mistakes I ever made, I got Bosser and put him on the scent, which led me right to the bird. Big mistake. Old Bosser got the scent in his nostrils, leading him to become a chicken killer. I came home from work on an evening and learned from Uncle Raymond that Bosser was no more. He had killed him after he had killed six of his chickens. My poor judgment cost Bosser his life, one more hard lesson learned. This led to the end of my hunting during this time of my life.

The times with Brother Bob, recalling the many areas of the country where we lived and the memory of names and faces recognized brought things to mind that were forgotten by both or alive to the one that could not be remembered by the other. Throughout our lives, I have always believed we were different due to the many moves influenced mostly by the death of our mother. Can you understand brothers who experience the death of their mother, yet speak seldom of her passing? Bob, to his dying day, had her picture visible in his room. I always felt her presence. Twenty years of my life have triggered my mind as to where we lived: "in the greatest country in the world."

I remember learning the Lord's Prayer, pledging allegiance to the flag of the United States of America, and the National Anthem: The Star Spangled Banner. I learned of the establishment of our unique government, the Declaration of Independence, the Constitution, the Bill of Rights, and the Amendments. There were the simple things such as the daily train of the Reading Railroad running on time through the rural countryside between Reading and Columbia at noon every day, which expressed to me the order in living in regularity of liberty and freedom of our lives. We had the open right to go state to state without identification with the exception of the examination of fruit transported between Pennsylvania and Maryland in the thirties due to a danger of pest infestation at that time. This is the only restriction I can recall in my life at that age. Your reaction? What are some of the likenesses or personal experiences you shared with folks in your life through it all? Places you've lived, the schooling, work and play you enjoyed, the friends you have had? Too personal? Maybe. That's okay. The Lord knows all about your life, including the things you are proud of and those you are proud of not need forgiveness. Okay, so you say we are rambling with the experiences of our lives? Think about these as relationships, actions, and stories contributing to who and what we have become.

Back to life as it was at this time of our life. An appliance known as cuboids was developed to distribute the weight-reducing pressure on developed corns and calluses, providing newfound foot comfort. For the sale of each one, the clerk received a PM of a dollar an incentive to introduce them to the customers. There was joy of learning later when customers expressed their gratitude for our introducing them. This was enlightening to me, once more learning the necessary parts of being a part of a successful business. What evaluation was recognized of my accomplishments? I received an increase in pay and was affirmatively told, "Good!"

My evenings were spent with the Boy Scouts or visiting with Betty and Jim Garber and their two children in their home. Rarely were they spent at home with the family in the farmhouse. Dad had given up on the cookware business and took a job in a furniture store in York for a short period of time. I would pick him up at the bus stop in Columbia with Rita and Jeannie riding along at times. He worked at that for a time, then went to work for Keim's Bakery, delivering bakery products in Columbia. The fellows previously mentioned in the test ride in the 1936 Ford to York and I spent time playing poker in a small eatery hangout for the guys, where the poker games were held at Chiques Rock. On Sundays I rode double on my buddy Tom's Indian motorcycle to Williams Grove Amusement Park and Speedway. These were the big car races that were very competitive. In September 1947, Uncle Harvey made his weekly trip to the Lancaster store. He took me aside to inform me of my reported progress with the offer of my going to work in the York store, which I considered an opportunity for advancement in the larger store. I would work under Bill Jones, head of the children's department. Considering the distance traveled from Columbia to Lancaster was the same as the distance from Columbia to York, my expenses would remain the same. I informed my family, and they approved.

In the spring of 1948, I was apprised of a room available for rent in York with Todd and Marie Beck and her mother at 110 South Duke Street. Marie worked weekends for the store. She was a wonderful saleslady in the women's department. It was a good financial move since the rent was less than operating the car. Work went well. I learned more working with children, learning of corrective measures used by children with prescription shoes and with the use of braces and wedges, developing straightening and strengthening of weak and, in some cases, deformed bones. Uncle Harvey introduced me to the full staff, beginning with Andy Shumaker, the store manager under Uncle Harvey. There was also Charlie Adams, Norman Myers, Frances Beaver, Bill Jones, and Dick Horton. The weekenders were Marie Beck, Norman Hanning, and Carl Dreisbach. Responsible for myself, I applied for insurance coverage. When having a physical, it was recommended I have surgery to correct my testicle. A decision was made to have it done in the Lancaster General Hospital. Similar to the experience of having had my appendix surgery, I was informed once more of the risks involved in having surgery. The danger of not surviving piqued my relationship with my Lord. In prayer, the likeness of the previous experience came over me with such a sense of peace and trust. The surgery was performed with a spinal injection, which was effective to some degree, but while conscious, I was watching the procedure in the overhead light until my reaction to their movements, when the surgeon said, "Put him under," and the lights went out. Upon my awakening, I discovered a large rubber band taped around my left leg above the knee and the other end attached to the cord to my testicle. I moved as little as was necessary due to the pain it caused. The purpose was to stretch the cord, restoring the testicle into the scrotum.

Upon healing, I was greeted once more with the invitation to serve my country in the military. Yes, I was found to be physically fit and classified as 1A. It caused excitement to think of the experience ahead of my being called to serve my country. Orders to report for induction came a week later. Then a week later, the news reported President Truman had discontinued the draft. I had mixed emotions between wanting to serve and then not being needed, which produced a letdown. This was after Harry Truman had been reelected to the presidency in 1948. I voted in my first opportunity to vote for the presidency for Thomas Dewey. I had read he was a shoe-in. Wrong! The headlines of the newspapers had been already printed, some already delivered for the following day. Surprise, surprise! Was it the termination of the theater of wars, Harry's decision to drop the nuclear bombs? Will we ever know the reasons taken by the majority of voters?

While reviewing the course of the Keesey family since Dad and Ruth's marriage, I believe Ruth influenced Dad to leave a most successful financial income for the purpose of Ruth being close to her family. As I see it, had Dad stayed with McCroy's stores, his finances were provided for his life. That was not the plan. His experience until that rainy day, his run-in with his district manager with little support from Ruth, ended it.

I learned the family was moving to Chester. Dad was going to work for Baldwin Locomotive Company in Eddystone. They took up residence on 22nd Street in Chester. Rita was now ten, attending classes at St. Robert School in the fifth grade. Jeannie was now five years of age. I was continuing to learn more of the shoe business in the children's department while picking up some men and boy customers. Yes, there were some young ladies and women customers, which helped me gain experience throughout the store. Children's experiences were dealt with under Bill Jones' direction, filling doctors' prescriptions for corrections such as wedges, buildups, and braces for a number of children. This had proven successful, gaining greater doctor interest in Bill Jones and Newswanger's Shoe Store. It was interesting to see the progress in helping to straighten ankles and knees with adjustments of walking habits and seeing children at an age going to bed at night in braces. In these later years, it is observed the poor practice in walking—in particular, the younger people. The general public is no longer served by the special personal care and fitting in shoe establishments today. It is too costly today. The shoe industry is out of the country, as are other businesses.

On January 19, 1949, Aunt Ina and Uncle Harvey invited me to go with them to Shaffner Jewelry Store, next door to Newswanger's. I was given my choice in selecting a wrist watch. I selected a self-winding Gerard-Perrago watch, a black-face, silver-hands timepiece, which I have treasured for years. My twenty-second birthday was celebrated with a fine dinner at the Yorktowne Hotel dining room.

In the spring of 1949, a phone call was received at work on Saturday afternoon for me. Ruth called to inform me that Dad had come home Friday after work and was abusive to her. Ruth requested I have a talk with her and Dad before she took action to prevent such abuse from ever happening again. I assured Ruth I would be there as soon as I finished work. Having known of their relationship over the years, there was evidence of Dad's jealousy of this beautiful young woman he had married twelve years ago. How would I get involved with family members I loved impartially? Would I favor one more than the other? Twenty-two years of life with Ruth turning to me as mediator gives evidence of trust in the fairness and judgment as to the confidence she had in me and my influence upon Dad.

As I drove those miles, my mind was moved to my Lord, praying he lead me right in these issues. My mind was opened to the two young girls involved in every aspect of their mother and father's relationship. Lord, help us. Upon arrival, they were seated in the living room. Dad was asleep and Ruth was reading. The girls were in bed. Dad awoke immediately upon hearing my voice. He asked why I was there. I explained the phone call from Ruth, to which he offered no denial about the situation Ruth had related to me. After rational discussion, with little input from Dad, I asked, "Do you love each other?" requesting an affirmative answer from them. Were they willing to provide a happy home for their girls? The most important issue was Rita and Jeannie experiencing a happy, loving home. It was agreed this was not a happy life in these circumstances, especially for the girls. They agreed to reconcile their differences or separate for the girls' wellbeing. My prayer life was of a personal practice at this time of my life. Had we prayed together, would the result have been different? I spoke of my love for them, bade them goodbye, and returned to York.

Brother Bob graduated from Oberlin College, impressing me with his accomplishments. He had received a baccalaureate and participated in graduation ceremonies, affording me an experience of higher education. It was at this time Bob introduced me to Eileen Moore, to whom he had proposed marriage with plans for the wedding on May 13, 1949. Eileen, a most attractive young lady, gave hope one day that I would find my love. After graduation, Bob was employed as secretary of the Alumni Association of the college. Several years later, Bob was installed in the Oberlin Football Hall of Fame, having served as captain of the team for two years. With his scholarship, Bob had worked his way through his four years of college. I am proud to be his brother.

My life in York was the first experience in regular church attendance. I attended a men's Sunday School class in addition to some programs during the week. A young man tasting my independence for the first time, I was free to make my own choices, yet spend some time with Aunt Ina and Uncle Harvey. When I wasn't in church on a Sunday morning, my aunt and uncle stopped by, often finding me still in bed. I was invited to have dinner with them. Appreciation of their interest and concern was felt and related to the commitment in Mother's request to look after her boys. I honored the commitment with respect and love toward them for the years we shared.

I was invited by friends to become a part of the York Little Theatre, a community playhouse. Most of my involvement was behind the scenes with props and staging. Two shows, *My Sister Eileen* and *The Corn Is Green*, offered small walk-on parts. Tryouts for *My Sister Eileen* had the need for two drunks passing the window of the sisters' basement apartment to make a pass at them. In tryouts, I was so convincing, it broke everyone up. I've been having fun at times amusing folks with that character. It was great fun, and I still do it today very convincingly.

The wedding of Eileen and Bob was approaching. I was asked to be my brother's best man. It pleased me to be asked, particularly knowing all of his close friends he had made. Dad and Ruth came to the agreement to separate. The decision was made considering the influence their present relationship had on Rita and Jeannie. Dad had convinced himself he would not go to the wedding. Our conversations were ongoing as to his need to be there for Bob. I told him the time I would be there to pick him up. Once more, he declined. He was not going. I did not accept his stance in the matter. The day of my planned arrival, he was still in the "no-go" frame of mind. I stood my ground that I was not going without him. He thought this over for a time, realizing I was serious. He got his belongings together, and we were off for Oberlin. I knew Dad did not have the finances to represent our family as he felt it was necessary. His fears never realized, his toast was meaningful. It was a wonderful wedding, meeting Eileen's family and friends.

On our return trip to Chester, we were going through one of the tunnels through the mountains on the Pennsylvania Turnpike. A Greyhound bus came up behind us in the tunnel. The driver was right on our bumper, continuing to gear down, causing the motor to roar in the tunnel. As we were exiting the tunnel, I said to Dad, "Keep an eye on the bus." The driver flashed the lights as he pulled to the left to pass. I gave it the gas, pulling steadily away until I saw the headlights in the rearview mirror before he was no longer in sight. I won't tell you how fast we were going. Dad remarked, "I would never have believed the speed we were going."

Arrived safely with Dad in Chester, I took a rest and headed home to York. I was happy for Eileen and Bob, who were on their honeymoon.

Attendance in church has taken more of my interest and time. I am forever thankful for the influence my aunt and uncle had shown in my life. Many friendships are of a lasting part of my life as will be shared on pages to come. The Reverend Dr. J. Edgar Skillington, Pastor of 1st Methodist Church, has had an influence on my life. Ike Aigeltinger, leader of the men's Bible Study class, has left an impression upon my developing faith in God, Christ, and a growing presence of the Holy Spirit. During this study of the Bible, I was learning of the presence of God and Christ in believers' lives. There are others. So many faces without names, even at this young age, moving as often as we did, staying briefly here and there, you learn to make acquaintances and friends readily. It has advantages coupled with the fact that few are lasting due to the brief time moved from place to place. You may keep in touch, eventually losing contact in time. A change had taken place in my life as I had experienced the close presence of God in my life. Scripture was probably heard earlier without acceptance of Jesus' words to his disciples: "Take up your cross and follow me." I asked myself, "Have I heard this before?" It is a searching still pursued to this day. You are a part in what has been my life to this time, reflecting upon your experiences to date at this age. No matter your age, we would enjoy the thoughts of your life.

Two years had continued in York, living much of my time after work with the Adams family. Charlie and Velma and daughters Joan, Shirley, and Nancy lived on Boundary Avenue. I spent time with the girls until bedtime, then we adults were joined by Hap and Haddie Leppo, the Adams' neighbors from across the street, playing canasta and other card games at times late in the evening. During these days when the weather and temperature was right, I played golf two or three evenings a week. I occasionally shot in the seventies. I had purchased a bag and a broken set of clubs.

June of 1950 news informed us North Korea had invaded South Korea, prompting the renewal of the military draft, which changed my life since I was classified as a 1A back in 1948. The greeting came in August for induction on September 19, 1950. Life with Uncle Harvey and Aunt Ina had grown warm as the family related. The support and interest they had given me were the evidence of our love for one another. In preparation to serve in the Army I sold the Ford.I gave notice to Uncle Harvey of my wanting time to spend with Eileen and Bob in Oberlin before induction. They were visiting family in Pennsylvania. I rode back to Oberlin with them. My visit with them was relaxing, plus supportive, as I prepared for what was ahead in the service of my country. Bob's experience in the previous war, as I remember, spoke little of his experiences. I suppose he felt I had grown, having good values to live by, and I knew their love was with me, never speaking of his faith. There were a few stories or accounts of his war experiences, but none he spoke of God's presence with him.

Returning to York, I flew out of the airport in Cleveland into Harrisburg. As the plane was circling over the Susquehanna River to land, I was sitting at the window, gawking at everything there was to see. A pressure built up in my head, and suddenly as it released, fluid flowed from my nostrils. Quickly, I put my handkerchief to my nose, thinking I'd had a nose bleed. A colorless clear fluid issued from my nose. This has great importance, for I have had hay fever ever since. An appointment with Dr. Trimmer suggested, jokingly, that I go up to rid it the same way I had gotten the problem. No, I did not and have lived with hay fever arriving each year around August 15.

In preparation for induction, I moved my belongings from the Beck home on Duke Street to Aunt Ina and Uncle Harvey's home at 170 Irving Road for storage in the attic. I met with Dr. Skillington in preparation for induction, and he encouraged me to trust my Savior and read His Word. He had prayed with me, assuring his prayers would continue for me. I thanked him.

September 19 arrived, and I spent several nights in Uncle Harvey and Aunt Ina's spare bedroom. They drove me to the draft board at the post office. We said our goodbyes, and I reported for induction. We were the first group leaving York since the renewal of the draft. We walked north on George Street to the train station. Salvation Army folks passed out Bibles while we were boarding the train to New Cumberland, Pennsylvania. We arrived at New Cumberland and were sworn in, receiving our first meal courtesy of the military. We boarded the train to Fort Dix, New Jersey, and spent three days with indoctrination and issue of our military clothing and gear. In civilian life, my shoe size was 13AAA. I stated this to the supply sergeant, who said, "You are in the Army," and issued me a pair of 11B. "I told you I wear 13AAA," I said, followed by, "You now wear size 11B." I spent the next two years wearing 11B combat boots and 11A dress shoes. David, you are in the Army NOW.

Lesson #1. "David, did you know?" Know what? Being a Phillies baseball fan most of my life, it was tough knowing the Philadelphia Phillies and the Yankees were playing the World Series not more than fifty miles away. My aunt and uncle were attending games I could have gone to except for Uncle Sam. Much to the sorrow of the Phillies fans, they lost all four games to the Yankees. Can't win them all. They could have at least won one. While at Dix,

I pulled KP in rotation of our numbers. It was ironic to learn that yours truly got the duty of pots, pans, and garbage cans. Soaking wet, sweated, and chilled, I ended up with pleurisy, lasting the remaining time at Fort Dix. Pleurisy involves the lining of the ribcage and is extremely painful with every breath as the cage expands and contracts. Our transport was by train to Fort Bragg, North Carolina, where we were assigned to receive our basic and advanced training. The first morning after the arrival at Bragg, I reported on sick call. I was told by medic, "You have pleurisy. Here are aspirins. Return to your barracks. You are on fire watch." After a day of fire watch, I was ready for duty. Having lived in Dunn, North Carolina, in the early forties, there is familiarity with climate and terrain. Living close to the ground, digging and crawling, gives one a different perspective. In basic training, one comes to grips with discipline. Use and care of equipment becomes more important than care of one's body and health. We learned early. The routine of Army life required each individual his turn on KP, which as you recall already was an experience at Fort Dix for Private David. Reporting to the mess hall, the cook said, "Keesey, pots, pans, and garbage cans." Who told him I was an expert at pots, pans, and garbage cans?

My Bible is important to me, though not a daily practice. What do I know? Not much at this point. May I make an observation at the age of twenty-three? I learned I was a senior citizen in age to the newly enlisted men, a reason to be given responsibility to lead the first floor of the personnel of "B" Battery 30th Field Artillery barracks. I was to oversee conduct, behavior, living habits, cleanliness of barracks, and individuals. I was given directions and orders by the cadre in charge of us. It was discovered on KP that one of the cooks had more in the flour can than flour. Would you believe he stashed his bottle of whiskey? No, he never shared it. I wouldn't have had any if he had. Basic training is conditioning people to take orders on command without question and to recognize authority. Basic training of six weeks is followed by four weeks of advance training, preparing us to become a fighting group familiarized with our personal weaponry and personal field equipment. We were the men of the 30th Field Artillery Battalion, activated to serve as a 155mm Howitzer outfit. The 30th was stationed in the Aleutian Island Group during the World War II, deactivated at the war's conclusion, and reactivated for the Korean War. Our draftee compliment and cadre were the 30th. According to the aptitude tests during indoctrination, my scores were best in communication, where I was assigned. Our responsibilities were running and maintaining ground and radio communications to all commands, headquarters, fire direction centers, firing gun batteries, and forward observers. Prepared to go into the field for training, Captain Henshaw met with personnel, giving strict orders to inventory equipment to ensure nothing was left behind in the areas of operation. The responsibility was mine to take charge of the three-fourths-ton wire truck driven by Richard Bolton. Sergeant Ripley, a training cadre, was our communications head, ordering our truck to turn an entrenching shovel to him when we entered the area. Having completed the exercise, the order was given to evacuate the area. Ripley ordered us to join the column. We refused, citing the lack of the entrenching shovel he had not returned. Word came down, asking why the column was not falling in line. Ripley ordered us again to join the column. If we did not obey his order, I would be written up for disobeying an order. Under protest, we pulled into the column. We turned our equipment in to the supply room and went to our barracks to care for our personal equipment. I was attending to my personal equipment when the orderly called me to the supply room. When I arrived, I was asked by the supply sergeant where the entrenching tool was on our truck. I asked, "Had it not been turned in to you?" In explaining what had taken place in the field, the supply sergeant insisted I personally would be charged for the shovel. An argument ensued and voices got higher and hotter, bringing Captain Henshaw into the fray. Not knowing he was behind me, I continued insisting we were not responsible for the tool. Everyone had come to attention. I turned around, discovering the Captain. I snapped to attention. We heard the sergeant starting to explain the reason for the ruckus. The Captain said, "Keesey, what's the problem?" The sergeant kept on talking. The Captain said, "Sergeant, I'm asking Keesey. Continue, Keesey." I related that the shovel incident was the reason we would not join the column. Captain heard my story related to Sergeant Ripley. The Captain said, "Keesey, you're dismissed." The orderly told me Sergeant Ripley was called to the supply room and made responsible for the shovel if never found. I never heard any more about the situation. Another lesson learned.

Military life is character building for those taking orders as commands of authority are given. Personalities are put aside in following instructions with direction, refusing to ask why with little time for explanation. I liked the discipline, the rigid order of command, so long as personal considerations were avoided. Inspection of equipment was found to be rewarding, meeting the fulfillment of requirements, which were often the key for weekend passes. Guard duty was an assignment we each pulled, rotating daily the complement of the battery of a hundred and thirty men, plus officers. As a rule, Nichols and I, upon appearance at inspection, were colonels, orderly or supernumerary. The orderly accompanied the colonel during his numerous routines. The supernumerary slept in the guard house, called upon to replace a guard taken ill, unable to walk his post. There were times replacement was necessary, and we were called upon to pull the duty. Two hours on, four hours off, two hitches in a twelve-hour night. The duty was required in all kinds of weather. At times our imagination had us seeing objects and movements of shapes that weren't present. It could be scary, and it made the hair on our necks stiffen. At times we heard ourselves challenge, "Who goes there?"

During our advanced training on the use of our equipment, and firing of our weapons, the 30-cal. carbine for the rating of our proficiency, the exercise of crawling through the infiltration course under live rounds fired overhead tested us under fire. Some found this to be a very trying experience. More than one would freeze under the fire, causing a ceasefire to get them off the course. You felt the threat causing to freeze. A tactical exercise required the squad to advance covering flanks using live ammunition.

There was much parading and close-order drilling, creating a particularly trying time for me. Our outfit was blessed with a First Lt. Speedman, new to our outfit. He would approach our formation, reviewing our appearance. He had us dress right dress, calling us to line up on the individual on our right. As he came down the line, he stopped in front of me and directed me to straighten my helmet liner. It was customary to place your forefinger and large finger together between your nose and the front rim of the helmet liner. After several formations, I was told to line up my helmet liner, never to his satisfaction, resulting in my being directed to give him twenty-five pushups. More than once it wasn't enough, causing twenty-five more pushups. At times I was unable to prevent a smile that come on my face, which didn't help me, I am sure. This went on for several formations, always me being the one singled out of our formation of some thirty men.

One evening Sergeant Green, our barracks NCO, called me into his quarters, asking me to close the door. He offered me a seat, asking if I knew Lieutenant Speedman. I told him I know him now but I never had seen him before he joined our unit. He questioned if I knew why I was the one he singled out in formation. I responded, "David didn't know." At a later time scuttlebutt had it, men from our outfit would be selected as replacements to Korea. Our training completed qualified our unit in specific areas of service to fill certain needs. Men from our barracks on the second floor were from communication personnel, firing battery personnel, fire direction personnel, and forward observers. In addition to the thirty-three of our enlisted people, two officers from our battery were ordered to pack their gear. In my area, Kohl to my right and Kershner to my left, were told to pack their personal equipment. We had lived together for four months. These were tough farewells. More than one night I lay awake, questioning how they were chosen. When might our names come to follow them? It came home to me this was why we were there, in defense of our people and our nation. The faces of several of our guys came to mind as to the lack of seriousness they placed on training. Had it never been realized or brought to mind before, it settled into our being witnesses watching our buddies depart. The question asked repeatedly was, what of those selected who lost their lives and those wounded? Why not me? I prayed for the others, giving thanks for the life given to us, to me, who lived. Am I in the plan of God?

The number leaving was thirty-three men, compliment of our "B" Battery. On their departure, the 1st Sergeant called me to the orderly room, presenting the request to have me take charge of thirty-three replacement rookies to fill those vacancies. I accepted the assignment, realizing at a later time I had been tested to determine my ability, my temperament of being capable to perform this assignment. Remember 1st Lt. Speedman? Thirty-three men were replacing those assigned for service in Korea. Would I be up to it? Responsibilities in training barracks life routine were making bunks, taking care of equipment, dressing for formations, scheduling of time, marching to and from formation areas, marching to mess hall, close order drill, and my assignment was marching with a drum, giving cadence to left, right cadence. The men hailed from different parts of the country: New York, Virginia, hills of West Virginia, Alabama, Georgia, Indiana, Illinois, and Washington State. A representation of many states coupled with different levels of learning. I was soon to learn the need for understanding and patience.

Evenings were often spent reading a letter for one or two who were unable to read fluently, at the same time requiring the writing of a letter or two for those in answer to the letter they had received. One evening when talking with our buddies, I was referred to as "Mother Keesey." You might know, the name stuck among the group. I felt like a mother hen enjoying the work that had to be done. Basic training went well except for those few who, for one reason or another, needed time and instruction in bonding as the team. Actually, the initial group I was trained with was more rebellious than this group, with one or two exceptions.

A New Yorker decided a month into training the Army was not for him, going AWOL, only to be brought back by MP's. He served his discipline and off he went again. Two fellows had to be reminded of cleanliness, which a trip to the shower, accompanied by the scrubbing brush, made the point necessary for improvement. One with heavy foot odor required help from the medics. Much time was spent on the parade field, learning your right foot from your left in cadence kept by the beating of a drum. I supplied the drum beat when the left foot was supposed to hit the ground. I was led to believe why I was chosen to serve in this capacity. I learned Private Keesey had the disposition to be in control of the problems confronting him. Basic training completed in six weeks, we moved ahead.

Advance training became another story, particularly in the handling of their weapons. We had a ceasefire in infiltration exercises twice, when two men froze, crawling under barbwire under fire of live ammunition. Ceasefire took place in the tactical exercise when a live round hit a tree not far from my head. A jammed chamber was the cause. Fortunately, we observed a soldier trip jamming his carbine muzzle into the ground, and we got to him before he attempted to fire the weapon again. An assignment to introduce communication line equipment was given me in a seminar out of doors, where small groups of enlisted men were familiarized with the specialties of an artillery battalion. A colonel observing the presentation questioned Sergeant Green as to my rank. There were no stripes on my uniform. Sergeant Green informed the colonel I was up for advancement. Sergeant Green informed me of the exchange between him and the colonel. In the colonel's opinion, I should be a recognized rank. At this point in their training, they were shown a film to impress them with the risks and the finality of war lying ahead of them. Their attitude was receptive to the need to learn everything they could in most individuals, for it could be the difference between life and death for them. Some of the people in the group I trained with either didn't take this seriously or they were covering up their fear of combat. The first person had been used in much of these experiences, for I was in most cases the one training. I lost some respect for areas of military life for the lack of rigid discipline. My military experience had given much growth to my life, acknowledging a need for a closer walk with God.

Having completed the assignment with the recruits, I was called to the orderly room to be complimented by 1st Sergeant Davis for the work with the recruits. He informed me it was the command's decision to send me to Camp Chaffee, at Fort Smith, Arkansas, for leadership training. Was I receptive to those orders? Given time and thought, I realized I was not being told what to do. It was my decision. The course was six weeks, beginning the last two weeks in May and all of June. Most of my life, I have waffled with the value one would have in God's intent to use that individual, me, to the capacity and effectiveness of representing His Kingdom. When we question our service for God, we question the Word of the Bible, acknowledging the many people God selected to bring his way of life into their living as examples for generations to come. Are we questioning our belief, our faith in God's Word?

Accepting the new assignment, I was driven to the train station in Fayettville, North Carolina, on Thursday. I traveled by train to Florence, South Carolina, where I changed trains for Birmingham, Alabama. I was unable to find the train scheduled to leave from Birmingham according to my timetable. I learned the train was leaving from a different station across the street, overlooking the rail line that was down an outside set of stairs about fifty feet to the platform below. I boarded the train for Memphis, Tennessee, then on to Arkansas. In the club car, I made acquaintances with several officers proving to be regular men to share their time and a drink with an enlisted man with the rank of corporal.

While asleep in my berth, I was awakened at 4 A.M., informed we were at my destination. Grabbing the duffle bag with all of my belongings, I debarked and watched the train go out of sight. A large brick unlit building was outlined by the night sky. There were no lights in sight in any direction. My question was, Lord, where am I? A good half-hour later, headlights appeared on the horizon to the west. I discovered it was a Jeep carrying a man and a German Shepherd dog. When asked where I was going, I responded, "Camp Chaffee, Fort Smith." I was told I would have to go in to town to the highway to catch a bus. "How far is the town from here?" "Three miles," he told me in the same breath. He said I was welcome to ride with him and Frank, the dog. On the way to town, Frank smelled me all over from the back seat. I behaved myself. I learned as we rode the mayor, postmaster, sheriff, and dogcatcher all in one was taxiing me to town. When we arrived in town, I thanked the man of many jobs who directed me to a restaurant for breakfast.

At breakfast I was told the highway to catch the bus was at the edge of town, about two blocks. I would purchase the ticket from the driver. Two hours later, the bus arrived and I headed for Fort Smith at 9 A.M. Since it had been five hours since I debarked from the train, I slept most of the way on the bus and arrived in Fort Smith at noon. Never having ever been in these parts before, I suppose it was written all over me. Guess what? I was across the street from a storefront advertised as the saloon. I forgot my ten-gallon hat and cowboy boots, but I went in anyway. Hungry, I ordered a salad, steak, and potatoes. The food was served, displaying in front of me the largest steak I had ever seen, let alone eaten. How big was it, you asked? The plate was the size of a table platter served in the center of the table at home for the entire family. It was a foot in length, eight inches across. The steak covered the entire plate, extending over the eight inches. I ate every morsel.

I asked how to get to the camp, and I was told a bus ran every half-hour across the street. I arrived at camp, was assigned to a bunk, and took a nap. That evening with a new friend, we went into town, looking it over. We had a walk around, enjoyed a sundae, and returned to camp. Three days later, a letter arrived, informing me that my Aunt Ina and Uncle Harvey were in the hotel in Fort Smith the night my friend and I were walking the streets. They planned a trip southwest with their friends, the Smysers, wanting to surprise me. They had inquired at the post, learning I had not arrived. They were told there was no listing by that name on the post. Disappointed, I sat down, answering their letter, explaining what had happened.

Life has many twists and turns, revealing circumstances we learn to accept. My church attendance had lessened during this time. In Bragg I attended regularly, at times Protestant and at times Catholic services. I was familiar with Catholic services, having attended with Ruth and family. The following Monday, our class received orientation to prepare for training. Mess, PT, and parade formations were daily routine, accompanied by classes on tactical field exercises. M1 rifles were issued. We were taught to tear them down, clean, and assemble. There were five weeks of routine before our field program. We dealt with the use of numerous clothing items, uses of gas mask, footwear, and foul-weather gear. We had protection against insects, poisonous plants, hot and cold elements, personal health, pure water, and good food intake. Class was on munitions use and affective deployment to get the most in application. The chain of command included the proper carrying out of orders providing for troops under your command. We handled personal troop attitudes and gripes. Reading assignments led to many tests determining abilities to maintain information and accuracy, the use of code words for ID, identifying friend or foe. Our final test covered twenty-four-hour assignments beginning at 1800 hours on Friday evening of the last week of training. We were divided into three squads of eight men each, not coming in count to include all since there were twenty-six in the compliment. I was assigned point man in our squad. Our task was to determine the strength of the aggressor force our outfit was opposing. Advancing down a road staggered the point man, right side second man, ten yards back, left side of the road, and so on, including the eight men. Very dark, discovered an individual crouched in the gutter to my right, I could make out the rise behind the person. In the open I was an easy target. I spun screaming, bolted over the form, hit the top of the rise, and rolled into the small gutter, lying still. Gunfire opened up on us from five locations, which gave good indications of forces for report. A signal was given to end the assignment, collecting around a bonfire to critique the results. The aggressor said whoever screamed, jumping over him, scared the bejabbers out of him. We did well in infiltrating the rest of the aggressors' line with the exception of crawling around the base of a farm silo in daylight. I came face to face with a snake. No problem, I gave him wide berth. After we completed that phase, we were again critiqued and given grades. For the last tactical problem, we were divided into squads of four to erect a footbridge for advancing troops. Logs were available to put in place, making it possible to complete. A problem developed. There were two of us left when they got to us, me and a young redheaded fellow, who was eighteen with a very slight build. His name was Frankie. We got into the task that Frankie felt was hopeless for the two of us to accomplish. He broke down. I took hold of him, encouraging him that we do the best we could because we were being observed. He bucked up to do the best we could, which we did. The final test called for the two of us to penetrate the aggressor line without detection to join our unit. Our final exercise completed, Frankie came to thank me for working with him. He was great; I liked him.

Four weeks into our training, I learned the 30th Field Artillery Battalion was alerted to go to Germany. We were assigned to support the 3rd Army Division Artillery. You can understand my concern to learn Camp Chaffee was staging area for Korean replacements. As had unfolded for me, events and changes had been a constant surprise and mystery. As you can imagine, my thoughts were on the unknown future. A week after being first notified of the 30th assignment to Germany, I received word from Sergeant Davis I would be returning to Fort Bragg. After the completion of our course of the last formation was the awarding of the certificates of our accomplishment. One soldier was recognized as first of the compliment. He was recognized as one of the good old boys.

I had applied for furlough upon completion of the training planning to visit Brother Bob and his wife, Eileen, in Durham, Ohio. Two friends in our class offered a ride to Indianapolis when they learned of my plans. I graciously accepted, offering to pay for gas. I thanked them for the time we had in training and their friendship and ride to Indianapolis. At the bus terminal, I bought a ticket to Durham and arrived midafternoon. I had a couple of days to visit before we drove to Chester, PA, to visit with the Keeseys. Dad was now living in an apartment but joined in the family time together at the 22nd Street home. During this visit, Bob, Eileen, Dad, and I decided to take in a fishing trip to

Lewes, DE. Dad had made contact with a skipper to go fishing. We arrived to learn the weather was not fit to go out in open water. The skipper offered fishing inside the breakwater, though it limited our prospects of catching fish. Though we were inside the breakwater, Eileen became seasick. I held the bucket, showing concern for her. No fish, though. Another boat was trolling as we were, and they caught several blues. In an effort to get us fish, the skipper positioned us near the breakwater rocks, attempting to catch black Tautog without success. No fish.

The visit in Chester over, Bob and Eileen drove me to York for a short visit with Uncle Harvey and Aunt Ina. I then returned to Fort Bragg. Back at Bragg, preparations were being made for our shipping overseas to Germany. My friend Chester King, a leader of one of our firing batteries, asked if I had ever done any coon hunting, to which I replied no. He had been offered an opportunity and needed lineman spikes to climb the tree. I said we had spikes available in our section we could use. Off we went, on an experience I will never forget. The coon dogs were great to hear as they chased the coon until treed. This was where the spikes came into play. I climbed the tree and went as high as I could. I shook the tree until the coon dropped to the ground. The trees were six to eight inches in diameter. Do you have any idea the care needed to keep from spiking oneself or spiking out? We were successful in this, my new venture. Both Chester and I had the worst poison oak we ever wanted to experience the next day upon arising. "David, did you know?" David found out!

The Battalion continued the readiness of equipment for our voyage overseas. When made ready, we traveled by train to Fort Dix, our jumping-off point to board ship. After two days at Dix, we approached the New York harbor to board a ship—a troop ship, as I recall, named "Hershey." I can't give you the full man's name. I had developed a cold, I thought, and it wasn't until two days at sea when it cleared up, leading me to believe it was my newly acquired "hay fever." I was happy that was over.

Having often heard Navy chow was good, I now had the opportunity to experience for myself. Food was plentiful for those who could keep it down. My favorite was cream-dried beef, better known in the Navy language as "shit on the shingle." Fortunately, I was one with a strong stomach, a reason to be assigned to the latrine or head. I remained head of the head detail all the way to the English Channel. The sight of the White Cliffs of Dover was great. The ship docked at Bremerhaven, Germany, ten days from the time we left New York. We debarked from the ship and boarded the train for Manheim, Germany. We learned our barracks were being refurbished in Erlangen, a former barracks for Luftwaffe pilots. We were assigned tents in Camp Y79, squad tents on cots, for two weeks. Our orientation introduction to Germany included what to expect from the populace: customs and areas off limits to military personnel, exchange of money, but no help with the German language, and above all beware of the intake of German beer since its octane was much higher than American beer. We soon learned by the number of guys who couldn't get home on their own. The location of the camp was at the end of a trolley line on the outskirts of Manheim. Three of us paid the fare and took our seats in the middle of the then-empty trolley. As the trolley got closer to town, the car filled up with people standing. A young pregnant woman boarded, and as Mother had taught me, I offered her my seat. There was great objection to my insisting until finally she accepted. The three of us moved to the rear of the trolley. We reached our destination in Downtown Manheim. We asked the conductor why there was such an objection to offering a seat to the pregnant woman. We were told that had been unheard of to this date by servicemen. We were pleased to have been one of the first to show chivalry in the country.

Our barracks were completed, affording living quarters we could not believe. The floors were hardwood, with a tile bathroom and shower room. I lived in a room with Harvey Manifold from West Virginia, an NCO, both receiving our staff sergeant stripes. Harvey was crew of one of our firing teams of a 155mm Howitzer. Harvey had purchased a German Mauser rifle he wanted to sell for one hundred dollars. Considering it, I bought it with the intent of going for wild boar. I had been told of hunts. In search of the Huntmeister, I asked a citizen where he lived, as the only German I knew having the individual respond in better English than I spoke, which was a surprise. I registered to hunt on a date in a group. I was assigned a stand receiving and was told not to leave the stand until I was given word that the hunt was over. I saw no boar or learned of anyone getting one. I sold the rifle. Getting accustomed to the new routine, new mess hall, motor pool, and climate was interesting. My MOS was changed to that of Supply Sergeant, Staff Sergeant of "B" Battery Supply. Most of my fieldwork came to an end. I made one trip to Grafenau for bivouac and firing mission of our big guns, the 155 Howitzers. The trip we made in January 1952 was not soon to be forgotten. We were cold; we had eight inches of snow on the ground, and we were living in pup tents, two men to a tent. Chow was served from portable stoves using mess kits, and we watched the steam diminish as the food cooled before we could mush it down. We learned to appreciate the sacrifices our men and women made at war.

While we were bivouacked, an alert was sounded. The Russians were rattling their sabers across the Czech border. Our outfit was dispatched to counter their movements. Nothing materialized, we returned to our position. A duty pulled was checking the guesthouses in the Erlangen community for personnel who would get out of hand due mostly to drunkenness. I resented being nursemaids for men who didn't know when to stop drinking. One night we had to use force to keep one of our charges from jumping out of our moving two-and-a-half-ton truck. We took them to their outfit orderly room and laid them on the floor. They became their worry.

My writing of the account of my life has been and continues to be witness of the presence and growth of my faith in God, and I am prayerfully inviting you, the reader, to recognize the growing of your faith.

On Sunday morning, our Chaplain conducted services. On Sunday evening, some of us gathered in the mess hall, singing hymns and sharing our faith, led by the Chaplain. I was twenty-five at this time of my life, giving thanks for the faith and trust I had in God, Christ, and the Holy Spirit. The Holy Spirit remains in my faith as somewhat of a mystery.

"B" Battery was informed of a two-hand touch football tournament within the battalion in competition with the 3rd Army Division units. Dick Barthold, our battery clerk, got the fellows together as to the interest to enter the tournament. The response was good for a full team and a couple reserves. "B" Battery won our battalion championship. We then played the winner of the 3rd Army Artillery. On Friday we played two teams, one in the morning and one in the afternoon. The first game we won 14-0, and the afternoon game we won 3-0 with a field goal kicked by our coach, Bill Williams. We were beat but anxious for the final on Saturday. Our Battalion CO treated us to sauna that evening, trying to be helpful. Saturday we had no pep, losing 18-0, and were awarded the runner-up trophy. I joined the bowling team and won the high single game, 255. I garnered a trophy. We had an NCO Club on the post, where we could go have a few drinks and food. Some gals had permits to come on the post to entertain and dance with the guys. One particular performance I remember was a young lady slight in build who was a contortionist; it was an absolutely impossible routine. One night as I was returning to the barracks, I passed one of our fellows sitting on one of the motorcycles parked outside of the 3rd Army barracks. The guys on the second floor were yelling at him to get away from their bikes. He was drunk, arguing with them. To keep him out of trouble, I told him to go to his barracks. He told me to get lost, at which time I threw him over my shoulder and carried him to our parade and recreation field. I put him down, listening to his abusive language. I told him to shut up and go to his barracks. He took a swing at me. I ducked, grabbed his jacket at the throat, and told him again to hit the barracks. The next morning, I put in a report. The First Sergeant called me in. He wanted to know why I didn't lower the boom on him. I told the top kick that wasn't my style. Later that evening, there was a rap on the door. It was the young fellow coming to apologize for his actions. I thanked God for the manner in which I conducted myself. Yep, I might be learning a thing or two of the leading of God. I believed I was walking with my Lord.

In March the scuttlebutt was that our enlistment was extended by three months to the initial twenty-one months. We were now to serve two years. Our outfit for the most part at that time was twenty-five percent who would have been shipped out in June for home and discharge. Our Commander-in-Chief, President Harry Truman, determined otherwise. Three of us decided to take leave for ten days to furlough in Switzerland. Paul Fitzgerald, Richard Harris, and I caught a train in Nuremburg, past Munich to the Rhine River basin. On to Baden-Baden, we crossed the Swiss border. We learned about the electrified rail transportation of the Swiss rail service. Our eyes were opened to the Swiss military individuals in full-battle dress going for training year 'round in full-combat dress individually on public transportation. Our destination was the City Hotel in Berne, the capital of Switzerland. The hotel was across the street, convenient from the station. Berne is a beautiful city in May. The Parliament building was surrounded by beautiful flowers and the park with a small pond, ducks, and more flowers. It was peaceful and restful to sit and relax. That was not why we came.

We took in the casino the first evening in Berne. We had dinner, and while having an after-dinner drink a young lady caught my eye, leading me to ask her for a dance. After a smile and a nod of her head, she proved to be a good dancer. I invited her to the table and introduced Paul and Richard. Emily spoke very good English. She took us under her wing.

After dancing, we joined her in the casino. A little roulette led to no wins. The four of us then took a walk in Berne, enjoying the midtown close to the Aare River. The city was breathtaking with the animated figures on the ledges of the façade of the buildings. The city clock produced figures of native dress of Switzerland, appearing out of the walls to proclaim the hour. The feature of the bear pit is a must in Berne. We sat and talked, speaking of the differences and the likenesses of our countries and life experiences while enjoying the evening. Through our conversations, we learned Emily was a model and an artist of some renown, traveling extensively at times. As it was getting late, we had a drink. I then walked Emily home, agreeing to meet her for lunch the next day.

Dawn the next day, while having breakfast in the hotel, we struck up a relationship with the young son of the manager, about five, in the dining room. We were shooting at him with our guns of fingers and thumbs, to which he responded. We then took a walk through the Parliament area and the park, and we then met Emily at the designated time and place. We toured the city in daylight, spending time at the bear pit. It was then that Emily floored us by inviting us to a nudist party. Was she kidding? No, she was serious. We declined the invitation. The three of us discovered further that Emily had an international flavor.

As the day ended, we had our meal with Emily, thanking her for her hospitality and bidding her a goodbye. Three mornings later at breakfast, after our shootout with our young opponent, the father and son came to our table. Over coffee we were invited to accompany Mr. Johnson and his son on a tour the next day. We happily accepted. At breakfast, we had our usual shootout with the son, whose name was Frederick (Freddie). We joined them. We were introduced to his black Buick Road Master sedan, and off we went.

Our travel brought us to Lake Thun. Circling the lake, we passed through the town of Thun, observing the picture of history in the buildings and homes. We drove past the Jungfrau Mountain, but it was shrouded by clouds so we were unable to view the peak. Next we approached the Interlaken Garden, where Summer International Music Festival Programs of competition were held throughout the summer. Traveling the north side of the lake, he pulled off the road to have us see a cave dating to the time of Christ with the legend of a hermit residing in the cave. The history was found on the walls. The approach was steep, winding back and forth across walk bridges over the small mountain stream and coursing down to the lake. It was an experience we were sure few people were afforded of the wonderful history related to the time of Christ. Today the experience then may have been less meaningful than my faith of today. "David, did you have any idea?"

Returning to the hotel, we expressed our appreciation for the wonderful day filled with sights we otherwise would not have enjoyed. It was a rather sad goodbye upon our leaving the son. We boarded the train headed for Zurich, the International City of Switzerland, which was modern, clean, very metropolitan, and busy. In route to Nuremberg, we enjoyed the countryside, in particular the city of Stuttgart. The rubble was cleaned up, though the blank slabs were evidence of the heavy bombing. This was 1952, seven years after the end of the war revealed the few buildings not yet replaced. In return, we had much to share with our buddies.

A month later, I had a call from the front gate from a young lady named Emily from Switzerland. Emily had a showing in Erlangen and decided to look me up. We had a nice visit over a bite to eat. I thanked her once more for all of our time together. We said goodbye.

In June I was awaiting the news of the arrival of my first niece or nephew bivouacked on the airstrip at Wiesbaden, Germany. I learned the event had taken place on June 26. I made a call to Bob and Eileen, congratulating them on their becoming parents. I had become an uncle to Kathleen Mary Keesey. Joy! Our time on the airstrip, we remember the June bugs came out of the ground at dusk, moving four of us to sit back to back, swatting the attacking bugs. After dusk they returned to the ground.

In July we learned of the policy to integrate the races in the military forces. Replacements for those of us fulfilling our enlistment would be filled with other than Caucasian races given time to train, maintaining our strength as a unit. The transition was well accepted by all.

In early August, I was called into Captain Dunn's office for an interview pertaining to reenlistment. My intentions were to leave the military, returning to civilian life. Captain Dunn made clear to me I needed additional training and schooling with the prospects of officer candidate school and promotions. He explained those possibilities should be considered. He asked if I intended to return to be a shoe salesman. To which I responded that I did.

I spoke of a young lady I had not yet met who might be looking for me to marry. Should I change my mind prior to my leaving, he would like to know at once. I further made it known of my satisfaction serving in the 30th under his command. I had no guaranteed future if I decided to reenlist. He responded, "It is true." I would be in another command. He thanked me and wished me well.

In early August, we prepared to turn in battery equipment issued for our departure to be discharged. Transported by train to Bremerhaven, we boarded ship on the ninth of August. U.S.A., here we come! It was great weather this return trip. We enjoyed watching the porpoises swimming beside the ship at night as the phosphorous in the water created sparkles in the water. Going through the English Channel, a series of pictures of the entire White Cliffs of Dover were taken. I have been razzed every time they have been shown, and with some they said not again.

We arrived in New York Harbor at dusk, spending the night sitting on the deck and looking at the skyline, plus the beautiful Statue of Liberty! What a sight! We realized we had been gone exactly one year, August 19, 1951, to August 19, 1952. We had our last mess aboard ship, cream dried beef once more, before debarking for Fort Dix. We spent a few days at Dix, then transported to Indiantown Gap for separation. We received separation pay and honorable discharge on the twenty-seventh with an invitation to join the Army Reserves. No thanks. I left Indiantown Gap bound for good old York, PA., on the twenty-eighth of August. Military life was behind me after two years of discipline. No more receiving orders telling one what to do and how to do it. Men were raised from all walks of life, with differing beliefs and varying educations, and they were thrust together in the service of our great country. We were able to set differences aside for the common purpose to learn how to work together in protecting our country and the people. I learned much as to who David Edward Keesey has grown to be. I like the results of the evidence.

At the age of twenty-five, the maturity truth searching reveals errors in decisions, judgments, actions, and words. Thirteen of these years have been lived knowing my life has changed since the evening I asked Jesus to come into my life. Experiences written about exploring the past have exposed reactions to situations, pointing out a life given credit to the presence of God in my life. Areas are now recognizable with the presence of God's influence and teaching called upon. Jesus is present in my daily life with decisions I have made. God is called upon as a daily practice, though His Spirit is a mystery. The growth in the two years in the service has been significant. "David, have another look at your life, a good look. What do you see?"

A further look shows little learning of God's Word. The full sacrifice Jesus has given for me, the Holy Spirit, a presence of God was totally unfamiliar to me. There is so much to learn.

While home in York, gathering my personal effects from my aunt and uncle's attic, I move to the YMCA. I was living in one room with a dresser, bed, and my radio-record player with records. Records produced the listening to the big-band music era, plus artists of yesterday and today of love ballads. It was a quiet time of thought and reminiscing, plus singing to the romance in songs looking to come into my life. The present includes the absence of Kathryn, my mother. I have spent time daily in spiritual time with memories.

I returned to employment with the Newswanger Shoe Store with the renewal of acquaintances with those I had known plus the new faces. I had to adjust to changes taken place in the two years of my absence. Personnel had remained much the same with the addition of a few. Mary Jane soon would marry to become a Kauffman to the man she had chosen. Ruth Sloat, the office secretary, had retired, and the position was filled by Yvonne Henry, daughter of the present pastor, Edgar Henry, of 1st Methodist Episcopal Church, which I had joined prior to military life. My interest in sports was renewed, following the Phillies baseball team and the Philadelphia Eagles football team. Long ago I forgave the Phillies for their flat performance in the World Series in 1950. Now came the era of the Pittsburgh Pirates to prominence. We, in the store, were followers of the York High School football and basketball teams in the seasons. Some of us would go to Small Athletic Field after work on Friday night to watch the football game. The marching band was outstanding. "The Saint Louis Blues March" was one of their specialties.

I became active in the York Little Theatre and active in the Coed Club, sponsored by the YM/YWCA. I met some nice young ladies and gentlemen at the dances and socials. I was friendly with Betty and Bill, who later married to be Betty and Bill Crumbling. Phyllis Seiker, Helen Kendig, Jeanette Schweitzer, Bob Sturman, Jim Hayman, and others were introduced and be-came friends.

The subject of electing the next president comes to mind while remembering the news that came to us while in Germany. Ike Eisenhower, his availability of whether he was a viable candidate, was willing to seek the office. Information reported about him was reason to vote for him. His family background influence was of a Republican nature. I do think for myself in final decisions weighed in this case the conservative verses the liberal philosophy. Books have been written on the differences. The difference I see is initiative of the platform by the conservative, government welfare handout for votes from the liberal. Enough said for the moment.

When I had returned home from service, Uncle Harvey introduced me to a used car dealer, a customer of the store and member of the Rotary Club they both attended. The purchase of a Chevrolet four-door sedan, 1948, green in color, was a gift celebrating my return from service. I received it graciously with thanks. As previously told, it is my belief at this time in our family relationship a love between Aunt Ina and Uncle Harvey and myself had grown. They may have wanted children, but that never was spoken of in my presence. I gave thought to the unfolding, perhaps a better way of expressing the subject, in the living of my God-directed life. My belief and trust in God gives evidence to the expression "Everything happens for a reason." Mother's request of Uncle Harvey and Aunt Ina comes to mind: "Look after my boys."

My return to church brought renewal of family and friends I had not seen for two years. I learned a class of young single and married folks was being established.

I met Beppy and Mary Baker, sisters who were dating two brothers, Bill and Don Baker. The girls were of no relation to the guys. Pastor Edgar Henry met with those interested in creating the class, determining the possibility. Pastor Henry gave approval. The prospective members of the couples and singles of Sunday Bible Study met. With the guidance received from Pastor Henry, a date was established to elect officers. At that time, Bill Baker was elected president, I was elected vice president, and Jeanette Sweitzer was elected secretary. Our next need was for one to teach the study. Several names were considered: Harrison B. Waltman; Lester Aigeltinger, presently teaching a men's Bible study during the same period Sunday morning; with most favorable being Dr. Lester Johnson, an educator employed by York Collegiate Institute, later to become York Junior College. He proved to be a fine choice, owing to his education of the Bible and human life experiences. The church family welcomed me home warmly, asking about my service experiences. I readily shared my thankfulness of being spared the need for battle combat.

I'm led to thoughts of God's presence and direction for my life. Life with God has given the need for arising on a Sunday morning and going to our Sunday adult class. Following the Bible Study, I joined Uncle Harvey and Aunt Ina in church. They have been that church influence in my life, which changed considerably since my return. Then we would have Sunday dinner out. One Sunday morning, I entered class early, marking the attendance book of those present. A young lady entered and took a seat in front of me. As officer of the class, I greeted her and learned her name was Juanita Hildebrand. She informed me she was a student at Dickinson College. She was home some weekends. I asked if she would like to join the class. She was pleased to join the class. Writing her name in the book, I discovered I had written "Quanita," to which she responded with a smile, "'Juanita' is spelled with a 'J.'" There may have been a slight blush on the part of this young man. "David, did you know?" I had no idea then.

That following Sunday, I suggested I might call for a date. Juanita responded favorably. The invitation was made with a friendly acceptance. During the conversation at dinner, Juanita was free in speaking of her life. After dinner and the movie, we drove around a bit, ending up in the driveway of her home. Juanita was relaxed and spoke of her early childhood, where she and her two sisters and brother were left in the care of an alcoholic father. Her mother had taken Ann, the youngest child, and left while they were in school. At the time, Juanita was eight years old. Juanita had discovered she found a listener. Trusted with this information, I found myself interested, seeking more of her life experiences. She continued. The children were taken to Chicago by their grandmother. They were passed from one relative to another. She and her sister Carol were placed in a foster home. Her eldest sister and brother, Paula and Arthur, were independent, making life on their own between visits with families. Juanita and Carol's adoptions were with different families. The Hildebrands experienced the death of little Warren Jr. at the age of three and felt need for adopting a child. Juanita was their choice. For the better part of an hour, we enjoyed our being in one another's company. I saw Juanita into the house and spent some time with Ethel and Warren, Juanita's parents. It was a short visit, bidding a goodnight, having already asked for another date. In my mind, I was now reviewing the happenings of the evening. I tried not to believe what I was looking to find. What reason had this young lady found to open her life to this fellow she had just met? "David, have you found you could care for Juanita?" Hold on, try not to get carried away.

Another date followed the previous evening. As before, we parked in the driveway, enjoying our own company. Juanita was seeking to know of my life, need you be bored with my life any further. Over several more dates of sitting in the car before saying goodnight, my thoughts endeavored to ascertain if there was a future in our lives together. "David, enjoy this time for its purpose."

During a pleasant evening of sitting on the side step of the house quite close to one another, I was moved to kiss Juanita. She responded with a warm kiss and a pleasant goodnight.

My ride home to the YMCA was one of joy. I was happy with our relationship. We continued dating when our time would permit on weekends. My thoughts during all this time being there for Juanita and enjoying her company prompted me to ask myself, "Okay, is this the girl for me?" I was jumping to any hopeful conclusions, but why not? On other occasions, Juanita spoke of the relationship she had with her adoptive mother since she was ten. She discovered little love from the spiteful person Ethel could be. Warren, her father, was all Ethel would let him be to Juanita.

Many more nights we were to talk, producing a greater fondness for this young lady. During that fall of 1952, I suggested I pick her up at college and we go to dinner, then to a movie in Harrisburg. My need to express my warm relationship with Juanita made me select a small diamond horseshoe pin. On our journey to Harrisburg, I presented the gift to her. She put it on, pleasing me. I came to believe Ethel and Warren approved of our relationship, though I learned Ethel was asking for details of our relationship after each date. I spoke of our first kiss as a beginning. Please don't get the wrong idea. It was not a common practice, as much as I would have liked it to become. You must understand this young lady. She could be very shy amidst her openness in speaking with me about her family life. Had the time arrived to reveal thoughts to Juanita? A big-brother relationship was the vibe I received from Juanita in her opening up to me. One, to share in her story looking for support. Honestly, at this time, could I tell her how much I cared? The word is "love." I was having difficulty after all this time of expressing it for fear of rejection. How does one know, never having been here before with one I cared for so much?

I had always had the greatest respect for Juanita, remaining free of pushing myself upon her. I made no overtures of more than a kiss to deepen our relationship. I never received any indication from Juanita that she expected more or was looking for more in our relationship. Early on, Ethel and Warren invited me to join them for dinner and a show at Allenberry Playhouse. It was a nice evening enjoying a closeness between the two of us in the backseat going and coming home. There had been no introduction other than mine to Ethel and Warren. The Newswangers knew I was dating Juanita because of her membership in the church. I had no idea how our togetherness might have buzzed about the congregation. I am sure Ethel aided and abetted the subject.

Juanita was dating the Newswangers' nephew, me. I was a member of our church. Reader, whoever you are, look at the life you have and are continuing to live. Have you discovered that reason for your life? You are precious to God. Every one of us is in His longing for an intimate life with each of us. Learning has taken place, experiences bearing the truth to the words coming to me from God's Book. God has a purpose for all of His creation, each one of us. How long until we each discover God's purpose? Life was good in my work. I enjoyed the people and experiences during my learning more of the shoe business. My sales included every department in the store. I hadn't placed any metatarsal pads backward as I did for Cousin Anna while working in the Lancaster store.

At Thanksgiving, the time with Juanita was enjoyable. In our friendship, questions asked about my life were answered as to where I lived, about my family, and how I came to be in York working for my uncle. An opportunity was offered at the YM to attend a class on public speaking. The study was titled: "The Dale Carnegie Study." The teacher was Attorney Burg Anstine, a well-known attorney in York. The basic principles became very important to me, being asked to speak at times on varies subjects. I had a need to know my subject, speaking slowly, audibly, and developing the practice of including everyone in the audience by eye contact. To this day, these principles are practiced without need to concentrate on them in speaking. There are occasions when someone may say, "I can't hear you," perhaps due to their hearing or loss of concentration.

Christmas was approaching, requiring longer store hours because of the increased volume of customers. I must tell you of the tremendous business Uncle Harvey and Aunt Ina had grown. On a Friday night, customers requiring service had waited as much as a half-hour before closing. On Saturday afternoon, we closed at 5 o'clock to find every seat particularly in the children's department until 6 P.M. There were times we left the store as late as 7 P.M. Today, little thought is given to foot care, of the nature and services rendered. Juanita had come home from school to my pleasure. We enjoyed being together when time permitted. We celebrated Christmas and New Year's, then came time for Juanita to return to Dickinson. I was pleased to have the pleasure of taking her to Dickinson. I took her things into her dorm, and I experienced a sudden change. Juanita had no time for me. She had introduced me to no one. She was cool, aloof, and disinterested as to my being with her. It didn't take a ton of bricks to fall on me; I just said goodbye. Needless to say, I was deeply disappointed and at a complete loss as to what had just taken place. The moment we entered the dorm, every enjoyable time we had together was gone. At a loss, I licked my wounds all the way home. By the time I arrived home, I asked, had I made more of our relationship believing in the faith I held Juanita had placed in me? My mind raced to the differences in the educational experience we had and were achieving on Juanita's part. Why the sudden change in Juanita as soon as she was removed from our togetherness setting? Words were not spoken taking a difference or offense. I best put it to rest. Was it possible?

I speak of the Lord, for I turned there, praying for understanding free of having malice toward Juanita, for my caring for her had not changed. Searching as I had done, nothing made sense to me relating to the change that had taken place in Juanita. Thank you, Lord, for the experience. I had time to look to the future. True, I was looking very hard for this woman. I came home from the service to find I wanted to fill my life to make her happy, for I too would be happy.

I have always enjoyed poetry of expression of thoughts put to paper. My thoughts return to age twelve, when I accepted Christ as my Savior, not knowing at the time what I really had done. I was growing into praying prayerfully, a life guided and directed by God's Word. Remembering the prayer I had offered, asking for a loving wife, children, and a house with a fireplace, came to mind. Lord, was I wrong to assume? I could not let this rest. Searching, I returned to Dickinson on an evening. Passing Juanita's dorm, I saw Juanita and a fellow sitting in the car parked at the curb. What influence did this have on Juanita's change when we returned her to school? I learned much later the fellow in the car was Ed, and Juanita was engaged to him. Learning this explained why she did not want my presence with her known to Ed. This, however, shed no light upon my puzzlement in my relationship with Juanita. I felt finality seeing the two of them in the car. Poetically, I share my expressions of my deep feelings for Juanita put to paper.

NOT YET!

In wonderment, Juanita could have been the girl.
Would I know that someone when she came on the scene?
I felt Juanita's friendliness with her needs might have been the one.
Her return to college revealed to me I was still alone.
I discovered with sadness the relationship was not right.
It was best knowing now these feelings had come to light.
The next girl I met, would my mind travel there?
Thinking of this past, I looked forward to see how I would fare.

The year of 1953 was an interesting time, only to mention trying to forget my time with Juanita. Young ladies were introduced to me, believing this single young man was in need of company. I went on dates, enjoying nights that ended at the door. "Thank you for a nice evening," we said, and "Goodnight." I never led to ask for another date, not that I would give them a call. These dates were fine but left me feeling unmoved to pursue a relationship. Was it Juanita? "David, did you know?"

I was included by invitation to join my Aunt Ina and Uncle Harvey when visiting Uncle Roy and Aunt Grace, Uncle Owen, and Aunt Edna. Visits would occur maybe once a month. Trips on Memorial Day, putting flowers on family graves and traveling sights in and around Lancaster County, brought stories of David Sylvester's craft of carpentry. David, aided by his sons, Roy, Harvey, and Owen, had built peg barns on numerous farms. Numerous family histories of the lives of those graves we visited. There was always a visit to Mother's grave in Quarryville Cemetery. Standing and looking upon the grave, my mind would turn to what might have been had she lived, thanking God for the time we had while she lived.

I knew of my family involvement in the Masonic Fraternity. My grandfather, Edward Keesey, lived in Columbia, PA, and he was a Mason. My father, Charles, became a Mason in Frederick, MD. Uncle Harvey was a Past Master of his York Lodge #266 in York, PA. In March of 1954, I asked my uncle what I should do to become a Mason like him. I was told I had just asked the right question. A petition was submitted to the Lodge, investigated by the committee as to my interest in joining the Masons. My response was to be associated with the caliber men I knew to be Masons. It passed the investigation and was balloted upon and approved. The next three months were spent learning the three degrees of the Blue Lodge. I was assigned an instructor aided by Uncle Harvey. I became a Master Mason in June of 1954.

In June 1954, Aunt Ina and Uncle Harvey invited me to drive them to West Point to witness the graduation and military wedding of Quay Snyder and his bride. I knew Quay was happy for the trip. It was a grand experience for the memory book. It was during our return to York when they invited me to come live with them at 170 Irving Road. I believed this was a continuation of Mother's request. I accepted the offer. This date as I write comes to mind; on April 7, 2014, Mother would have been one hundred nineteen years of age. Mother has been with me in spirit of all this time after her death these many years.

During the summer of 1954, when Joyce Smedley was married to Kasimir Kociatyn, I had an opportunity to see Juanita. We spoke briefly as to how each were doing. My mind went to what might have been. The warm affection I felt for her was still with me. Were she carrying less of a burden in her life, would things be different? I recognized her indecision concerning matters in her life and thought it was best to forget her. She looked fine since returning her books loaned to me when she was ill. She was now graduated from Dickinson College.

Sunday morning at 170 Irving Road included breakfast and a ride to church with Meritt Wells, our neighbor next door. I recall the stop sign at Queen Street. Mr. Wells told Uncle Harvey to sit back, "I'll do the looking." After church, Aunt Ina, having driven herself to church, we went out to dinner. I was the driver in these outings. It was a family affair, including me in their usual schedule of events. I was comfortable in our relationship. The store was open until 9 P.M. Friday. I often accompanied them going to Fisher's Restaurant for the evening meal and returning to work. During my return from work in early December, I received a letter postmarked "Chicago, Illinois, November 30, 1954." It was from Juanita. She was living with her Aunt Mattie, Ethel's sister. She was working for the Continental Assurance Company. She had gone to the Chicago in order to sort out her life, free of unwanted influence. Question number one: Why after this time was Juanita moved to write to me? Good question? How did I feel over these past months? I was hesitant to respond to the letter. Juanita was not sure how she felt toward me. Maybe she was cautious about facing me. If she spoke of being unsure of me, why was she writing to me? "David," I said," let's not be hasty. Give it time." *Good idea*, I thought.

Christmas and New Year's came and went. Turning over and over in my mind, and remembering the last several months spent, January 1953 to December 1954, I realized the feelings I had for Juanita. Dates with others proved of no interest in pursuing a relationship. It convinced me I had a great interest to determine where this was leading.

Aunt Ina asked when I received the letter if I intended to answer it. I remarked, "That will take some deep thought." She responded, "You know your previous experience. Be careful."

Before answering her letter, I considered her words. I reflected on what I had learned of her life in our previous time together. Reviewing Juanita's life as told to me, there was found on my part a will to address her need for me, her discovering the deep interest shown to her in our relationship. I asked myself, "Are you in love with this young woman to risk the unknown, based on the strength of not knowing, for sure it exists in her unknown love she may have for you?" Explore further your known information as to how the two of us had been brought into each other's lives.

Warren, Juanita's father, was employed by the Colorado Iron and Fuel Company. They had hired him at the American Wire Fabric Company of Mt. Wolf, PA, and transferred him to their operation in the Chicago area. Warren and Ethel met, married, and had Warren Jr. He died at age three and they, being childless, decided upon adoption and chose Juanita. Juanita shared that Ethel wanted to change Juanita's name since she felt it was a name for a black child. The tone of this story gave me all the more reason to reach out to Juanita. I wanted to embrace her needs and be there for her. Shortly after the adoption, Warren was transferred to Mt. Wolf, where he had originally been hired, explaining Juanita's presence in York. He gave evidence of how Juanita, born in Montana, was now a resident in York, PA.

Was I a believer in the leading of God in my life? Would I turn my back on this outreach Juanita had made, seeking to learn my present regard for her? Prayers had been offered for guidance as to pursuing a relationship at this time. What had changed in two months, producing a need to respond to Juanita's letter? December and January had given me time to search Juanita's letter. Question: Was I doing the right thing after two years and now the two months since receiving her letter? Juanita wrote of confusion, needing time to sort out her life, free from the pressure from her mother. I asked again, was I doing the right thing? If I didn't, I would always wonder if the door closed was God's will or mine. In all this time, I had spent these past months trying to forget Juanita. Dates I had with other young ladies left me with thoughts of Juanita. The evidence spoke loudly, and I had a strong urge to pursue this now. I was sensitive to not fall all over myself, expressing the open love I had and had found for Juanita in the months in 1952. The letter was sent the end of January and responded to in three days. Juanita's letter indicated a desire to continue the correspondence on the strength Juanita needed time to learn more about me. Juanita's desire to know more of me prompted my immediate reply. The many letters exchanged brought little disclosure as to the personal regard either of us had for the other. Juanita's letters are now still in my protective care, and I was moved to review them this evening. I discovered a reason to believe Juanita disclosed her feelings clearly, revealing her warm affection for me, feared to embrace. Both protective to prevent being hurt, letters continued. Juanita informed me she would be coming home for Easter. I asked her parents if I might meet her at the Harrisburg airport. Her parents were pleased to have me meet Juanita. The letters did not lead to filling in blanks that existed. Her letters continued to hold me at bay as to her feelings. Her responses to my letters indicated my cautious words left her at odds as to my feelings. Could I tell her how I felt about her? Would it lead to a like experience with her after the holidays in 1953? I didn't need that again.

Letters continued, aimed toward her return to York at Easter. Our letters continued, providing an open door as to what might be revealed next. Her letters in the beginning were signed "Sincerely," then "Always," and the final six letters were signed "Love." In the March 1 letter, Juanita had disclosed a call from Ed. She had an opportunity to tell him it was finished and not to contact her again. A letter revealed the hold Ed had upon Juanita. I was led to believe the relationship Juanita experienced with him gave evidence in her mind to the respect and desire I had shown of taking care of her. This was an indication Juanita had eliminated one of the questions in her mind as to her future.

I learned of a better understanding of Juanita's letters to me. In the same letter her first beau, Paul, stirred a desire to see her again. He flew into Chicago for a get-together, which she described as a final meeting. This letter led me to believe these experiences gave an understanding in her mind. Question: Was these coming together with these two men in her life witness to the comparison of her understanding as to the life I had to offer her? She remained in a quandary as to her feelings toward me. Caution was to her unsettled mind in her knowing how she felt toward me.

We continued writing twenty letters during this time. It is my belief that both of us knew we had love for the other but were unwilling to venture to disclose that truth in the relationship.

April 6 had arrived. I contacted Juanita's parents, informing them I was on my way to meet Juanita. Here she came toward me. I was not sure what to expect, so I said a cool "hello." My mind was trying to handle the thoughts she expressed of being afraid and unsure of me. There was a shy "Hi, good to see you." I responded with a "Hi, how was the flight?" Our drive to York was filled with "Glad to have you in York. You look great. Good to talk with you rather than letter writing." Juanita followed, "You look as I remembered you." We spoke of the weather. How my aunt and uncle were doing was a subject. I was hoping for more, but it wasn't to be. There was evidence of feeling one another out. I took her at her word of being unsure of how she felt toward me. "David, did you know?"

The following evening at dinner, we enjoyed conversation, being together, and looking at one another. We sat in the driveway as we had done before this time, speaking of Ed and Paul and how she had no reason to continue either relationship. I learned at this time she and Ed were engaged at the time I drove her to Dickinson. She feared someone would tell Ed about me. I was really surprised to learn about their engagement. I spoke of my trip to Carlisle, seeing her and Ed in the car in front of her dorm and decided our relationship was ended. I confessed a lack of interest in young ladies I met and dated, coming away from them with her on my mind. I felt a relaxing of her toward me, learning of my thoughts for her. I told her in my letters. I hinted of these feelings, afraid to witness outright to my true affection for her. Juanita admitted a similar feeling of not wanting to be hurt after she related her feelings toward me. Her writings of caring for me later in a letter would change, revealing a vagueness of thought as to what she had already written. At this point of conversation, I asked myself, was I missing between the lines of her expressions as to her feelings for me? In answer to my questions on my mind, Juanita spoke of the encouragement she received from me, giving her an insight to her self-value. Having listened to her own voice speak of her life, she lived knowing I was supportive, not critical. She was given strength and trust in me. I told Juanita of my fondness for her when I would leave her on my way home to the YM. I was excited and filled with the joy of our conversations. I recognized she was comfortable to speak openly with me without reservation, the trust, the confidence she felt to speak her mind to me in our conversations. During these evenings we were talking, she said she felt my feelings toward her as more like a big brother in whom to confide. The evening we sat on the outside step at the side door, I risked to kiss her, learning of her response. Could I call it love or infatuation? Whatever I felt, it was wonderful.

We were unable to speak of these things in the house for fear her mother would enter into our relationship in wanting to know the details of our conversations. This led to our sitting in the car. We went in the house, visited with her parents, and left by the side door, and Juanita kissed me goodnight. Did I have to wait until the next day to see her? Our dating continued several nights a week, growing closer to each other. A Saturday night in early May, while driving through the square in York, she spied Marie, a college friend, with her gentleman friend, Ed Fisher. We pulled up next to their car, passenger door to passenger door for the two girls to talk. As they were talking, Juanita turned toward me and slapped me. I had no idea the cause for her actions other than to think she was showing off in front of Marie. Their conversation finished, we drove out of the square. I turned the radio up so loud, it was impossible for conversation. We drove around in silence. I was not looking at her for an hour, then decided to drive her home. We parked in the driveway. I turned the motor off, which silenced the radio. I turned and looked at her. "Juanita," I said, "you will never slap me again. You will never, ever do that to me again. In whatever state of mind I might find myself in any future relationship our coming together again will produce, I would never think of treating you in that manner. I have much too much respect for you. I care much too much for you to think of striking you." She apologized, downcast, avoiding my look. I took her hand in mine, leaned over, and kissed her. She was reluctant to respond. I asked her if she had any idea how much I cared for her. She said she was learning.

I walked her to the door, and we kissed goodnight. I called her the next day for an evening out. She agreed to dinner and a movie. I went to the door to say hi to Warren and Ethel. We walked to the car, seeing her seated. As I entered the car, I discovered Juanita sitting closer to me. As our dates continued, a noticeable change in Juanita had taken place. She sat closer to me in the car and spoke freely concerning our relationship. I found I was in love with Juanita. I wanted to be with her more. Juanita was responding to those feelings, the wanting to be there for one another. The firmness of my talk after the incident of the slap revealed convictions I had for life, perhaps giving her a sense of what she was looking for in me. No matter what, I was there to take care of her. Our words became free with warmth.

One June night, we had come home to the house and we were sitting in the living room on the couch. I turned to Juanita, looked into her eyes, and asked, "Juanita, will you marry me?" What did I expect? I had no idea. She gazed into my eyes and said, "Yes." She asked, "Will you answer a question?" "I will if I have the answer." "You are twenty-eight years old. How many girls have you asked to marry you before you asked me?" My answer: "You are the first and only one I cared for to even think of asking." She kissed me, expressing her love for me. We sat holding hands. I told her my proposal was not planned, so there was no ring in preparation for her positive response. I wanted to linger longer. We kissed again, and I saw in her what I had been looking for since I first met her. A warm smile and the shyness of our being close made me want to stay.

We walked to the door, and we kissed goodnight. Going to the car, she waved to me from the kitchen window. It was difficult to sleep. In my sleeplessness, my mind was of God, praying our evening would be forever and thanking Him for bringing Juanita into my life. I announced my wonderful news to my aunt and uncle, receiving reserved congratulations, especially from Aunt Ina. Her question challenged me to be sure this was the girl for me. I wondered if she felt any girl was the right one. The ring issue became a subject of concern for Mother Hildebrand. Juanita told me how she was questioned after our being together. The ring was purchased about a week after the proposal, giving Juanita some peace when she would go home after our being together. Was Juanita happy? Was I happy? Just look at us; the answer was all over us. In our affections, we respected our passions until the special night when we married. I believe Juanita developed a greater respect witnessing the respect I had for her and her body. I have been thankful, believing this to be directed in my faith and trust in my Lord. Ethel, being true to form, made up the engagement announcement for the paper, spelling my mother's name incorrectly as Catherine. She never asked the spelling, which was Kathryn, prompting hurtful words from Aunt Ina directed to me, which tore me up. These were words at a time in my life I would find unforgivable, but today God is teaching me to be forgiving. These two women became an influence in our lives, forging a stronger togetherness, owing to the two of them pushing and pulling for a say in our lives, which brought Juanita and me closer in our love. Juanita's birthday is September 17, contributing to the wedding date of September 24, 1955. The question by the family, the two women, was, what is the rush to set the date? Our response had to do with our love for one another and desiring to be together. There was little reason to delay what we both longed to enjoy: our togetherness. I was surprised, for I looked at myself as being easily influenced. Look how Juanita had strengthened me. I spoke to

Juanita of my brother and his wife, Eileen, and my only niece, Kathy, who was three years old. I had seen Little Curly Top in 1954 at the age of two, when Dad and I had made a trip to Oberlin for a visit. "Cute" did not describe her. I loved her before I first saw her. I expressed the desire to ask Bob to be my best man and wanted to do it in person. Juanita agreed, and we attended a party earlier, leaving for Ohio late Saturday night. I will always remember our ride. Juanita, tired, stretched out in the front seat with her head on my leg. This was the woman I felt God had intended mine from the beginning. She was perfectly relaxed with me, not unsure or fearing to trust me completely. My heart was singing. I was totally in love with her.

We arrived early in the morning, and I introduced Juanita to Bob and Eileen. Juanita fell in love with Kathy the moment she saw her. They were pleased to hear of our plans to wed. Bob was honored in my asking him to be my best man. This was my girl. I was looking at her every chance I got. Our ride home was special, hearing her speak of my family. Could I love her any more than I did? We both were smokers and decided to quit the habit. My decision to cut back came about having carried the pack for two weeks. I found one cigarette at supper with Aunt Ina and Uncle Harvey. I lit it up, and it tasted terrible, putting my head in a spin. I put the smoke out, declaring it to be my last cigarette. Uncle Harvey challenged me. He bet I couldn't quit until December. Aunt Ina said, "Harvey, make it worth his while," to which he responded, "Fifty cents." Aunt Ina said, "Harvey, you are the last of the big-time spenders."

Juanita gave up her habit of smoking shortly thereafter. In church one morning, while seated with Aunt Ina and Uncle Harvey, Aunt Ina struck up a conversation with Colonel Haines, an advocate against smoking. He had the reputation of paying folks twenty dollars to quit. The fact that Juanita had already quit didn't stop Aunt Ina; she had twenty dollars handed over from the colonel for Juanita. Juanita stated she had already quit but it had nothing to do with the fact that she had quit. We often walked in the neighborhood, walking hand in hand, discussing our family relationships with our two families, namely the two women. Riding in the car, we sought the privacy in the intimacy of our future. It was a private time, with happy dates of dining and movies, discovering more and more our lives were meant to be together. Juanita and I found our likes and dislikes for our wedding became Mother Ethel's wedding in the planning. There was no opposition owing to our love for each other. Wedding plans continued with Juanita purchasing her gown. Juanita chose Beverly Klock as her maid of honor and Nancy Hildebrand and Elaine Hildebrand, her cousins, as bridesmaids. Brother Bob was my best man, and Bob Romito and Charlie Martin were members of the wedding party. Romito was a church friend and Martin a coworker at Newswanger's. Had Bob Sturman been in York at the time, he would have been my choice rather than Charlie Martin. I was disappointed learning my bride was to sleep in the attic the night before our wedding due to the placing of wedding gifts in her bedroom. Time was enjoyed, knowing we belonged to each other. God had brought us together for life.

Our talk continued being happy with the apartment we found at 33 South Hartley Street, third floor. The furniture was ready for us on our return from our honeymoon, especially the new cherry bedroom furniture, which was a wedding present from Aunt Ina and Uncle Harvey. A garage was rented to get the car off the street at night. We were pleased as we observed everything coming together without a hitch. Would we ever know one another for sure? Juanita's warmth gave evidence of wanting to be with me. I discovered a willingness to accept the ideas and the suggestions offered. When asked her desires, she would respond, "What do you want to do?" The realization Juanita had lived following directions for most of her life convinced me of the sensitive love she needed free of criticism, accompanied by encouragement to speak her mind about all things with me as she had done in our first time spent on our early dates. My prayer was to be the understanding love of her life. This was the role, with all sincerity: to bring happiness in her life. Willingly, I was ready to bring this into her life. I have said my reasons for coming home from the military. At least the main one had been met. Thank you, Lord.

As stated before, bringing wholeness and happiness to the woman God had brought into my life, in the happiness she found my happiness was whole.

It Has Happened!
Once again, this woman had come into my life,
Her willingness was to discover the possible oversight;
To give it a try, to learn what might have been,
Hoping to discover in that something unseen.
Circumstances, diversions prompting heart to tarry.
The time might have been wrong, our interest varied.
It is another day we go forward,Let us two marry.

As I confessed in the beginning what I felt in my heart,
Was real beyond question I had known from the start.

I am so grateful we're afforded this our second chance,
Knowing in our hearts we have found our romance.
Thanks be to our Father and our God for He knows best,
The results were that we had ventured, the journey with success.

I honestly believed this marriage was to be made in heaven. Heaven, my faith was experiencing a deepening beyond all expectations I had. My trust was in God, knowing this was right for Juanita and me. The day of our coming together after the slap incident in the square left not a doubt that Juanita had arrested the uncertainties as to our relationship being right without question.

The day had arrived, Juanita's and my wedding day. The day dawned wet with rain falling and heavy overcast. Bob and I shopped for a few last items for the honeymoon, enjoying our time to be together on this special day. I thanked Bob for our lives shared, his influence, his guidance, and his patience, and most of all for his love he had always had difficulty expressing. Two o'clock was approaching. The weather had lifted, allowing family and friends a dry entrance into the church. Pastor Henry was to perform the service. Bob and I were in the church secretary's office just off the sanctuary when Charlie Martin entered from the basement, informing us the bride's father had forgotten his tie. I recall telling Charlie, "Don't tell us. Tell the pastor." Uncle Earl, Dad's brother, was sent home to get the tie. After the small delay, the service began. Bob and I assumed our positions as the music began. Enter the bridesmaids, Elaine Hildebrand and Nancy Hildebrand, and the maid of honor, Beverly Klock. I was looking for Juanita. She came down the aisle on the arm of her father, Warren. It was a beautiful sight I had pictured since the night she said yes to my proposal. Warren said those expected words: "Her mother and I do." I took hold of her hand, squeezing it lightly as I looked at her through the veil. Pastor Henry began the exchange of vows on the main floor. We moved to the altar, and it came time to turn to one another. I looked into her beautiful eyes, a question in my mind. What did this pretty young lady see in me? God was strong in the commitment I made to Juanita. I felt moisture in my eyes as I gazed at her, feeling the oneness joining us together in complete belief God willed this to be right. God had brought us together for a lifetime. I heard, "You may kiss the bride." I needed no second invitation. We were married. We were one before God and everyone present.

The reception line brought love and good wishes from all family and many friends alike. The reception was held in the large classroom on the second floor of the education section of the church. Brother Bob's toast cemented the joy of the day. Jim Hayman was our photographer. Pictures have been reviewed many times, which was his wedding gift. The Hildebrand family was well represented, Grandmother Lilley and Grandfather John. Also was Uncle Earl and Aunt Mary, Uncle Les and Aunt Edna Conrad, Aunt Anna and Uncle John Krebs, and Aunt Ruth and Uncle Raymond Warner. Uncle Harvey and Aunt Ina represented as my mother and dad. Dad was not present. There was also Aunt Pearl and Uncle Raymond, Uncle Roy and Aunt Grace, and Uncle Owen and Aunt Edna. Velma Adams, with daughters Shirley and Nancy, was present. Joan wouldn't come; she had made up her mind I was to marry her. I was to wait for her to grow up. Many church friends from both families attended.

The reception over, both of us went to our respective homes to change for our trip to New York. Reservations were made at the Taft Hotel. The 1950 Buick was in the garage at 170 Irving Road under lock and key. As I backed the car out of the garage with much supervision, I heard the rattle of stones in the hubcaps of the wheels. I learned Pastor Henry convinced Aunt Ina and Uncle Harvey to produce the key to satisfy the need to remember this, our day. With bag packed and loaded in the trunk, off I went with an escort to 1309 South Queen Street to pick up my bride. She was wearing a tan tweed jacket and skirt as lovely as ever. I loaded her bag and off we went, followed by several cars blowing their horns. We were driving out Rathton Road to Ogontz Street and applied brakes at a stop sign. I slid into the intersection, but nothing was coming. We left town out the East Prospect Road, discovering our escort went another route. We turned left onto Valley View Road to Route 30. We learned upon our return Jim Hayman was friendly with a state trooper, and he had posted to intercept us on Route 30. We had passed where he waited, having traveled East Prospect Road beyond where he lay in wait. We were on the New Jersey Turnpike when we stopped to get supper and heard on the radio in the car that President Eisenhower had a heart attack. I took the time to remove the stones from the hubcaps at this time.

We arrived at the hotel just before eleven. In this entire day, I felt so right with this woman who consented to become my bride. We were and are so a part of each other. Writing about the uniting of the two of us today fills me with love and gratitude to God. God is so good, all the time.

We entered our room and closed the door. I took Juanita in my arms, kissed her, and asked if she was happy. The kiss I received gave me my answer, revealing her happiness. We prepared to change for bed. I discovered my pajama legs were sewn closed at the ankles. Could I believe Aunt Ina would do such a thing? I supposed I could, for she did it. Having changed, Juanita came from the bathroom to a rap on our door. There stood the bellhop with a bottle of champagne, wishing us congratulations. My love and devotion to this woman, my wife had come about in answer to my prayers for a second chance with Juanita. I did not believe God would bring her into my life a second time, though I felt so strongly from the beginning we had every reason to believe our lives were made for each other.

Our coming together as husband and wife and the excitement in our becoming one missed the endearment I wanted for our intimacy. It came later. We enjoyed the shows for which we had received tickets in advance. We saw Red Skeleton's rehearsal preparation for his appearance for the *Dave Garroway Show*. We visited the Kelly Restaurant to enjoy their famous Reuben sandwich, which I had enjoyed on a previous trip with Aunt Ina and Uncle Harvey. We enjoyed our trip to the Empire State Building. On the one hundredth floor, we took in the view and entered the elevator, thinking we were on the top floor, then we discovered we were going up. Juanita looked at me with disbelief, but to the tower we went, the 108th floor, a view unbelievable from that height. We passed the Little Church around the Corner, St. Patrick's Cathedral, and passed Grant's Tomb in our travels along the Hudson River.

On Tuesday, we called for the car and drove to Battery Park. We took the boat to the Statue of Liberty and climbed the steps up into the head. The arm and torch were under repair, preventing us from going higher. On the boat returning to Battery Park, the foreign-language-speaking folks and the big city prompted Juanita to say, "Let's get out of this town. I've heard and seen enough." We called for the car. As the attendant brought the car and spied the rice in the back seat, he said, "What have we here?" with a big smile on his face. We decided to go north to Watkins Glen and stopped at a Chalet Restaurant for dinner. We spent the night at a motel overlooking Seneca Lake.

The next morning, I arose and looked out the window. Seeing nothing, I rubbed my eyes, discovering fog so thick the lake was not visible. After breakfast in the motel restaurant, we drove to Watkins Glen. Walking the distance up the grade to the top, we enjoyed our stroll hand in hand.

On Thursday, we journeyed through Corning, where the glass company is located, down Route 15, and there was a sign directing us to Shikellamy State Park, which caught our attention. While exploring, we found grounds that had burros and other animals roaming around. It was a beautiful view looking out across the valley over the Susquehanna River. Relaxed, we drove for York and home.

We arrived home to our third-floor apartment at 33 South Hartley Street. We discovered some groceries had been brought in by family, which perturbed me a bit. Lord, help me with my attitude. They wanted to be a part of our lives, so I shouldn't shut them out. The rest of the weekend was ours, shopping for a few things and enjoying our time together.

On Sunday morning, we drove to church for the first time as husband and wife enjoying the weekend together. Going to work Monday morning would be difficult. You might have guessed the reception I received the first morning back at work. The comment about my going home for lunch was introduced with smiles and raised eyebrows. We decided I would come home for lunch. While eating I wanted to linger a little longer, and longer could have been the rest of the afternoon. Dinners on Sunday were often spent with Juanita's parents or Aunt Ina and Uncle Harvey. Juanita wanted to prepare a meal for the six of us. She did a wonderful job. We learned having the women together was not very desirable. It was enjoyable recognizing the pleasing expressions they witnessed in our love. I was amazed to find we were free of mentioning or calling attention to those little quirks or habits we might have that would have led to remarks or comments. I found happiness in every moment that was ours ever since the episode in the square that evening with Marie and Ed. I was free of being fearful of saying the wrong words, a free openness on the part of both of us convinced of our joy of togetherness.

In October of 1955, after our marriage, Juanita petitioned the Eastern Star, the women's organization in likeness to the men's Masonic body. She was approved, becoming a member. Juanita made an application to York School District to substitute teach, working in the Hannah Penn Middle School when needed. She would come home, sharing some of the scary experiences that were not to my likeness. Life moved on, living in our Hartley Street address until spring of 1956. While visiting Aunt Ina and Uncle Harvey on a Friday night after Juanita had picked us up after work, we spent some time before going home. One particular evening, the subject of buying a home was brought up, introduced by Aunt Ina. They said they had put aside the money I had been paying them for room and board. Those funds available, they suggested we look for a house if we were in agreement with their offer. We thanked them, intimating we were interested. The search was on, looking at several homes for sale. We learned of the Pyle home, Charles and Lillian, members of 1st Methodist Church, who were moving out of town. Charles' firm was transferring him to another district. It was a Cape Cod-style with dormer windows, six rooms, a bath and a half, and a finished basement with an attached garage. It was nice with an acceptable price. The address was 777 Grandview Road.

I was home from the service and returned to my previous job, and I met a beautiful woman, discovering she was the love of my life, resulting in our marriage after my third year home. My mind recalls the discussion I had with Captain Dunn prior to my return home from Germany. I was looking forward to my previous job and the prospects of finding the girl of my dreams, realizing in this short time the Lord had provided the answer to my prayers. I believe with all my heart faithfulness to the Word of God produces fulfillment and happiness. We bow, thanking God for His blessings. He continues to pour blessings upon our marriage. I am unable to measure in the history of my life the lessons of love God has showered on me.

We wanted a family. Juanita was learning of friends having children, which increased the desire for us. In July 1956, we learned Juanita was pregnant. The search for names began: Cynthia Louise for a girl, Timothy Blaine for a boy. Our families were excited with the anticipation that lasted but a short time. Juanita experienced a miscarriage after two months. Dr. Trimmer came to the house, confirming a miscarriage had taken place and offering at the time his encouragement to try again. There was a problem; this was the body addressing it.

In the summer of 1956, my friend Bob Sturman returned from his employment in Washington, D.C., to take a job with the Bon Ton Department Store. In our discussion of retail work, we kicked the idea around of going into business for ourselves. I discussed the idea with Juanita, finding support should this be our decision. Once more, there was evidence of the confidence my wife had for me. To carry this idea further, we discussed it with Uncle Harvey and Aunt Ina. I heard Aunt Ina remind Uncle Harvey the words his father, David Sylvester, told him when he spoke with him about going into business. He had said, "Nothing ventured, nothing gained." Our decision was a technical business of television sales and service. More discussion led to contacting DeVry Technical Institute in Chicago, inquiring about more information. Returning from work one evening, Juanita informed me a representative from DeVry had stopped to talk to me personally. Juanita impressed him so with her high confidence in her husband that he wanted to talk to me in person. He made arrangements to stop back that evening. He arrived around 8 P.M., conversing several hours over two pots of coffee. I signed up for courses in basic electricity and electronics. When informed of my tenth-grade education, it did not influence his decision to sign us up. The cost of the correspondence course was five hundred dollars. We gave him a check for fifty dollars, agreeing to pay fifty dollars a month. He gave Juanita and I every assurance from his experience I would complete the course just in speaking with both of us. Might I speak my mind, knowing of the confidence Juanita had shown in our decision? I realize the continued reference to the love Juanita and I have represents the faith in God we have spread upon these pages, meaningful in the manner our Lord brought us together in our lives. I must speak of this woman in my life. She has shown so much faith in this man she has married. Her encouragement in the months and the three years taken to complete the studies was constant without criticism or doubt. I am in love!

The fall of 1956, Juanita went to work in the Red Lion School District at Windsor Manor Elementary Building. Juanita was pleased with the position she was hired to fill. In April of 1957, Juanita learned she was pregnant. She completed the year teaching at Windsor Manor. During vacation time for me in the summer, we planned a trip to Blue Island, Illinois, to visit her Aunt Mattie. I mentioned to the folks at Roupas Shoe Repair next to Newswanger's we were going to Chicago. Al, an employee with contacts in Chicago, having been a boxer there in his day got two tickets for us to see the Chicago White Sox play. On our trip to Chicago, we visited with Brother Bob, Eileen, Kathy, and Kevin. Kevin was a little over a year old. Kathy was as cute as ever, and redhead Kevin was full of it. Juanita enjoyed the visit, becoming warm and comfortable with our family. During our trip, the first maternity clothes were worn. Rejoice!

We arrived at Aunt Mattie's and enjoyed the visit with her. We attended the ballgame between the White Sox and Detroit, and we visited Grant Park, examining a submarine in the park on display. Juanita pointed out where she worked while living with Aunt Mattie before our marriage. I enjoyed Juanita showing me the sights, discovering no desire on my part to live there. We visited the birthplace of Thomas Edison in Milan, Ohio, a beautiful community, then we were homeward bound. We visited Bob and Eileen, Kathy, and Kevin again on our return to York. During our time awaiting the arrival of the birth of our child, we were at the Visiting Nurse Association in a parental care program. Birthing today appears to be much different, including the father being involved. In our day, I was waiting patiently until told the baby had arrived. I don't recall the pacing of the floor, nor the going for hot water. Oh, that is only in the movies.

Our Christmas that year was spent with the Hildebrand clan in the Jefferson Fire Hall in Jefferson, a small town where Aunt Anna and Uncle John Krebs had a grocery store on the square. The family gathering numbered between forty to fifty. Prior to my meeting Juanita, the family had a collie—a full-blood registered collie named Frederick Alert Collie. I never met him. Ethel and Warren, after Ricky had died, said they would get a collie for Juanita when she had her own home. When we had moved into our home, a litter of collies in the West York area was advertised. An appointment was made, and a male was selected. A cost was agreed upon. The selection of the one Juanita chose we picked up at the appropriate time. We named him Prince; his registered name was Prince of Grandview. As a puppy, he was discovered in our neighbor's yard behind us. With newspaper in hand, I marched into the yard. The neighbors, believing I was going to take the paper to him, pleaded on his behalf. Prince saw me coming and rolled over on his back, his little eyes rolling in his head. I struck my leg with the paper, commanding Prince to go home. They were amazed to see this little dog obey the commands. We never needed to be physical with Prince. Another dog there never was or ever will be. He accepted training and obedience with the use of a rolled-up newspaper applied to the thigh of our leg, creating the loud sound, telling him to stay in the perimeter of the yard. His response to command was immediate. A neighbor, Chuck Robison, at one point tried to coax Prince to go to him across the street, which Prince ignored. Chuck was a good neighbor, only needing to be told there would be consequences should he try it again. There were no future problems.

The birth of our child was expected around my birthday, which is January 19. The nineteenth came and went without great disappointment. The morning of the twenty-second, about 7 A.M., labor pains announced the need to get to the hospital. The day was long. Our baby girl, seven pounds, four ounces, arrived at 9 P.M., a very long day, especially for Juanita. I came out of the waiting room and confronted the nurse carrying our Cynthia Louise. I looked at Cynthia, who had come right from delivery and had not been cleaned up. I looked into her face and saw those little hands and little feet. I never had given thought to our child other than perfect. Suddenly, I was overcome with the miracle of it. The tears began to flow, causing my vision to become blurred. The nurse asked, "Are you all right?" I replied, "I think so." I thanked God, a prayer of thanksgiving that mother and child were fine. Juanita had spent the day in labor due to medication slowing the birth. She was extremely tired. She had a need for care for a time in the home. My prayer offered upon my return from service for a wonderful wife, child, and a home with a fireplace was answered by age thirty-one.

Prince, having grown to full size by the time of Cindy's birth, showed his displeasure by rolling in the mud in the backyard when Cindy made her appearance in the Keesey family. Prince did not like the competition. Juanita took to motherhood lovingly. I enjoyed watching her feed and bathe Cindy. Diaper changing was something I had done with my sister Jeanne when she was born. I renewed the technique of handling the child. God blessed Juanita and me to love raising her with our nurturing. Fatherhood is wonderful in the love for our own child. I was so pleased Juanita was able to be a fulltime mother.

Sitting with this little bundle in my arms, I asked myself, what kind of father will I be?

Our First Born

Cindy, at birth she appeared so new and tiny,
Her little blue eyes, bright and shiny;
Fingers and toes, to me never doubted, all are there,
Her skin so pale and pink, her hair light and fair.
Had I taken too much for granted she'd be complete,
Hope by faith, our God blessed us in this His fete.
I looked upon my likeness, familiar with the features,
In prayer, the Spirit related this to be God's plan.
Will there be a time we truly come to understand,
God's creation, we will see in our lifespan, He is, "I AM."
My eyes filled with tears, she was Juanita's and mine,
Only this is possible with the presence of the Devine.

Much of my drive was derived from having three mouths to provide for in the work in daily life. I had the responsibility of providing for wife and child, house payments, utilities, food, clothing, and a car with a greater potential to determine our income. Understand I had gone into this venture knowing full well. My wife was in full support, encouraging, always observing the determination to succeed, and offering her love. It was a joy looking forward to greeting Juanita and our new baby, Cindy, on my return from work each evening. Fatherhood is great, trying to learn to provide help for the new mother.

At lunch in Peoples Drug Store at the counter, I was seated next to a young lady who asked why I wasn't on my TV show, *Noon Day on 8*. I asked who she thought I was. She replied, "Bob Malik, the news announcer on WGAL 8. You look just like him." This led to sometime later our sending in my picture as a lookalike in the contest they held. I won, appearing with Bob when he presented me with a check for fifty dollars on *Noon Day on 8*. Thanks to the young lady at lunch.

I enjoyed the shoe business and could have spent the rest of my working years satisfied with running stock closing up the shelve holes as shoes were sold out of stock, trimming windows during each change of season. New styles and color I also enjoyed. Yes, a right offer to go into the shoe business for myself would be tempting, but not in competition with the best shoe store I believed existed. E. T. Wright Arch Preservers was my choice. The greatest satisfaction was providing comfort for the customer. "Shift gears, Dave. Your interest is now in learning electricity and electronics to provide for your family." Speaking of family, the Hildebrand and the Newswanger families enjoyed the arrival of Cindy Lou. It was a joy to see the women and the men sitting from time to time, holding this little mite in their arms, looking into her cute little face. Juanita and I were filled with love, providing God's gift to us in sharing her baptism with family and friends.

Time was flying. We were watching the growth of Cindy, my studies every day; my Juanita's involvement in Eastern Star chapter. Happy, I was pleased Juanita was able to be a fulltime mother. God was providing our income to make this possible. Our church attendance each Sunday with Cindy in the pew with us was a delight. She was usually quiet, often sleeping and leaving her in the nursery during services at times.

One Sunday morning, Maude Shope asked if I would consider teaching in the children's area in Sunday School. Juanita and I discussed the possibility. Acting on Juanita's acknowledgement of my ability and knowledge of the Bible, I decided to accept the challenge. Maude's son, Bobby, became our greatest challenge. More than once, he was sent to his mother because of his behavior. At this time, Fred Krsek, our good church friend, was invited to teach in the same department. Much to my pleasure, he accepted the call to serve the Lord.

The year 1960 was near. The DeVry course was nearly complete, presenting a concern in giving notice to the store I would be leaving. It was difficult to know how Uncle Harvey felt since he seldom revealed his personal feelings. I left early November, the week of Armistice Day, fourteen years from the time I started working in the Lancaster Store, November 11, 1946. Probably placing more pressure on myself, I had become involved in serving in the line of chairs in my Masonic Lodge, working to advance to the chair as Worshipful Master. I was following Uncle Harvey's lead where he had served as Master in 1927, the year I was born.

Bob and I had come to the agreement to meet the need of beginning our business of investing $2500 each, $5000 for starters, testing the waters. Our initial purchases were a 1954 Dodge panel truck, two tube testers, a forty-foot wooden ladder, replacement tubes, a picture tube tester rejuvenator, and tools and brackets on the truck to carry the ladders. We agreed I would start by resigning my job until we learned of the acceptance of folks to take us on to service their needs to get the business off the ground. Amazing as it seemed, prospective customers I had made friends with in the shoe business were willing to call us, knowing we recently had schooled for an entirely different technical line of work. It was gratifying, instilling a confidence, convincing us we had made right decisions in our venture.

Juanita learned she was pregnant with our second child in October of 1960. We were getting a late start, recognizing I was thirty-three and Juanita became twenty-eight that September. Cindy was two years old. There is much joy in the families at the prospect of another baby in the family. We learned that Doctors George and Lois Kushner, members of our church, husband and wife, had established an office accepting new patients. We were pleased to have them as doctors for Cindy and for Juanita during her pregnancy and the birth of our second child.

Keesey-Sturman Electronics was off the ground, discovering plenty of business for the two of us. Bob gave notice to the Bon Ton that he was quitting. He was single, living with his parents. The two of us wrestled with adopting techniques of servicing various manufactured products. We learned the little secrets of how things were assembled to be able to return them to their original state. We analyzed problems to reduce the time in producing the acceptable cost of repair. Learning the purchasing of parts, suppliers, and technical data was a plus. Juanita and I were in conversation when she expressed her feelings about a matter never before mentioned. She asked, "Don't you think it is time for your wife and daughter to meet her father in-law and her grandfather?" That was my wonderful wife, who never ceases to surprise me. We made arrangements on a weekend to look Dad up. He was living on Upland Street in Chester, PA.

We arrived early afternoon that Saturday, announcing, "Dad, meet your daughter-in-law, Juanita, and your granddaughter, Cindy." He was surprised, never asking what took so long or why after all this time we came into his life. He was pleased we were together as family. There was an understanding in my mind that Dad did not have a high regard about his success in life. This understanding came from his unwillingness to attend Bob and Eileen's wedding that I practically had to force him to attend. I believe it was how he looked at his financial picture. This was the beginning of a continued enjoyable family relationship encouraged by my wonderful, loving wife, Juanita.

My sister Rita had graduated from high school and made the decision to enter the Catholic Convent. I met this news with mixed emotions, loving her as I do. I questioned the limited opportunities of our having family time together to continue visiting her. Being Protestant, these changes were not known to me. Seeing her in her habit for the first time in Ilchester, MD, caused me to reflect on her decision from my point of view. I observed little change except for my quietness I had toward my sister, Sister Rita Ann Keesey. Attending Catholic services with Ruth and Dad on special holidays or family observances of weddings and funerals told little. Rita was preparing for teaching in a parochial school in the completion of her vows. Cindy was now two years old by Christmas of 1960, and we had the celebrations of her first and second birthdays. Those present included Ethel and Warren, grandmother and grandfather, and Aunt Ina and Uncle Harvey, her Granny and Gramps. Both birthdays were great, especially seeing Cindy in her highchair on the first birthday as she dove into her cake. She had it in her hair and all over her face. Her second birthday was much the same, with the singing of "Happy Birthday." Both families were providing much of Cindy's needs. It was a wonderful experience to see the love and joy they had for Cindy.

On January 22, 1961, we celebrated Cindy's third birthday, enjoying the excitement in watching her unwrap her gifts. Juanita learned her June delivery date was wrong. The doctors were going to be away in July without any indication of delivery when they left on their vacation. Dr. Herr was the doctor on call. July first had come and gone, still no delivery of child number two. On our awakening on the twenty-seventh of July, Juanita informed me it was time to go to the hospital. We arrived at 7:30 to learn I would be in the first-floor waiting room due to renovation work on the third floor. Waiting patiently until nine, I went to the desk on the first floor and asked if there was information on Juanita Keesey's delivery. Told there was no word, I returned to the waiting room. At ten I inquired again, but still nothing. I returned to wait, at which time a nurse from the third floor asked for Mr. Keesey. She informed me our baby daughter was born and in the nursery. She accompanied me to the window to gaze upon Lynn Ellen Keesey. She was a honey, with a shock of dark hair I could hardly believe. Once more the miracle of birth came over me as I prayed with thankfulness that both were well. I entered Juanita's room to find her crying. She believed my mind was set on having a boy. I asked, "Have you seen Lynn Ellen? You can't be sad with such a beautiful little girl." Was there something missing in my manhood that there was no drive on my part that said the Keesey family had to have a boy?

Our Second Child Born

Blessings keep coming so close they're together,
In birth we give thanks to our Lord today, forever.
This small bundle from heaven by name, an infant,
The joy and the love for each we'll never recant.
Lynn's wonderful features the distinct hair on top,
It remains in our memories the long curly dark crop.
Our family has grown numbering a total of four,
Yes, only the Lord knows, shall there be any more.
We bow in reverence as our minds jump ahead,
Asking God to direct and guide us in her life we be led.

With the new arrival of Lynn, my sister Jeanne asked to come help with Cindy, the household chores, and assisting Juanita with Lynn. It was pleasant having Jeanne with us. You might know there would be that incident to be told in the storytelling of life. Well, here it is. Juanita volunteered to make her delicious butterscotch pie that I really like. The pie was made, and our supper was over except for dessert. Standing at the counter, Juanita inquired how large a piece of pie I would like. In reply, I said, "You and Jeanne have a piece. I'll eat the rest." I knew I shouldn't have said it, for she started toward me. Not knowing how close she was, I put up my elbow as though warding her off and knocked the pie out of her hand. It did a flip, ending upside down in the middle of my lap. In disbelief, I stood up and turned the pie plate, catching as much of the pie in the plate as possible. I went into the garage to scrape the residue of pie into the garbage can. The expressions on both Jeanne's and Juanita's faces that I looked at were frozen. I stomped through the kitchen on the way upstairs to change my clothes. It was very quiet downstairs until the humor of this experience had time to sink in. I started to laugh. I then heard things come back to life in the rest of the house. You wouldn't believe it; Juanita set about baking another butterscotch pie. I ask you, did I get the right girl? She's marvelous!

The Keesey family was now a family of five, including our wonderful collie, Prince. I have known Juanita since 1952, living the experiences of setting life right between us. Since September 24, 1955, the day of our marriage, I realize there is every reason to believe God has intended us to be one in Him. In the six years of marriage, we were in our own home, blessed with the birth of two healthy, wonderful daughters, including the love and provisions from time to time from our families unsolicited. I understand the scripture in its

Word of two people becoming one before God. There are no doubts.

A good spring continued with increased work. Word of mouth was the best advertising we could hope for indicating customer satisfaction with our work, bringing us new customers. We were not setting the house afire with income, realizing Bob should be receiving more from the business. Also, he had not put in the study time I had prior to his starting the job. I spoke with the officers of the lodge considering relinquishing my station in line due to time restraints of family, work, and church responsibilities. My brothers had me reconsider my actions, receiving assurance they would provide the time I needed to be proficient in the work, assuring me they would give of their time to accomplish our purpose. The beginning of 1962, Bob and I did an evaluation of Keesey-Sturman, which revealed Bob's dissatisfaction with his return from his work. He considered ending the partnership. I understood exactly his position. An attorney was hired to draw up the necessary papers to dissolve the partnership. In support of Bob, his father was present.

My work in Keesey Electronics had changed little in the absence of Bob. I missed him. The equipment and the operation were now Juanita and David's business. In Rosen's for parts one day, a fellow approached me and introduced himself as Dale Shephard. He said Henry Rosen mentioned I was working alone and that I possibly would consider using his help. I discussed the matter with Juanita, giving thought to our turning out more work, lessening the labor on me on some jobs, especially the installation of antennas. Dale and I worked together for about two years, then he indicated he wanted to end our arrangement. He was fully employed, working with me in his spare time. I questioned, were we fair with Bob and Dale? Juanita and I were owners.

In September of 1962, Juanita found we were expecting our third child. It was good news in a difficult time. That fall I visited and carried Aunt Ina down and up the steps, she being too weak on her own. She was so frail, it was little effort for me. I called upon my faith in this time, giving love and smiles for them both, Aunt Ina and Uncle Harvey. On Halloween, Cindy, Lynn, small as she was, and I dressed up to trick-or-treat Aunt Ina in her bed. She laughed, bringing laughter from us all. I explained to the girls the need for her to be in bed was difficult. We would visit with them when she agreed to see us. She was a strong-willed person who knew how her last days would be spent. We felt she quit eating, wanting as little lingering as possible.

Christmas was a different time, owing to Aunt Ina's illness. With Cindy, Lynn, Mother, and Dad Hildebrand, we spent our Christmas in our home. Juanita and I prepared the family meal, mostly Juanita. Reviewing this period of our lives, we ask once more how it all got done. God is in our midst, provid-ing love, strength of faith in His promise never to leave us. We live with family memories these past years. I had gone for parts on January 8 in the morning, and on my return Juanita told me Uncle Harvey called, telling us Aunt Ina died. I immediately went to 170 Irving Road to console Uncle Harvey, including my-self in that need. The funeral was conducted at Small Mortuary. Bill Small was a member of First Methodist Church. The service was well attended, owing to the family and many friends Uncle Harvey and Aunt Ina had made over the years. After the service, while in the car waiting for the procession to begin, I was overcome with grief. Was the memory of my mother's passing renewed? I was not sure. My love for Aunt Ina and her death consumed me. Was it the lack of faith I witnessed in her? Brother Bob asked if he might drive. I assured him I was all right; it was just a moment needed to come to grips with my grief. Brother Bob came for the funeral in support of Uncle Harvey and family. Aunt Ina's burial was in Quarryville Cemetery, where Mother was buried twenty-eight years ago; it was March of 1935. Bob and I coming together at Mother's grave brought back the memories of those experiences. While we were together in this time, we discovered more of our thoughts and emotions that had not come to mind during those younger years. Bob had come alone; Eileen chose to remain at home in Durham with the children, Kathy, Kevin, and Kimberly.

On Sunday morning, Uncle Harvey and I were driving Bob to the airport in Harrisburg for his return home to New Hampshire. Traveling on snow-covered I-83, I lost control of the car at the Newberry interchange when I moved into the passing lane to avoid a car exiting 83. The car rotated and backed into the guardrail, rupturing the gas tank. Fortunately the motor was turned off at once, avoiding the possibility of fire. We got Bob's suitcase out of the car and observed a passing car, which stopped, asking if they could be of help. They were going to church but volunteered to take Bob to the airport, permitting him to make his flight. Uncle Harvey's car was towed back to York, the two of us as passengers. Juanita, when told of the accident and learning none of us were injured, suggested the accident might be providential, con-suming Uncle Harvey's mind in the repair of the car, giving less time to grieve. God moves in our lives, bringing learning of His presence in experiences we often miss. It's true, God is always with us.

The expected birth of our third child was approaching. We continued with the name Timothy Blaine for a boy while I was pleasantly surprised to hear Juanita suggest a girl be named Kathryn Elizabeth, honoring my mother. I admit, I tear up when touched by the Spirit, and this moved me greatly. I looked at this woman, counting the blessings and continuing to fill our lives, my life. Uncle Harvey decided to take up residence in the Yorktowne Hotel Suite of rooms, a sensible move providing in-town access to activities and near the shoe store. I was pleased to help in his move, providing more time to be together, realizing the move from 170 Irving Road would be helpful in his future years. His loss of interest in the store after the death of Aunt Ina gave me reason to believe he would turn the ownership to Andy Shoemaker. I had no knowledge if there were any agreements made at a time such as this. The idea most had was that Andy would assume the ownership. But an agreement could not be reached, thus ending the friendship between these two men because Andy assumed the store would be his. The buyer, the Damasheck father and son, came to an agreement with Uncle Harvey. I will have you know, this was no ordinary shoe store. My uncle began his store in 1920. He and Aunt Ina sacrificed much to bring success to this business that began when he ask his dad, David Sylvester, for his advice about going into business for himself and wife. Aunt Ina repeated his words: "Nothing ventured, nothing gained." As you may remember previously, this was the expression we heard when we asked what they thought of Juanita and me starting our business. Newswanger Shoe Store became a run-of-the-mill business for the simple reason the people buying it did not sell quality and service. Uncle Harvey called me into the store, presenting three pairs of 13AAA Wright Arch Preserver shoes before the sale was closed. Yes, I have always felt they are my adoptive parents. The relationship has been that we are their children, our children their grandchildren.

On the morning of May 1, Juanita announced labor pains had begun. Mother Hildebrand wasn't available to be with the girls. Jo Graber, our neighbor next door, came in to be with the girls. Off we went to the hospital. The day was overcast, quite chilly for a spring day. Arriving at the hospital, Juanita was received in preparation for the birth of our third child. Would this be our boy, Timothy Blaine, or our third girl, Kathryn Elizabeth? Standing in the waiting room, gazing out the window, snowflakes were blowing around, and I remember this often in reference to our third little girl, Kathryn Elizabeth. Yes, Kathryn was a fair-haired light-skinned little one, much like her sister Cindy, with pretty blue eyes acknowledged later like the first two. She had blonde short hair, unlike the crop Lynn was wearing at birth. Kathryn weighed in at 7 pounds, 6 ounces. We were blessed with Kathryn Elizabeth's arrival and quite pleased with our three young ladies. There were no tears when I joined mother and child as with Lynn. We were pleased with God's gift of a healthy bundle of joy, complete in every way.

Happy with Three

Juanita, before wedded, wanted children,
the number six.
How many boys, how many girls
would be a perfect mix?
Considering the blessings realized,
we were blessed with three:
Cindy, Lynn, and Kathryn.
Beautiful and healthy is enough, we agree.
There was no mention, no discussion of wanting or needing a boy.
Life is a wonder. The challenge of teaching these three was a joy.
There were moments we encountered.
Was this right or was it wrong?
Times were spent in prayer, asking,
searching in the night and daybreak,
asking how long.
We had found the understanding;
our mindsets in decision were one.
With God's direction,
faith in common sense helped us get the job done.

Pastor Paul Myers had filled the pulpit, replacing Edgar Henry. Pastor Myers approached me after some time of service, asking my willingness to fill the pulpit as a Layspeaker on a Sunday. Surprised, I asked the pastor why he believed I had Bible knowledge or the ability to preach. The pastor witnessed the teaching, the speaking gift, and message he saw in me, which gave him confidence to ask. I expressed my appreciation and my willingness when called upon. This raised a question in my mind as to how others looked at me. What did they see? I had not thought much about the time spent in homes during service work. The ministry developed in listening, sharing time and prayer with some customers. There was a willingness to speak intimately about their problems with me ending in prayer as we parted. It was a revelation revealing a quality I hadn't considered.

We still owned the 1950 Super Buick. One day when I was with Uncle Harvey, he suggested it would be good for us to have a larger car to accommodate our growing family. He suggested we go to Bashore & Kohler in Manchester. He was friends with Mr. Bashore, a Rotary Club member. He purchased a 1963 white Ford Falcon station wagon for us. Uncle Harvey heard us speak of the need of an outside entrance into our basement, where our shop was located. Deitz Construction came out and gave an estimate, and Uncle Harvey contracted them for the construction. It involved a sidewalk around the house and excavation outside to the basement floor, opening the wall with a ramp and an oversized door. Uncle Harvey had been so thoughtful toward us.

In September 1963, Cindy was off to school, picture taking on this first day of first grade, our first child growing up before our eyes. The effect this had on Mother and Dad exhibited the question: "How will Cindy fair among an unfamiliar teacher and other children?" She had done well.

Uncle Harvey grieved for some time the loss of Aunt Ina until invitations were accepted with friends leading to him meeting a fine woman named Evelyn Speakman. Her sister, Jerry Thompson, was a member of First Methodist Church. He and Evelyn became fond of one another, enjoying playing cards with friends, church functions, and shows. I am uncertain where Uncle Harvey and I were going in the car when he asked what I thought of him getting married. I assured him it would be fine with the right person, but only he could determine she was that person. He spoke of his fondness for Evelyn, of the happiness they shared being together. I asked, "What is more important than the happiness the two of you enjoy together?" He asked if I would be his best man in the wedding. I was proud and honored. The question came up, was it too soon since Aunt Ina's death? The answer to the question was his and Evelyn's, no others.

In June of 1964, they were married in First Methodist Church. I was the best man. They purchased a home on Club House Road, enjoying their happiness for life together in York. The newlyweds journeyed to Florida, purchasing a condo in the Fountainhead Condominium in Fort Lauderdale. The purchase of the condo introduced the question as to my availability to drive their car to Florida in the fall. It required driving them to BWI Airport in Baltimore, seeing them on the plane, then me continuing to Fort Lauderdale in the car. The first trip in 1964, we got permission to have Cindy excused from school to make the trip. We believed the trip to be educational. Cindy and I stopped in Vera Beach at the New England Seafood Restaurant for dinner. Cindy saw softshell crabs on the menu and asked if she could have them. The answer, naturally, was yes. Was she surprised to see four on the platter! Her eyes opened wide, but she ate every one.

Before returning by plane, we spent two days enjoying some sightseeing and helping them to get settled. Uncle Harvey, Cindy, and I had fun putting on the putting green. It was a good experience for Cindy and me. We enjoyed the flight to BWI, where we were picked up by Juanita, Lynn, and Kathryn. During the summer of 1965, we made our first camping trip to Zack's Campground at Indian River, Delaware. We enjoyed fishing, crabbing, and clamming. Our seafood meals included fresh tomatoes, corn on the cob, and potatoes. It was our first experience camping, bathing in the ocean, and enjoying the sun. We purchased a used tent, a truck tarp using telescoping pipe to mount the tarp, giving us protection from the sun. The next four years, we spent at least five days at Indian River in the summer. The Ritter family, Larry and Doris, with their three daughters, joined us. Hope and Fred Krsek joined us another year. The Masonic Lodge advancement came a year at a time, Junior Warden, Senior Warden, and then Master of my Lodge. Conducting those meetings and scheduling programs had been an education as was continuing use in speaking and governing the Brethren in the Fellowship of Brotherly Love and Affection. The first Sunday in the month of September, the family had gone on a drive through Apple Country around Arendtsville, through Adams and Franklin Counties. Juanita was uncomfortable; we had no idea how ill she was. Dad Keesey was with us. Juanita's illness was diagnosed on Monday after the trip to the doctor. Juanita had a very deep mastoid infection of the left ear. The seriousness required surgery scheduled for Tuesday night at the same time our Lodge meeting was conducted. Knowing I would be of no known support for Juanita during surgery, I chose to conduct the meeting. I had conceived the time to be with Juanita would coincide with the end of the meeting. The meeting completed, I drove to the hospital to be with Juanita as she gained consciousness. The surgery was very serious. The mastoid bone had deteriorated, requiring a period of time for recovery. I felt responsible not sensing earlier the quietness of Juanita revealed the seriousness of her condition. She came home heavily bandaged. Our friend Hope Krsek came to our need, enabling me to work. She cared for the girls, Lynn and Kathryn, who were too young to be in school. It was a week until Juanita was able to resume her motherly and household chores once she returned home. Blessings come in unexplainable manners, having friends like the Krseks and our thoughtful neighbors. Jo Graber next door was available. I held the fort with the girls.

After the year as Master, I was asked to serve as chaplain of the lodge. I served six years as chaplain of the lodge, offering prayers in meetings and funeral services for departed brethren. In September of 1965, our Newswanger family said farewell to Aunt Grace, Uncle Roy's wife. Her service was held in the Quarryville Church, where Mother's service was held in 1935. Where had the time gone? Thirty years of life found me at the age of thirty-eight. My life had been enriched learning to walk closer with my Lord. These deaths are difficult, receiving strength, knowing the faith and trust our family members have in God. Our love and prayers sustain comfort and bring peace to each believer. Every visit to Quarryville is time to visit Mother's gravesite. Our family's faith was witnessed by church attendance.

Juanita made the trip in 1965 on our drive to Florida for Uncle Harvey. Juanita and I had a wonderful time together, focusing our attention on one another. The girls were cared for by Mrs. Jamison from church. Lynn made the trip in 1966. In 1966 the ship *Queen Elizabeth* was berthed in Fort Lauderdale harbor. Uncle Harvey, Lynn, and I were happy for the opportunity to board her for a look around. Cindy had difficulty starting school early due to her birthdate in January. The teacher told us Cindy needed to repeat the second grade. Juanita and I decided it was the best thing for Cindy. Lynn's first day in school was in September 1966. Juanita took pictures as we had of Cindy on her first day off to school. We have reviewed them often.

In 1967 we decided it would be good to have more bedrooms. We learned of a home on the corner of Midland and Woodberry Road, the home of the George Lauer family, members of First Methodist Church. Our house was listed with a realtor, and a buyer was found, agreeing to sell 777 Grandview, with a down payment accompanied by monthly payments. Juanita and I were pleased with the arrangements.

The move was interesting, involving the disassembly of the TV antenna and tower to install it at our new address. I placed the concrete base on the appliance mover, fastened it to the back of the van, and drove three blocks to Woodberry Road. Arriving, Juanita wanted to be helpful. She took hold of the tower section with the concrete base to roll it into place for mounting. The base was lopsided, making it unruly to roll. Unbalanced, it spun and struck Juanita in the head when it swiveled rapidly, knocking her to the ground. She sat in an upright position, dazed, unable to respond immediately to my questions. She was really dazed. Looking into her eyes, it was easy to see she was stunned. After a period of time, she was able to focus on me and spoke. I was concerned there might be a lasting injury, but that did not occur. The move from Grandview Road had mixed emotions for all of us. Concern about the investment Uncle Harvey had made in the entrance to the basement into our shop area gave me the idea that Uncle Harvey would feel we didn't appreciate his help. We certainly had to let him know this was not a whim without recognizing his support. You might know he was pleased with our decision, knowing the need we had for more space for the growing family. Cindy had a room of her own, and Lynn and Kathryn shared their room. It provided better bathroom facilities. It was a nice full basement with fireplace, finished recreation room, a divided basement, providing space for the workshop, with toilet facilities, and the laundry was a great improvement. Our move to the new address presented a retraining of Prince on his boundaries. Since he was almost blind, it took a little time. Prince had reached the age of ten, and we created the idea of getting another dog as we realized he might not have many more years. A trip to the SPCA produced another addition to the Keesey family, a young lady we chose to name Fluffy. She was a mixed predominant collie. The two dogs got along well, giving little concern for Fluffy, learning her boundaries in the yard as she followed Prince's lead. The girls liked both dogs, keeping them both filled with their attention. Prince developed kidney problems. He died the first year after the move.

Aunt Pearl and Uncle Raymond Garber, Dad's sister and her husband, turned their farm over to their daughter, Cousin Ann, when they moved to Lancaster in an apartment complex near Millersville. Uncle Raymond was quite an amusing uncle. When we were small children, he would entertain the three of us, Ann, Bob, and I, mostly every evening. In the late sixties, he became ill, needing transportation to the hospital. In the experience, he was true blue to his rowdiness, constantly throwing his leg off the litter, giving the attendants real problems going down the steps. Later he snickered as he usually did, speaking of the hard time he gave them. Uncle Raymond died on July 18, 1968. He was buried in Habecker's Mennonite Cemetery near Columbia. Aunt Pearl took Raymond's death well. At times we would take Dad to spend several days with her. They always had tales to tell each time. Aunt Pearl remembered experiences they had. Often Dad told us Aunt Pearl remembered things that never happened. They both enjoyed Italian subs we bought at Furillo's in Chester when we picked up Dad. We had a sub feast, Juanita and daughters included, or else we were in trouble.

After Uncle Raymond's death, Aunt Pearl moved to the Brethren Home near Lititz. Business was progressing, giving reason to replace the 1954 Dodge truck with a new 1968 Dodge van, with manual transmission and green and white in color. At our new home, we enjoyed entertaining family and friends, Uncle Harvey, Aunt Evelyn, Aunt Edna, Uncle Don and, at times, Uncle Roy, when he had free time. On one of the Durham Keesey visits, Dad, Aunt Pearl, Ruth, Rita, and Jeannie were with us. It was during that visit the fellows had a fishing trip to Harrison's on the Chesapeake. Aunt Evelyn showed great interest in the relationship Uncle Harvey had with Bob's and my families. It is my belief she had quite an influence on Uncle Harvey, planning his will on our families' future after he was gone. The future results gave evidence to support that belief.

In September 1968, Kathryn was off to kindergarten. The first day, Kathryn was to come home with Lynn for lunch. Lynn said, "I couldn't find her." We learned Kathryn's teacher asked who had money for lunch. Kathryn had none, so the teacher gave Kathryn money so she went to lunch. When she got home that evening after school, she was told again to come home with Lynn. It is wonderful being parents of three lovely daughters. We are learning sometimes by experience. Juanita was a great mother with the girls.

Our time living at Woodberry Road included continued Sunday School and church every week, steady business, camping in the summer at Indian River, Delaware, and continued Eastern Star and Lodge meetings. Daily thanks be to God for the blessings in our lives, for the health we had and the necessities of life.

The visits from Brother Bob and family and the visit to New Hampshire visiting them on family occasions had been blessed with our children getting to know each other. In my return from work one evening, Juanita informed me a customer called, being very disrespectful to her. I called and informed him of my displeasure at his rudeness to my wife. His TV would be delivered when properly repaired. The next day I called to deliver the set and handed him the bill for $25. He complained the price was too high. I asked for the bill and added $2.00 for the insult. I handed him the bill. When he asked why the $2 was added, I told him it was for the insult. He paid it.

Uncle Harvey and Aunt Evelyn were an enjoyable part of our family involved with the girls, our activities, and our needs. He invited the two of us to accompany him to Beasley Ford to select a new car. After the fact, one of the greatest blunders I confessed to was the selection on my part of the light blue 1968 Thunderbird. It was not a family vehicle for five, and using the van for family was no excuse. I heard no objections from Juanita or Uncle Harvey. We were the family Aunt Ina and Uncle Harvey wanted in their lives as evidenced by the wonderful needs and care they provided. Aunt Evelyn was a wonderful friend to Uncle Harvey, as well as his wife. It is our belief they lived every day for each other, always considering the thoughts of the other. Our lives lived and shared with them, we always expressed our love we had as family. In our family times together, with the girls active in church and school programs, we were blessed that Juanita was a stay-at-home mom, which brings me to the thought once more as to how it all was done. Our girls were good students, like their mother, who was pleased with the reports brought home. Dad Keesey had come to be with us from time to time. He would go with me on service calls, helping, visiting with the customers on whose sets I was working. He always minimized the help he was. I was unable to convince him of the help he provided. Dad moved to New Hampshire and took a room, enjoying Bob and family. He and Bob spent time playing the game cribbage and going fishing in Bob's boat in the Atlantic Ocean out of Portsmouth. On a visit with them, Dad and Bob purchased a rod and reel for my use. Dad had hooked a shark, and I put my rod down to assist him. The next thing we heard was Bob saying, "There goes your rod." He made a dive but couldn't save it. They both offered theirs to me, but I refused. Sister Jeannie, upon graduation from high school, followed Rita's example and applied to the convent to become a nun. Having visited with Rita from time to time most often with Ruth, Jeannie, Dad, and our family, I no longer felt any apprehension. They were in Ilchester, Maryland, for their training, and their wedding with Jesus we learned. Love has grown among us, giving an understanding each time we are together. Through good conversations of our Christian faith, we have learned in the Word of God and His love for us all. We receive continued blessings, knowing we are not separated by the different theologies existing in the varied man-adopted principles. God, Christ, and the Holy Spirit are our common relationships and focus.

An exciting time in history took place in the landing of the astronauts on the moon. Juanita's cousin, Mary Liz, with her three children, Jennie, Freddy, and Elizabeth, and our three were spread out on blankets on the basement floor to watch a first. Some were so tired, they fell asleep. As the space program has continued, that night lasts for us as part of history.

Our life at Woodberry Road saw many happy family observances. Mother and Dad Hildebrand celebrated their 45th Anniversary with family and friends. Juanita did a wonderful preparation of our food. We presented them with a small color TV, which they used in the bookcase in their living room. Bob and family visited us from New Hampshire, joined by Dad, who was already with us, and we brought Aunt Pearl for the day. We were complete family members for the first time since all came into the world. Bob, Kevin, Dad, Fred Krsek, Bob Stover, Larry Ritter, Larry's Pastor Rohrbaugh, and I went to Tilghman Island on the Chesapeake fishing at Harrison's. It proved to be too many for one boat. We all had a great time. We took pictures of the group and the catch in front of the garage at Woodberry. Bob, Dad, and I went to Baltimore to see the Mets beat the Orioles in the World Series game. The Mets took the series, much to my disappointment. The trip to Baltimore came about when on our return from church, we called the ticket office to see if there were any seats available. Surprisingly we got tickets at the gate to find they were behind supports for the upper deck.

I mentioned fishing at Lapidium in Maryland previously. One fall day, I asked Juanita if she would object to my going fishing since she had plans for the day with the girls. With her permission I could go without her, she consented as long as I returned, meaning be careful. What a day it was! Beginning by putting the boat in the water, I motored over to the Perryville Marina for gas and bait. I filled up the tank and bought two dozen minnows. I hooked up the gas line to discover the hose was leaking. I had my tools handy, so before I fixed the hose I baited a hook with no weight and dropped it over the side. I fed the line for the minnow to take it away from the boat. I finished the hose job and decided to untie the boat drift with the current to where I wanted to fish. I picked up the rod with the minnow, and as I reeled it in, it suddenly tightened and took off, away from the boat. I set the hook and reeled in an eighteen-inch smallmouth bass. Thank you, Lord, for the unexpected. I drifted down between the shore and a stone base for a bridge that had been dismantled. I put a bobber on, fishing for crappie bass. I had seen a young fellow standing in a canoe, catching crappies during a previous outing. I fished in that one spot all day. The day coming to a close, I looked west to see the red ball, the sun, heading toward sunset. There were two stringers over the side of the boat, and counting them I had twenty-three crappie bass and one small-mouth bass I caught with the minnows, a fish for each minnow. Arriving home, being greeted by Juanita, she asked if I had any luck. I lifted the one stringer out of the boat with half the catch. Her eyes got wide when I showed her the second stringer. She said, "Why does this happen when I am not along?" I am disappointed when things take place such as this, as I like to see Juanita get excited in such cases. I thanked the Lord again for my wonderful wife and for my safety and wonderful day.

Fred Krsek and I continue the teaching of our Children's Bible Study every Sunday. We continue to hear from them, "This is boring." Fred and I taught the class from 1958 to 1983, twenty-five years in that time our four girls had their Uncle Fred, as they called him, and their dad as their teachers for two years. In that time, we experienced some of the students grown returning, having graduated from college, thanking us for providing them the opportunity of learning the value of faith in God, Christ, and the Holy Spirit in their lives. Susan Boner, an outspoken one about how "boring" it was, having finished college and preparing to join the working world, came to us expressing her thoughts of not having taken it seriously. During those years, we were never sure of the learning that took place. We were pleased to learn they had grown from the seeds of God's Word we served in the planting. We offered prayers spoken for their future. Fred and I often spoke in our private time together of the growth the two of us had obtained in those years. I filled the pulpit for Pastor Myers, speaking on the subject of "Answering God's Call." I referenced scriptures of forefathers who answered their call: Abraham, early in the Old Testament, Moses, Jeremiah, the Prophets, and all men called by God, filling God's plan. I asked the question, "Is our call any less meaningful?" Church members serving I referred to by name were Pastor Myers and Ralph Wooley, two in particular, prominent as Pastor and Choir Director, and others, recognizing them for answering the call they had received. The message was well received. Several members felt I should consider pursuing the ministry. Among them were Uncle Harvey and Aunt Evelyn. They inquired as to my thoughts of fulltime ministry. They both knew of my limited formal education of completing the tenth grade. If I had the call to ministry, they were prepared to fill the needs. I spoke of the layperson ministry I was serving in my daily life, the comfortable freedom a layperson has witnessing the gospel message with individuals seeking assurance of spiritual need. I felt more open and receptive as a Lay Speaker than a pastor. As a layperson, people respond in an uninhibited friendly manner. In my relationships with those who know me best, family and friends, as well as newly made acquaintances, I find this to be true. An assurance in prayer with my Lord, I am convinced God has called me to service where I live. My wife, children, teaching, opportunities to preach, and leading in services and among business customers are the examples upon which I base my decision. In a time of reflection, the following are thoughts about my relationship with my God. Quiet time reviewing spiritual presences of late in my life reveal to me the presence of the Holy Spirit. Information I have sought learning of the presence and power of the Holy Spirit assumed recognition of thoughts, actions, and words out of my mouth, teaching, preaching, and singing. Asking Jesus into my life in the little Brethren Church in Ironville revealed the expression of the indwelling of the Holy Spirit. A period of thirty-three years of living, knowing of the words "Holy Spirit," absent from the knowledge of the power and significance as the third part of the Holy Trinity. To know the words, only unlearned, spoken of it having read of it. Until now, I never had recognized the words I spoke were rarely mine. Upon continued reflection of my life, the Bible reading, teaching of the Word, sensing the influence of the Christian growth represented in every area of my life. My life with my God assumed a more meaningful personal direction that was absorbed. The family, my family, Juanita and the girls, grew dearer. Was that possible? May I interject an experience at an earlier time in my life?

Our newly established Sunday School on my return from military service, I led our evening Wednesday night service. Upon the completion of the service, Aunt Ina said to me, "Don't be too good." What she meant to this day, I am not certain of or the inference intended. Was I recognized as being proud, prideful in the manner I conducted myself? On the other hand, experiences have proven to me we are judged at times by the lack of faith some are hesitant to witness of having themselves. The assurance one has of the faith and trust you walk with our Lord give the image of being perfect, lacking the ability to sin projected to others. Never a part of my being. Oft times we fail to act upon, to seize upon the actions, challenging us to follow Jesus when spoken of in Matthew 11:12: "From the days of John the Baptist until now, the kingdom of heaven has been forcefully advancing, and forceful men lay hold of it." Where is our faith to read of the forceful men laying hold to continue to advance the kingdom of heaven that has brought it to us today, lacking faith to continue the advancement? The disciples came to Jesus and asked, "Who is the greatest in the kingdom of heaven?" Jesus called a little child and had him stand among them. Jesus said, "I tell you the truth, unless you change and become like little children, you will never enter the kingdom of heaven. Therefore, whoever humbles himself like this child is the greatest in the kingdom of heaven" (Matthew 18:1-4). Where is our belief, where is our faith? Time and time again, we hear we human beings are incapable of living as Jesus because of our human nature. Ignoring the fact we have asked Jesus into our hearts, receiving the power of the Holy Spirit, we continue to live a spiritless life for the simple reason we refuse to follow Jesus and His Word. Having spoken in this manner, I was spiritually moved to express my belief and faith in the following words:

Who Am I Lord?

Who am I Lord, that you should give me life?
Who am I Lord, that you should love me, too?
Who am I Lord, that you should call me by name?
Who am I Lord, that you should call me unto yourself?
Who am I Lord, to love you, trust you and depend on you?
Who am I Lord?

Who am I Lord, that I should hear your words?
Who am I Lord, that I should take them unto my heart?
Who am I Lord, that I am to search for their meaning?
Who am I Lord, that I should believe you intended them for me?
Who am I Lord, that life's experiences are to draw me nearer unto thee?
Who am I Lord?

Who am I Lord, that when life's ways bring sorrow and pain,
Who am I Lord, that when anxiety, sadness and loss, you are near?;
Who am I Lord, that I expect your presence, your love and your peace?
Who am I Lord, when the sun is shining and all is well with my world,
Who am I Lord, that I should expect that you would be near, too?
Who am I Lord?

Who am I Lord, when I have offended one of yours?
Who am I Lord, that quick word born of short temper?
Who am I Lord, that have brought me low?
Who am I Lord, that I expect your forgiveness?
Who am I Lord, being forgiven you would forget?
Who am I Lord?

Who am I Lord, that those sad and depressed you use me to arrest?
Who am I Lord, that I should think you use me to attest?
Who am I Lord, that I should speak your Word, my faith to profess?
Who am I Lord, that faith indwelt in my heart I am led to confess?
Who am I Lord?

Who am I Lord, that you hung on a cross?
Who am I Lord, that you suffered and died?
Who am I Lord, that you arose just for me?
Who am I Lord, that you want my company?
Who am I Lord, when times I cannot stand myself?
Who am I Lord?

Thank you God, we know who I am,
You've made me as you want me to be,
With blemishes, defects and short comings, too
You're hard at work improving my lot to be cooperative

To stop being something or someone I'm not.
So Lord, you know me better than I know myself,
Keep working with me don't put me on the shelf.
Mold me and make me as only you can,
When I come to judgment we'll know whom I am.

Sadness in 1970 with the illness and death of Aunt Evelyn was sudden for us, not realizing her weakness. We knew of the friendship between Evelyn and Josephine but were not aware of Josephine's intent until Aunt Evelyn's death. There was no need for Uncle Harvey's loneliness, for Josephine was in his life the day Aunt Evelyn died. When we returned to the Club House Road home after the funeral, there was little privacy with him, Uncle Harvey. Brother Bob and I agreed she at this time isolated him from his family in particular. It was not too long until Josephine became Aunt Jo. No question of if it was too soon after Evelyn's death or what people would think. The marriage was a private service we believe performed in Maryland. In fairness to Aunt Jo, Uncle Harvey wanted for nothing, for she cared for him in every way for his happiness. I continued to do TV work for them at times and some jobs around their new home on Elliott Lane. In conversation with Uncle Harvey after work for them in the study, he told me of trusts he had made for Bob, me, and our children. Cindy was completing the sixth grade and was going on a trip to Washington, D.C. Juanita and I were invited to accompany the class as chaperones, to which we agreed. We had a group picture taken on the Capitol steps with our congressman, George Goodling. Visiting the FBI building, the students were looking at a vendors' wares when they were rudely told to move on, to which I responded, "Back off. They may be a customer." I received just a glare, no response, one of our wonderful citizens.

At the age I am in writing this account of my life and the blessings overwhelming, the impression I can sense one might get from reading these accounts would get the idea I am the hero type with an ego as big as a barn. I give God the glory in it all, recognizing always the part I find myself playing in God's plan for us. I was forty-three in this history of my story. I wondered, had it happened? I know it has, for the blessings in our families lives are true. The relatives, friends, and acquaintances in all these years continue to grow. You may believe we are coming to the end of this life's story. Wrong. It goes on and on and on.

The Dodge van purchased after our move to Woodberry Road had two electrical voltage shorts, burning the harness supplying voltage to all units. Covered by warrantee and serving notice to prevent it from happening again, we traded it on a less finished van practical for work, less costly at $3000. After we traded in the van, I liked so much was offered at $990. I countered, asked for more. The second offer was $1100. We were not satisfied, pointing out we only used the van two years, so we wanted $1300. It was agreed upon as a done deal.

780 Woodberry Road was a quiet, neat neighborhood where we had lived for over three years. A morning in May, the question came up as to why we were living in this neighborhood. This prompted Juanita and me to evaluate our situation. Our thoughts were triggered due to the gathering of old TVs and other discarded materials of yesterday. Our thoughts coincided with arriving at a plan of moving to the country and becoming farmers, but not really. We had a sales agreement to the folks at Grandview Road, satisfying their debt to us. The Woodberry home was up for sale before having a prospect for our next home. A buyer being found required us to find another place to live. We discovered an ad for a small place in the Thomasville area to be auctioned that weekend. We asked Uncle Harvey to look at it for his advice. He was not too pleased with the move from our present home to the country. It was difficult for him to recognize our motivation. On our return to York, he suggested we stop for lunch. That lunch Uncle Harvey introduced me to my first Burger King Whopper. For further advice, I invited Dan McElwain with York Bank to take a look at the Thomasville place. Dan agreed $!5,000 was a good buy. We went to the auction, the five of us. We discovered Lynn found the place undesirable since there was an outhouse with no hot water. That didn't present a problem, for the biding began at $15,000. That price ended our interest much to Lynn's satisfaction. The place sold for $18,000. Uncle Harvey suggested we be interested in Aunt Jo's home on Bonbar Road in York. Juanita's and my purpose of moving out of the residential area was, as explained, the eye sore the business created. Our desire to become rural land owners was difficult to have Uncle Harvey understand. We had no home when our settlement on Woodberry took place. Did we run ahead of our Lord, failing to call upon his leading? Prayer surely was a need for direction as to where we were going to move.

Keeping the faith, we returned to our home, or what was our home until we signed the paper that sold it. Returning from the auction, we found an ad in the paper for a twelve-room log farmhouse on fifteen acres of ground in Lower Windsor Township, located between East Prospect and Craley. Sunday after church, the five of us loaded up in the van to look at this property. It was a damp, wet day with light rain. We had directions and a contact in East

Prospect to get the key to check it inside and out. Well, it had a bathroom, much to Lynn's liking. Plus plumbing, hot and cold water, and lots of room. The kitchen was in the basement, furnished with an electric stove, meeting Juanita's approval. We had cleaning from basement to attic, being vacant for some time. The acreage was overgrown in weeds, creating a need for a riding mower. Bird dirt was throughout the attic, not a pleasant job. We evaluated necessary work to make it livable and workable. Oh, yes, I'm getting the cart before the horse. Seeing it, the five of us could see the advantage of living out here in the wilds. At that time, we could see at most two homes at a distance. There was a large barn, corncrib attached to a chicken coop, and a pigpen with additional buildings that previously were used for chickens, as well as an area of elevated enclosure for raising turkeys. It was evident the family held small attachments to the finer luxuries of residential housing. Was it the excitement of country living, realizing the work necessary to make the house our home? We heard no opposition to make the move. The price was $20,900 dollars. It was acceptable, so we took option to purchase with a trip to the bank for approval for a $15,000 mortgage. Prayers were offered in thankful praise for the answered provisions and direction of God in our lives. God works in our lives in such manners, we often fail to recognize His presence.

One of the examples is the friendship with the Robison family: Greg and Beverly, sons John and Larry, and later, daughter Ann. I met them having done TV work for them in York. This friendship had been made previous to our move to the country. Greg worked for Goodling Heating and Air Conditioning, which provided a truck with a hydraulic tailgate for our move. It was a fine friendship with Greg and family. They pitched right in with the move. The move was much easier having Greg with the truck, which made an impossible task doable. Juanita might have had thoughts of her life in Montana, though I never heard her express it likened to that life experience.

We had the necessary utilities and were surprised at the willingness of the children to become a part of this adventure. The time had come to move from Woodberry Road on Memorial Day weekend in 1971, our third home in sixteen years. Believe us when we tell you everyone was involved in getting things in place. The kitchen was set up for preparing meals and bedrooms set up for the first night. Cindy was thirteen at the time of our move; in the fall, she would start seventh grade at Eastern Middle School. Lynn was ten and would begin fifth grade. Kathryn was eight and would begin third grade. She and Lynn would attend Canadochly Elementary School, south of East Prospect, which was visible from the farm. Greg and I began installing central baseboard heating throughout the first and second floors, the kitchen, and the basement shop. The furnace, baseboard heat units, pipes, and fittings were purchased from Raub Supply, the company we dealt with for our Sylvania TVs, appliances, and other household supplies. Forge Hill Road R.D.#1 Wrightsville was our new address as we were now country folks. The girls had no school since it was summer, affording them the time to work, getting our digs in order. Our change of address for business was complete, and directions as to how we could be found including our new phone number. We discovered local neighbors learned who you were and what you were about. It was the move in the right direction from indications of the family. Praises and thanksgiving are offered to the Lord. Immediately the God-given talent comes into play in the numerous needs called upon to be met. I am blessed in the knowledge of electricity, plumbing, painting, plaster, and the butchering of wood, of which I am an expert. Some folks call it carpentry, but finished it is a butcher job. "Okay, Dave, keep trying."

The pots and pans had found their place in the cupboards, the plates, cups and saucers, the refrigerator and all the rest. The chef was at work daily with a smile, accompanied by those delicious vitals. The repair shop was set up in the add-on off the kitchen, along with the laundry. Filing cabinets lined the wall with the technical schematics and business records. Our garden area was all laid out for us, providing Juanita with her expertise of fresh vegetables and the canning, providing food all year 'round. The wide-open spaces enabled us the freedom of keeping animals. The size of the house was in need of updating with possibilities of making changes of our liking. A question comes to mind: Had we given this move sufficient thought and planning? Once more, had this been the leading of our Lord? We enjoyed the clean, fresh air of the outdoors. The nice front porch we learned was great for watching the thunderstorms. Our wooded grounds surrounded the small valley with the spring-fed brook running off our land to the lower valley stream called Cabin Creek. Wonderful foliage afforded cover and natural food for the wildlife that was bountiful. We had small game rabbits, squirrels, and pheasants. Deer were plentiful, which I had never hunted in my life. It was a wonderful area for Fluffy to roam, learning of her skill in ridding the area of unwanted groundhogs. She was a great pet, fun not only for the girls. Juanita and I too loved to have her at our feet. Farm offered a beautiful birdwatching experience. We began to get subtle comments from family and friends as to the move into our log house. The nice part in this move was the ones who count continued to be in our life. Lesson learned, it is who you are, no matter where you are. Our Lord is the same

Lord, everywhere we are. He has been and always will be faithful and true. May we speak of the wonderful Christian church we attend, 1st Methodist Church? It became Asbury United Methodist Church in 1968, with the merger of the Evangelical United Brethren Church and the Methodist Episcopal Church. Juanita and I questioned if we should make a change, owing to the issues with the reading of the discipline governing Methodism, particularly in the General Conference meetings every four years. The issues of gay marriage and gays in the pulpit ministry were constantly presented for a vote to accept the lifestyle we felt was in opposition to God's Word. In our deliberation in this year, 1972, our decision was to remain in our loving, faithful church family, constantly in prayer and love with each and every one of the members and friends of friends and relatives. The question often heard was, how do folks get along in this world in the absence of God in their lives? The continued Bible studies ongoing in church and private homes call us to be faithful to the Word of God by our faith, witnessing by the lives we live. We have family history in Asbury, calling us to be faithful to God, continuing to witness with our presence while in prayer support of the issues of sinful ways in conflict with God's Word.

An issue came up in church involving a woman hired as coordinator of youth and activities during the ministry of Pastor Paul Myers. Pastor Paul had moved on, resulting in the appointment of Pastor Martin Hopkins, better known as Marty Hopkins. During Marty's ministry, the coordinator assumed positions in every ministry of the church, becoming more the role as pastor of the church. She was approached by the pastor, the Chairman of Ad Council, the Pastor Parish-Relations Chairman, and asked to relinquish her assumed role on these committees without any acceptance on her part. It was learned the pastor was visiting homes, seeking support to oppose her position and her unwillingness to cooperate. Time and prayers on my part were given, experiencing many nights of interrupted sleep. Scripture searching, I was requesting guidance and direction as to whether I was called to address the matter as a member of God's Church. On a given night in the Ad Council meeting, I was moved to address the problem moving upon powers to be for action in the matter. Chairman of Council, my close brother in Christ, Smedley Craig, stated this was not the place for such actions to be taken, that the Pastor Parish Committee should have jurisdiction. During the meeting, those in support of the individual stood up, questioning how I could speak of this person in this manner. Following the meeting, the conversations intimated I spoke with anger and contempt for this woman. I must confess, when I believe in my convictions, my tone is firm. There is no questioning my intent. A letter was written to the Pastor Parish Relations Committee to enlighten them of the facts. The love and high regard I personally had for the individual had little to do with the need to write the letter. The committee took action by vote to resolve the matter, removing her from the position she held. I had weighed the position I was led to follow, knowing it was right. Talk was the issue that could split the church to some degree with some displaying coolness toward me personally, in addition to those who spoke openly about the issue with me. In most cases, the end result, differences were resolved with few strained relationships. I came away from the experience with little satisfaction other than knowing it was a direction given me to take prayerfully, believing it was of God.

Friends of ours, the Franchios, learned of our living on the farm and spoke of friends having a horse needing a good home. This was something enjoyed with Brother Bob several times, and he had enjoyed the excitement and challenge of horseback riding. It is an adventure challenging areas of life in which we have no experience. Yes, on the farm with Aunt Pearl and Uncle Raymond, I was able to handle Calvin the mule. Horses are different. Thoughts were this was early to be getting involved with horses when we were hardly settled in our new surroundings. The family discussed the possibility of having a horse; we had the barn and pasture, and the three girls were ecstatic at the prospects and ready to go, so bring on the horse. It was decided we should look at this horse before making our decision. Off we went horse hunting to look her over. Her name was Ajax, white like the foaming cleanser, ten years old, spoiled by having come in the pasture to the back door of the house, where corralled to receive sugar cubes as a treat. Were we sure this was a good move? The girls commented, "She's free, doesn't cost anything." Mom and Dad agreed.

Finding the person with a horse trailer, Ajax was delivered to the farm. We learned she could be temperamental at times, consenting to the saddle once we all had made friends. A saddle and bridle were purchased, left only to get them on this beast. There were three girls champing at their bits to get on for a ride. Naturally, father had to be first to see if she was safe to ride. Much to our surprise, she responded without a hitch. A hitch, get it? So up they went, one at a time, Cindy first without a problem, being walked about before having rein control. Lynn followed successfully, then Kathryn, who was eight at this time in 1971. Juanita was busy with Eastern Star meetings in evenings from time to time. On such meetings, Father was holding down the fort. One evening Juanita was attending a meeting, Father got the bright idea to take in a livestock auction near New Freedom, looking for ponies for Lynn and

Kathryn to ride with Cindy. We arrived at the sale, which began with the farm animals, steers, dairy cows, sheep, and goats. The girls and I found it interesting taking in the prices, the farmers paying, watching them check them over before they came into the show ring. During a break in the farm animals, there were several ponies we had looked at in their pens. Several had been shown, surprising us at the low price they sold for. A dark gray almost black Shetland mare pony was being shown, prompting the girls to ask if we were going to bid on her. Did they like her, I asked? Nods from the three of them indicated yes. The bid began at seven dollars, bringing looks from the girls. Our bid was against one other person, reaching fourteen dollars; we offered fifteen. By golly, we got her for that price. Next was a brown-and-white pinto male pony as long legged as the mare but not as heavy through the body. Bidding started at five dollars. We bid six, there was a bid of seven, followed by our bid of eight dollars. Guess what? He was ours. The girls wondered. We bought them, so how were we going to get them home? Would you believe I heard myself say, "In the van." We were going to try this since there was just the one seat behind the front seats, leaving at least six feet to the door in the rear. I paid for the ponies and backed the van up to an embankment the height of the floor of the van. A crowd started to gather. We could hear from the crowd, "This is going to be good." The girls held each pony while Cindy knelt on the seat facing the back door. We took the mare first. She stepped up into the van. I handed the halter to Cindy, kneeling on the seat. I led the pinto into the van, handed Lynn the halter, and got out and closed the door. The girls were in the van, kneeling on the seat, petting the ponies to the ponies' delight. I got into the driver's seat and drove off, watching the people standing there with wide eyes and opened mouths. We drove home, careful to make slow turns, even slower stops at signs without a hitch. Everything was fine. All we had to do was break the news to Mom when she arrived home. The girls could hardly wait for her arrival. Juanita arrived in her white gown and shoes worn for the meetings. The girls told her she had to come out and see what was in the barn. Juanita dressed as she arrived home, satisfying their requests. Yes, she said we were nuts. We already knew, and she accepted it well. Moms are understanding.

Once more we were meeting new people, with new faces and new names to match the faces. We lived in a community comfortable with those they have lived with over the years, scrutinizing any and all moving into the area. A relationship that blossomed was at the grocery store we passed just before we entered East Prospect. The owner's name was Sedon Ritz, of Ritz Store. As mentioned before, the recognition of what makes a person tick comes across in the way two people look upon one another and the choice of words expressed. Sedon was an older man than I, probably in his sixties. I recognized immediately he was a Christian. We had known each other a short time when he asked if I preached and taught the Bible. I responded affirmatively, expressing interest should he have a need for service. A door opened to Juanita and me to serve in East Prospect United Methodist Church when called to teach and preach. We traveled these many years twelve miles every Sunday, plus weekly meetings and Bible Study at Asbury in York, as faithful members. We as a family were active in Sunday School, youth group, and the children's lives and the lives of the members of the church. In July of that first year in our new old home, Juanita's Eastern Star had the opportunity to attend meetings in the Pittsburgh area. I was pleased she wanted to be a part of that trip. Her absence was felt by me realizing the times we were not together was during her childbearing and the surgery she had on her mastoid infection. It was lonely with her absence, short as it was. I emphasized much happiness having her home. We missed her the three days she was gone. Absence does make the heart grow fonder.

It wasn't much later when we learned we were to be blessed with our fourth child. This was going to take some getting used to at our ages. I have suggested, on more than one occasion, you can never tell with this well water. HE! HE! Juanita, when asked how she felt about another child, spoke of her age, praying she could carry it to term, producing a complete and healthy child. She spoke of the obligation she had to her Eastern Star as Worthy Matron. My concern was for Juanita's health at her age, thirty-nine. I would be forty-five at the birth. We spoke of this child being our boy. Then it hit me; I would be in my sixties by the time of high school graduation with this child. God is good, always knowing of our faith, our trust in him. Though never mentioned to Juanita, the age of thirty-nine brought memories of Mother and the age she was at her death, prompting me once more to recount that period of my life with her.

The summer was great, with plenty of work in the business, a garden, working on the heating, installing another wood stove, mowing the grass, riding ponies and the horse, and getting acquainted with neighbors. In retrospect, how did it all get done? Sound familiar?

Bob, Eileen, Kathy, Kevin, and Kim paid us a visit, made special by having Dad and Aunt Pearl with us. We had an enjoyable time visiting, eating, and playing games. You may start to believe me in my telling you of the wonderful girl I married. She does everything so well. She is a good mother, a great cook, in addition to being my wonderful wife. It is more than luck, for I put little store in luck. God has meant it to be; He is given thanks every day of our lives.

Whoever you are reading the account of this family at this time, surely you recognize the presence of our God, our Christ, and the Holy Spirit. The faith and trust is present, the understanding is searched for, though the surrender had not taken place in my life, still living the life of the world being. Writing today, the presence and direction of the Spirit with the perspective of the power present in the obedience direction fills me with a joy, bringing me to my knees.

In the fall of 1971, the incoming Master of the Lodge approached, inviting me to become Chairman of the Charity Committee of York Lodge. Once again Juanita, in understanding the responsibility it required, asked me what I could contribute. Was I moved to serve in this capacity? I had spoken with her of my relinquishing the chaplain responsibilities. I learned the Master wanted me to continue serving as chaplain his year. Since he recalled the prayer given at Mike Cassimatis's installation as District Deputy of the 42nd Masonic District, receiving such a compliment from Mike led me to accept.

Our expected child was to be born in April of 1972. A boy would be named Timothy Blaine, which was considered in all of our previous expected children. Juanita, the girls, and I went 'round and 'round, choosing the name for another girl. Juanita liked Joyce Celeste. I held out for Melanie Sue, receiving the honor of naming Melanie Sue. I believe being outnumbered four to one, they relented in considering my choice because they loved me. The girls were in the Wrightsville Schools. Lynn and Kathryn were bused to the elementary school. Cindy was bused to the middle/senior high. We questioned as to whether we had made a right decision with our move for our children. It was a suburban district with high academia compared to the Wrightsville District, being a rural country area with fewer expectations of the students. Just perhaps our girls would fare better in this slower pace of social aspects. Our church affiliations were to continue at Asbury Church, even with the twelve-mile distance, acknowledging the family ties and our years of service. Juanita at this time had been a member of the church since 1942. I had joined the church in 1948, having moved to York the previous year. It is fair to make this observation our coming together had our memory of meeting and falling in love and our marriage. Our relationships with the members of the church are our lives these many years worshiped together.

Thanksgiving and Christmas included Grandmother and Grandfather Hildebrand. Aunt Hope and Uncle Fred Krsek were usually included for Thanksgiving. The menu included turkey, which was at the center of the table, with filling, mashed potatoes, sweet potatoes, vegetables, cranberry sauce, olives (don't forget the gravy!), pumpkin pie, and mincemeat pie, pleasing me as usual. Yes, you know I am speaking of my wonderful wife. She does most of it, particularly the mincemeat pie for me, the one who is usually eating it.

The expectant mother was beginning to show evidence of the upcoming event. Our children's doctor was Lamon, the Kushners having gone to a specialty practice. Juanita's pregnancy and delivery doctor was Dr. Herr, the doctor who delivered Lynn in her late arrival in 1961. The season of Lent produced a Spiritual awareness while giving a talk before the Men's Lenten Breakfast at Asbury U.M. Church. The fact that no two of us have the exact same fingerprints brought to my mind the fact that God has given each one of us our own individuality. God knows each of us, having given us the uniqueness of His creation. I have lived the years since knowing God as always in my life, my reason to believe the people warm to me. I found myself riding in my work vehicle, saying to the Lord, "These folks I gaze upon are all your creation. You call upon me to love them all." I felt then, and to this day, God calls me to this practice, tough as it is. Yes, I believe at moments I fall short.

A most important experience in the Keesey family would be the arrival, the birth of our fourth child on April 23, 1972. It was a quiet Sunday afternoon when Mother announced a trip to the hospital was necessary at once. The girls at their ages, Cindy now fourteen, was comfortable caring for them until my return. They were excited to know if the baby would be a boy or a girl. The twelve-mile journey was uneventful. On arrival, we were directed to the labor room. We met with Dr. Herr and learned I would not be present during the delivery. I was not disappointed in not witnessing the birth but assumed the doctor knew best. Dr. Herr, having delivered Lynn, may have believed Juanita would do well, believing I might be a less-than-good risk. Labor was about two hours when we were informed we were parents of our fourth daughter, Melanie Sue. I looked upon this child, seeing features and coloring much like Lynn, but lacking the shock of hair Lynn had displayed. She was a pretty, healthy, fully developed child with no evidence of our concern related to Juanita's age. I recognized the demands made upon Juanita's carrying Melanie when I looked at Juanita's lack of color and her hair. God intended Melanie Sue to fill us with His love and expressions for all us. Thank you, God.

The blessings continue.
On April 23, 1972,

This surprise blessing has come from God,
Yes, born from above the product of our love.
The responsibility relished receiving this girl,
The joy the three lovelies kept us in a whirl.
One more added after a period of nine years,
In our experience of parenting will bring us cheer.
Melanie Sue, you've made our family complete,
The growth of our faith in God fulfills all our fetes.

Juanita, unlike the previous three births, showed her age, coloring, hair, and most of all, the slow return of her energy. I made no mention to her. I realized this pregnancy at her age, the birthing of Melanie, was more difficult. Juanita reading this may say she had no idea of my concern. The girls were great in handling and caring for our little one. I was helpful if able to get near Melanie.

Juanita was serving her year as Worthy Matron of her Eastern Star Chapter, fulfilling the obligation well despite the additional experience of bringing Melanie into the world. Her sisters in Star were like surrogate mothers in their involvement of the experience. Ah, yes, we were on the farm for a year Memorial Day weekend of 1972. Melanie was a month old. We learned of the approaching hurricane coming up the coast of the Atlantic named Agnes. It came inland across the North Carolina-Virginia coast, across Maryland into Pennsylvania, over the Susquehanna River to New York State, and it looped around, returning over the same route it had taken northwest, now heading southeast. For three days, we experienced downpours of rain flooding the Susquehanna River. It rose from the New York border to the Chesapeake Bay. Daughter Cindy and I went to the river, aiding in the removal of boats to high ground. The sight of seeing buildings, boats, and debris in indescribable amounts floating toward the Safe Harbor Dam was overwhelming. We returned home for supper, tired, with the satisfaction we had helped.

Family visits were enjoyed with Dad Keesey when we would visit him and have him return with us when Brother Bob and family would visit. Times brought Ruth, Rita, and Jeannie to visit. Dad and Jeannie were there on a day I got a hankering to get a horse for myself, enabling me to ride with the girls. We visited a stable in West York on Taxville Road known for having reasonably priced animals. Spying an unusually colored horse called strawberry roan, I asked the price. It was $100. It prompted me to want to ride him. Saddled and ready to go, I took to the saddle, learning after a few steps he didn't care to have me on his back. He bucked like a bronco until I brought him under control with strong pressure on the reins. The pasture was about an acre. I proceeded to ride him into each corner until he yielded to my commands. This was the horse I wanted. I paid for him on the spot and named him Shane. He was delivered that afternoon. Four animals were now in our care. Ajax, our first, was Cindy's; Lady was Lynn's; Bam-Bam was Kathryn's; and Shane was mine. Our girls were growing.

Cindy decided to become a member of Asbury United Methodist Church and had completed the preparatory class. The service was a moving experience for Juanita and me. Greg Robison became interested in riding and asked permission to board a horse with us were he to buy one. The answer was yes, our relationship being much like father and son in our time spent together. His moving us, installing the heating system in our house, we grew to be family. He purchased a horse and named her Candy. Our riding was a great time, so much that Greg and wife Beverly sold their home in York. They purchased a farm with a facility to board horses along the East Prospect Road. Living in the wilds of the country with my interest in hunting small game, pheasants, rabbits, and squirrels, I invited my friend made in the Masons, Larry Ritter, to join me in small game hunting. I owned the two German .22 caliber rifles Brother Bob had sent home while in Germany were not good for our game. I purchased a Springfield twelve-gauge pump gun to hunt on our ground and joining properties with land owners' permission. Fluffy wasn't a small game dog, though she was death on groundhogs. The presence of deer led to hunting for them on and around our property. I began the experience in using the 12-gauge pump with slugs called pumpkin-balls.

The winter of 1972 began my first experience of hunting deer. Early the first day at dawn, hunting for deer sitting in a likely spot at daybreak across the land, I heard cock bird cackles for miles around. That was the first and last time I ever heard such a sound. Larry came out to hunt the first Saturday of that year on the hunt for deer. I was out roaming in the woods and became so involved, I forgot completely Juanita planned on grocery shopping. Knowing Larry was experienced in feeding babies, she left knowing I would be home soon. On my return, I found Larry sitting on the sofa, feeding Melanie her bottle. No deer, but I sure got kidded about Larry feeding Melanie. I was bothered with my thoughtlessness in my absence, not being there for Juanita in her shopping and the care of our Melanie.

Farm life had been welcomed, owing to our being of one mind in the change made. Our lifestyle remained the same. Sunday morning, it was off to

Sunday School and church, twelve miles going and coming. Our commitment to God had been faithful in our life together. We have never heard our girls complain about going to church. Church was important. They never questioned as to our family joining with friends for worship and fellowship. Dad, being reminded regularly then and today as to his coming out the door last, greeted by everyone in the van, ready to go, accompanied by snickers from the back seat. New customers were coming our way, living in the Craley-East Prospect communities. News travels in the community where everyone knows about their neighbors' business, your neighbor in particular. They know about it before you know about it yourselves. They are caring, coming to meet the needs of their neighbors regardless of what they might be. Juanita's interest and involvement in Eastern Star was important to her, just as my faithfulness to my Lodge was important to me. The girls showed every indication of being happy, with their church, school, family activities, and observances, friends, and neighborhood friends living close by. Oh, yes, don't forget the horses. The sister relationships coupled with family time at home proved to be happy times, interesting to us all with an occasional uprising with the troops, troops being the girls. Our family life with Mother and Dad Hildebrand have been enjoyed and focused in celebrating occasions. The coming together of the Hildebrand, Newswanger, and Keesey families were never joined as one because of Mother Hildebrand's jealousy and unwillingness to being less than the center of attention. As members of the Lodge Charity Committee, we received a call from Jerry Bupp, secretary of the Lodge, requesting our committee to interview our first applicant for entrance as resident to Masonic Home at Elizabethtown, PA. The committee of Larry Ritter, pharmacist; Dr. Howard McDougal; and I received a fulfillment of service, making possible a better life for another. Our experiences in our lives prepared us for the responsibility required in speaking with the applicant. The application completed, we submitted it to secretary, Jerry Bupp. Upon approval, our responsibility was to present the new resident and properties to admissions at the home. Once received, we then enjoyed their first meal with the other residence and the new resident in a most impressive dining room. It was so impressive; every time you entered, you had to take in the dining room's entire grandeur. Our family at times made visits with the residents, becoming friends. The chaplain responsibilities serving in the ritual and the Lodge's brethren performed with a reverent sense of God's presence. Serving as chaplain in the last words in laying brothers to rest was a most meaningful service for families and friends, offering peace and assurance bringing gratitude for the brotherhood. In many instances, it was an entirely new experience for many families. Serving as Master of my Lodge afforded much growth, including memory work of ritual and confidence in presenting the message in an impressive manner. Our Newswanger family joined us on invitations: Uncle Harvey, Aunt Jo, Uncle Don, and Aunt Edna. On one occasion, Uncle Roy was among the family on the farm in the old farmhouse. There were memories we felt sure came to mind, having been raised in the Newswanger home across the road from the Mount Hope Methodist Church in the Quarryville region. Many family memories came to mind to be shared as family treasures. Aunt Jo joined in the day with great interest on her part. The girls were growing up, bringing great joy to their parents. Their school accomplishments in the grades coming home, most of all the principles we acknowledged in their growth. We witnessed the expression of right and wrong in the ongoing happenings of the days.

Once Lynn, invited to a Friday night party in a private home, called around nine o'clock, asking us to come pick her up. On the way home, she spoke of the unacceptable behavior she witnessed, causing her to feel uncomfortable. We learned from her she was looked upon as a prude, a "goodie-goodie." We expressed our happiness with her moral choices.

In the seventies, Dad Hildebrand, Warren Cake, a friend from church, and Charlie Adams, a good friend I worked with in the shoe business since 1946, and I made up the foursome for golf on Thursday mornings. Dad enjoyed the game to the point he was heard to say more than once on the eighteenth fairway, "I wish we were just starting instead of ending the play." We had a grand time each week, looking forward to our time together. There were times I felt guilty about putting golf ahead of my family and work. Moments in our lives being brought up short in surveying our purpose we have for life becomes clear as to who we are serving. At the time I may have said my Lord, family, and those I love near and dear to me. I rationalize the hours of the day, soothing the savage beast within me by starting my day with the Lord, calling upon Him through the day. Work hours outnumbered golf. Was I being honest with myself?

Juanita had regained her strength, her former appearance, and giving role of mother, wife, and her important role with Keesey Electronics. Her year as Worthy Matron of her Chapter had all but come to an end. The blessings enjoyed with this new member of the Keesey family, Melanie Sue, were many. Another beautiful daughter full of life, she has kidded us at times that she was an unwanted child, which was far from the truth. The expectation of our new family member was exciting, anticipating this could be our Timothy Blaine or Melanie Sue. Either way we were thankful for her.

The purchase of the Wheel-Horse mower provided the means of making a garden for vegetables, as well as mowing the expanse of grass and pasture. These wanted and enjoyed chores gave much satisfaction, including the fruits of our labors. The garden, as well as the nature and surroundings in our country setting. Family, friends, and neighbors filled our lives as the girls grew involved in the school and friends they had made in our rural home. Our riding of the horses was not an activity that took us away from chores, and duties needed to be attended. The tackle for supplying comfortable riding was not costly. The needs were met in some surprising manners, helping us to say this life was meant to be for us. Our summers were not routine with occasional visits from family members and friends. There were the unexpected repairs, replacement of the water pump and the electric fuse box, owing to the lightning strike that fused the connection in the original box, which brought the need and opportunity to replace it. A more adequate circuit breaker box provided better grounding to the bypass box. Blessed we are, God has blessed us with talents and gifts to be capable to perform these services for ourselves.

Our family attendance and activities in church were first place in our lives, providing the learning and opportunities of Bible knowledge, recognizing our decisions and actions with others witnessing our Christian faith in all aspects of our lives. For Juanita and me, the practice in following the belief, faith, honesty, and fairness toward the customer produced the growth of business, serving our customers on the principles of the Bible. I mentioned previously Uncle Harvey spoke to me of his providing for Bob and me in his will. He as much as told me we were well provided for in the proceeds. This was not any surprise, knowing Aunt Ina had told Brother Bob in their conversations our family would be well cared for after they were gone. In our relationship in their lives, never was there a request for anything. They always introduced their offer, beginning with the purchase of our first home on Grandview Road. All of the vehicles purchased for us when we accepted the offer, the question followed: "Are you happy with your selection?" It is true, I assumed the relationship as their son. That relationship could have changed with Uncle Harvey marrying Aunt Evelyn. We learned Aunt Evelyn was the strong factor in Uncle Harvey's making of his will. In later thought, it was possible Uncle Harvey was establishing this fact when the will was made to include trusts for each girl.

We had a surprise when we learned Lady was with foal. This would be an entirely new experience for us and anticipated by all of us. Inexperienced, we kept close attention only to learn on our return on an evening with sadness when we found Lady standing over the delivered foal, which was wrapped in the umbilical cord and the sack, not breathing. We tried blowing in the mouth and pressing on the chest in our effort to get the lungs to inflate without success. Cindy and I, in the rain, wrapped the foal in plastic and dug the grave, our eyes filled with tears, laying it in the grave. We all thought of what might have been had this gray pony survived, which was another episode in the Keesey family.

In 1974 we received a phone call from Dad, who needed assistance returning from his trip from the food store. We responded by going to the highrise, where he lived, in Chester. We learned of his weakness, leading to our determining he should not live alone. The visit resulted in inviting him to come to live with us. Juanita and I had discussed this possibility when the time would arrive. We moved Dad with all of his belongings to the farm in the van. You should have seen the van loaded to the hilt with the carpet tied on the roof. We looked like the Beverly Hillbillies. We moved the dining room furniture into the back room, establishing Dad in the dining room as his living and bedroom. Juanita's good cooking and family activities proved to be the nourishment Dad needed to respond, as he regained much of his strength and outlook on life. There were adjustments for all of us, particularly in the use of the bathroom on the first floor. The seven of us did well with experiences we had day to day, and I relive the humor today. Fortunately, we had few disagreements that tried one's soul. Dad got quiet at times. Dad, the person he was, picked up the small bow he saw we had. He asked me to supply the wood and he would cut it up. We had three wood stoves we burned during the cold weather. We all marveled at his strengthening and endurance, owing to the regular meals of Juanita's cooking.

Juanita continued her interest in Eastern Star, along with her home and family, caring for Melanie. We worked as a team, maintaining the house and grounds. We entertained ourselves, playing games, watching TV and, on occasions, participating in activities at church and community involvement. Dad attended church regularly on Sunday, including many of the children's and other programs.

The spring of 1975 was our fourth year living on the farm. The summer afforded Dad and me several fishing trips to Kent Island Narrows, fishing for anything biting. Most catches were white perch. During an experience one trip, yacht-sized boats were passing by with the beauties in bikini on the bow. Dad looked at me, asking, "Are they having more fun than we are?" "No, without a doubt" was the answer. Having enjoyed the day, on our way home, a beautiful, clear night, Dad spoke of the stars, of God's awesome universe, prompting me to speak of Christ. Dad became quiet for a time, then turning toward me, he laid his hand on my leg and told me, "David, you are my best friend, as well as my son,. If you continue to speak in those words, it could ruin our friendship." That ended the discussion. A further thought later, when at prayer, the Spirit brought to mind a session Dad had had visiting Aunt Pearl. Jim Garber, Jim, the son of Ethel, who had invited me to the Ironville Church when I received Christ as Savior, and his wife, Betty, visiting Aunt Pearl, were outspoken in their commitment to Christ. They pressed Dad to receive Christ as his Savior. This revealed to me a possible reason Dad no longer attended church with us on occasions. Aunt Pearl and Dad spent many Sundays singing in church choirs in more than one church in their childhood. Had Dad not accepted Christ as his Lord and Savior? I found that hard to believe.

Cindy had become sixteen, the age to start driving. Permit in hand, the practice with Juanita gave her time behind the wheel. On a shopping trip, approaching the need to make a left turn, Cindy turned in front of an approaching school bus, which would have been bad if the distance between them had been less. Juanita pointed out to Cindy the school bus had the right of way. It was a lesson well learned by Cindy. Cindy was ready to take her driver's test. Standing by, I was watching the test. Cindy was doing well. As they came off the course, the officer had her stop at the stop sign before turning right to a stop sign before turning right again. To my disappointment, I watched Cindy turn right, but she did not stop at the second stop sign. Cindy was disappointed as well. I made an effort to encourage her. Her next test, she did great; she passed and went on to become a very good driver.

Busy as we were, our family time was not neglected. Had it been, I am sure Juanita would have brought it to our attention. This was our special marriage we have had since the day God joined us together as one. Everything has always been open and free, evidence of the understanding we have of each other. We learned at a point in our lives that should either of us look upon another, it would be the end.

Dad's reading and his sureness of walking had lessened. Inquiring about his sight, we made an appointment for his eye examination with the Veterans Administration in Philadelphia, where he had had previous care. The examination determined the need for cataract surgery. An appointment made, we returned later. Dad had successful surgery and returned to doing his usual routine of cutting wood.

Winter had arrived. Dad bundled up and continued his outside work. We were invited out for dinner. Dad did not choose to go. He was in bed on our return. On return from church, I went into Dad's room to visit. I immediately noticed he was holding his wrist in his lap. When asked, he said he had fallen on the ice while sawing wood, landing on his wrist. I suggested we go to the emergency room at the hospital. He refused. On Monday we were scheduled to go to the Philadelphia VA Hospital for his final eye appointment. Dad was in pain, still refusing to go to the local hospital for his wrist. On Monday morning, we ate breakfast. Dad and I headed for his appointment. Dad was very quiet. I suggested his wrist be looked at in Philadelphia. No response for several miles before he broke the silence, agreeing to have them look at it. Arriving early, we went to emergency, explaining why we were there. I was asked why I had not taken better care of my father. Dad spoke up, explaining he refused to go. The attendant then turned his anger on Dad. After an x-ray, his arm was splinted. The eye exam was good, and Dad was released.

In the summer of 1975, the Bob Keeseys paid us a visit. While they were with us, Dad, Bob, and I made a trip to Tilghman Island, Harrison's, for a fishing trip on the Chesapeake Bay. We had moderate success coupled with the excitement of the first mate aboard the ship, who went into the water between the boat and the dock on our return. He swam under the boat and was pulled out with no injury. Harrison's was a real treat. We arrived and had dinner that evening, breakfast in the morning, and a basket lunch on the boat. In the evening, we had an enjoyable meal, eating fish we had caught that day. It was during this summer of 1975 that our foursome for golf came to an end. Dad Hildebrand was experiencing a loss of thought process, and his endurance had lessened.

Family visits with Mother and Dad Hildebrand, including Dad Keesey, were more often. Thanksgiving of 1975 was held as usual at the Keeseys'. Mother and Dad Hildebrand were present, enjoying the wonderful meal Juanita made with my aid, served to everyone's pleasure. Comments included, "I am too full." We all went upstairs, leaving the two grandfathers in the basement kitchen doing the dishes. It sounded as though they were having a wonderful visit, probably telling their yarns of the time spent during the war in France. Dad Hildebrand served in France in the Army. Dad Keesey had leave of ship when docked in port in France. I sure would have liked to been a little mouse.

Christmas of 1975 was our time for family togetherness. On Christmas Eve, Mother and Dad Hildebrand arrived for supper, joining in the activities and to care for Melanie as the rest of the family went to our church. The three girls were in choirs in the early service and late service; 11 to 12 was one of the highlights of the year. As we left church, the steam whistle at the New York Wire Cloth plant was playing Christmas carols you could hear all over downtown. Christmas was an exciting time for the entire family. There was a wonderful opening of presents with thank-yous all around. Santa Claus was generous to us each and every one. Santa Claus was important for our three-year-old, knowing she was also learning the reason for the season was Jesus. There is no question the purpose of the Keesey family in celebrating Christmas is God, Jesus, and the Holy Spirit. This Christmas contributed to the influence of my wife, Juanita, in addition to my two sisters. Upon opening the gift from Juanita, I discovered a necklace with a three-by-two-inch wooden cross. A gift from Rita contained an olivewood beaded necklace with the hand-carved Jerusalem cross attached. A third gift from Jeannie contained two carpenter nails connected as a cross. I mentioned the influence the first cross from Juanita, followed by the two from Rita and Jeannie, gave me reason to look within myself, asking, "What is evidenced by those I love in my life?" The cross Juanita had given me I put over my head, resting on my chest. A day or two later, very conscious it was there, came a heavy responsibility of the need of conducting myself in accordance of the representation of the cross. When folks were speaking to me, I sensed their looking at the cross. In the thirty-seven years since I have worn my crosses, there are so many folks who have identified with it, many asking if I was a preacher. My response was, "Yes, but not ordained."

Many spiritual blessings are present and in the future to come in my life. My walk is as close at this age as I have ever been in my belief and faith in my Almighty God. As we grow in our walk with God, why is it we doubt ourselves so often? My greatest growth in my life with God, Jesus, and the Holy Spirit has come from the study of the Bible, living as best as I can the lessons learned living the forty-eight years of life. The experiences one has with those we know to be believers by the words they speak, their response to the words, and treatment they receive from those they associate in their lives. Actions come into play as we assess those places they frequent and the treatment expressed to those they associate. As these relationships are observed, they give real purpose to analyze one's character, revealing the witness I portray to others as to my walk with God.

Spring 1976 presented a very special time in our Cindy's life as graduation day from Eastern High School was celebrated. We had great plans for an outdoor ceremony. We invited Aunt Pearl to come be with her family, especially Cindy and Cindy's grandfather, Charles, her brother. The weather was perfect,

the experience to be one for the memory book. It was the only graduation outdoor to that time at Eastern High School. During the summer, Cindy did not
make any effort to find work. Juanita put it to Cindy that she was taking her
downtown to fill out applications for employment in as many stores as she
could in a day's time. This moved Cindy to search for work. She learned of
the Avalong Horse Stables in East York. She applied and was hired as handler
of horses. I took her to work and picked her up with Granddad and Melanie.
On June 20, 1976, Uncle Harvey celebrated his eighty-seventh birthday. Aunt
Jo prepared an outdoor yard party for his family, including Uncle Owen and
Aunt Edna, Bob and family, and me and my family, including Dad Keesey. Tables and lounge chairs were placed around the side and backyard. It was a wonderful time of sharing the happenings in our lives as we remembered our days
of our past, particularly those with special memories in our hearts. The children livened the party up for a very busy time with much action and chatter.
Melanie was receiving almost as much attention as Uncle Harvey as he enjoyed
the wonderful day.

Fourth of July 1976 brought Aunt Pearl and the Keesey family together
once more. We had a wonderful day with good food as usual, then went driving
high on a river hill overlooking the bridge across the Susquehanna River between Columbia and Wrightsville as we viewed the fireworks. They were outstanding, providing a wonderful close to our day.

As Aunt Pearl and Dad watched, what were there thoughts of years gone
by? Early November, Uncle Harvey and Aunt Jo had gone downtown to the
bank. Uncle Harvey had gone to the parking garage on Philadelphia Street,
and as Aunt Jo waited for him she heard an emergency vehicle in the area.
Alarmed that Uncle Harvey had not appeared, she walked to the garage, learning the ambulance was there to care for Uncle Harvey. He had a stroke and
was transported to the York Hospital. Aunt Jo did not want to see him, for he
was not conscious. Several days later, she asked Ken Hendershot, her son-in-
law, and me to meet with Dr. Knoch, a heart specialist. Dr. Knoch informed
us the damage Uncle Harvey had suffered was such that he would not survive
in the absence of support systems. Dr. Knoch knew Uncle Harvey as a boy,
being brought into the store for his new shoes. Knowing my uncle, he assured
Ken and me that Uncle Harvey would not want an existence such as this. I was
well aware of his wishes were he able to speak. He loved life. The decision was
made at this time to remove the support system. He lived until the nineteenth,
then died. "David, did you know? Have any idea you would be a part of the
decision made in the life of your Uncle Harvey?" In my solitude later with my

Lord, I asked in prayer: Have I been prepared in belief and faith to meet life's purpose for living? Uncle Harvey was very much his own person in his belief and faith but never shared to another to my knowledge living his faith. His actions in attending his church in giving generously to the lives of others led little doubt as to his faith. I would add, Aunt Ina was of this same witness to her faith, rarely if ever speaking of it. They surely were one in their Lord. I was not moved to tears as I was for Aunt Ina. I never heard the name of Jesus ever witnessed. Their lives said it all. This was an observation on my part about the generation of many adults of my parents' age. I loved this man, respected him, acknowledging he and Aunt Ina missed the opportunities of developing the warmth of relationships not having children of their own. Reading this, I asked myself, "Is my sharing these thoughts altering my true love for these two people so important to me and our families' lives?" Sincerely not, for their love for me, leading me to the call of the church when I first came into their lives. My church life for the first time was established with them.

Services for Uncle Harvey were planned by Aunt Jo only. She sought little if any information concerning the life of Harvey Newswanger or his family and his life with the family members. She requested Pastor Martin Hopkins to conduct the service. As family were completely ignored, I was asked to serve to be a pallbearer. Not a word of the twenty-nine years we lived as family being looked upon as their son, Juanita, daughter, and grandchildren dearly loved, given a place of family recognition as family. Aunt Jo accomplished the purpose for her marriage to Uncle Harvey and her desire for Uncle Harvey's estate.

I have no reason to believe a change had taken place in the relationship of love and respect enjoyed through the years, especially during Uncle Harvey's marriage to Aunt Jo. We received no information of the reception after the graveside service. At graveside she banged her fist on the coffin, audibly stating, "Had I had more time, I would have gotten it all." Evidence was given of Aunt Jo's determination of moving in on Uncle Harvey at the death of Aunt Evelyn, proving Bob and I were right. Bob chose not to attend the funeral. In the years they had together, Aunt Jo devoted her time to caring and making Uncle Harvey's life worth living, a necessary need in his life. In all honesty, it was witnessed after Aunt Ina's death. I am sure it would have been the case with the passing of Aunt Evelyn, he needed companionship. We witness to the faith and trust we have in our Lord without any malice toward Aunt Jo. Juanita may have had reservations about having the same relationship prior to Aunt Jo's actions. In life we discover as individuals we are motivated by our different needs and desires. Needs, many times we classify them in such a matter, though they are more our wants than necessities. What are we willing to endure to accomplish the desires we have for life? I would never have felt comfortable depriving loving families that honor and right to be recognized, witnessing the lifetime of relationships. I would be depriving the wishes of another person. Being thankful for the love and memories of the past, all was put to rest in my life. Uncle Harvey was no more put to rest when we learned Uncle Roy Newswanger had surgery the first week of December. The surgery was successful, but Uncle Roy died on the ninth of December, 1976, due to complications. Uncle Roy's funeral was conducted in the same church where Aunt Grace and Mother's services were conducted in Quarryville. As the service was concluded, Melanie, four years of age, took hold of my hand, asking to go to the open casket to say goodbye to Uncle Roy. A wave of grief swept over me, causing me to commence sobbing uncontrollably for a short period of time. Melanie looked up at me, saying, "Daddy, it is all right, don't cry." My faith was strong, though Melanie, in her innocence and love, touched me deeply, releasing many held-in emotions over time. Once more we visited Mother's grave.

The Newswanger family was dwindling. Uncle Don, a brother, and Aunt Louella, a sister, the eldest of the children of David Sylvester and Dora Ella Reese Newswanger, are the remaining living children. Christmas of 1976 brought reflection and thanksgiving for the members of our departed families. Blessings and lessons learned in life enjoyed and put to practice prepared me well in speaking to the Word of God, the practices of those family members abiding in God's Word. Times such as these in life bring me up short, moving my mind to ask, "What does God have in store for us in the future?" The presence of the Lord was very strong in my life at this time. The message received was to continue where I was, doing the things I had been doing in His Name, witnessing, teaching, and preaching as opportunities continued to call me to serve.

Blessings continued, directing the growth of our family's spiritual lives. Juanita, Cindy, Lynn, Kathryn, and Melanie, young as she was, gave evidence of the unity we had as a family of faith and trust in our God. Living memories of the past enable the younger members to enjoy some family history. I have grown and am growing. I pray in the way my God would have me go. Having reached the age of fifty, the question comes to mind, "What have I learned?" I have learned there are folks in my life more important to me than myself. Jesus speaks of laying down one's life for a friend. Most especially, my family are my dearest friends. As you read these words, you surely must still be with me.

Dad continued to saw kindling wood right through the coldest of days. We had had a snow that didn't slow him down one bit. He donned his heavy winter coat with hood attached, and out he would go. In early spring, Dad had developed a bronchial congestion, prompting us to make an appointment with Dr. Trimmer on Tuesday after Easter. On Monday he was worse. Juanita and I felt he should see the doctor now or go to the emergency room then. He felt he would be fine to see the doctor the next day. Melanie would go spend time with him, talking about many things. She was full of questions, providing visiting time for them. We retired at our usual time, preparing for the coming day. At about 4 A.M., I made a trip to the bathroom and decided to go down to check on how Dad was resting. I walked into his room to find him lying on the floor. I tried to rouse him, discovering his body to be cold. I felt for his pulse, but there was none. Juanita came down together. We picked him up, placing him on his bed, and called the medics. They confirmed he was dead, notifying the coroner, and we waited until she arrived. She confirmed the death, listing the cause as congestive heart failure, noting the expansion of his chest. We were informed the body could be released to an undertaker. We chose Kraft's in Columbia; they had had Uncle Raymond's funeral and service in 1973. When faced with the unexpected, how would we handle it? In this experience, the entire proceedings followed the course of the immediate need. I can't say I was in limbo or unaware of all that was necessary to be done. God's presence was with each of us, knowing calmness and peace. The family members and friends were notified of arrangements for the service. We requested Pastor Marty Hopkins to perform the service for Dad. Aunt Pearl and Brother Bob represented he and his family, Ruth, Dad's wife of separation, their children, Rita and Jeannie, and our family, Juanita, Cindy, Lynn, Kathryn, and Melanie attended. The mood was light, taking in the presence of Dad being with us. Remembering days gone by brought smiles and laughter, prompted by experiences with Dad. Pastor Marty's scripture referred to tents to which I at the time was puzzled, having thought he had been told Dad was in the Navy. He had a good service, not having known Dad any length of time.

As we gathered after the service, Aunt Pearl spoke of their experiences during the summers spent in tents on an island in the middle of the Susquehanna River. Pastor Marty's scripture was appropriate. After all, I never mentioned this to him, only thanked him for his service. We proceeded to the Quarryville Cemetery, where Dad was laid to rest beside his Kathryn Elizabeth Newswanger Keesey. Services completed at the cemetery, a luncheon was served at the Willow Valley Restaurant, south of Lancaster. A good coming together of family and friends, we lived and relived days lived and this one in particular. We learned from Melanie that the evening before Dad died, as they sat together in her granddad's room, he was talking about the little people on the floor of his room, showing surprise in what she said, making no issue of it. In the separation of family members by death, there are three for whom I had remorse, that sense of loss. Mother's was the deepest, lasting some four years, learning to let her go upon inviting Christ into my life. The second, Aunt Ina's death, a question came to me in wonderment as to whom she knew herself to be. She was a generous person, never opening herself to you for fear she would have you learn of her inner thoughts and beliefs. May I be in error of her life's self-image? The third was with Melanie at Uncle Roy's service, asking to say goodbye at the casket, holding her hand. I'm not sure if it was the finality of the moment or the impact of all we had been going through these past months. Three deaths in the period of six months. In the seventh month, we learned of the death of Aunt Louella on May 2, 1977. Uncle Owen, we called him most of our lives, Bob and I, until we learned in his business life and his marriage he was called Don, owing to the initials of his three names: David Owen Newswanger. With Aunt Louella's death, he became the remaining living child of David Sylvester and Dora Reese Newswanger's family.

Cindy had gained good experience in working with horses, developing a good relationship with a young lady trainer who selected Cindy to prepare her horse for showing. The friendship grew to the point of her asking Cindy if she cared to join her at the stable she once worked for in New Jersey. Cindy asked how we felt about her accepting the offer. Should she take the offer? In discussing the matter, we informed her it had to be her decision. We could tell it was an uneasy decision for her to make, striking out on her own, to which she decided to do. It was our first experience of cutting loose our first child. We were never sure, but we felt Cindy believed we wanted her out of the house. This was never true, though it distanced our relationship. A shortcoming on my part in particular was when we learned Cindy had an accident with a riding mower and had broken and burned her right ankle and leg when mowing on un-level ground. The mower toppled over, pinning her leg underneath. We did not go to New Jersey at the time; I regret that decision to this day.

At this time we were informed Aunt Jo had gone to court, taking against Uncle Harvey's will. We might have supposed this action would be forthcoming, having witnessed her demonstration at the cemetery at graveside. The court reached a decision in several months, ruling in favor of the request against the will. The findings reduced the will of twenty-five percent from each principal, including charities as best we learned. We were awarded $75,000 of the $100,000 to be paid $10,000 dollars each year, plus interest, accrued over the period of time. When the will was satisfied, we received in payment over $100,000 with interest. Thanks to our Lord for the love served in our family. Uncle Harvey's will was settled when we learned our girls each had a trust established in their names for the purpose of furthering their education. They were provided a $5,000 trust fund each with interest, which we were informed were not taken against in the court action.

In June of 1977, five of the Keeseys joined Pastor Marty Hopkins, his wife Betty, and Associate Pastor Brad Brown, his wife Jane, and the youth group of Asbury United Methodist Church, bound for a missions trip to Cherokee, North Carolina, and to Red Bird Mission in Kentucky. It was our belief this was to be a working mission trip, but it was more the likes of a vacation. Swimming, volleyball, and horseshoes was not our idea of a mission working trip. There was good sightseeing and education for the children at Red Bird Mission, a mission supported by Asbury U.M. Church.

In the fall of 1977, I learned of the program to Certify Lay Speakers in the United Methodist Church. I enrolled in the basic course led by Pastor Norman Marden with plans to be certified at a later time, which was accomplished as planned. Learning included a good review of the public speaking, presence of mind, and personal bearing standing before an audience. Being a student of the Bible, learning and teaching the past thirty years in close allegiance with God, I was drawn up short in assessing my living with my Lord. Was there evidence of my witness of life for God's kingdom in a right relationship? Please forgive me should you believe I think too highly of myself.

I later learned Pastor Marden, whom I looked upon as a friend, became in his counseling intimate while counseling a member of his congregation, which resulted in his divorce. Our experience learning about the commitment to follow Christ can come up short in our absence of the Holy Spirit directing us. For example, the belief and presence of the Holy Spirit monitoring one's faith. More than one person has challenged my faithfulness for Juanita due to my strong statement of faith. Truthfully, neither my head nor my heart ever strayed.

Later in 1977, we received our first payment from Uncle Harvey's will of $10,000. Juanita and I agreed a vacation to Disney World in Florida was good for our family, especially for the girls at their present ages. The idea was to rent an RV large enough to accommodate the eight of us. The eight included Rita and Jeannie. The invite was made to Ruth, which she refused. We learned of a Coachman RV in Red Lion available for rent. The cost was reasonable, accommodating our number, and reserved it for December 26, 1977, through January 2, 1978. The time arrived to pick up the RV on Christmas Eve to have it available Christmas evening to drive to Glenolden to pick up Rita and Jeannie. We picked up the sisters and left Glenolden around 8:00 P.M. The trip to Florida was not uneventful. Traveling on Route 95 South approaching Baltimore, I missed the bypass, avoiding the tunnel under the bay. Realizing propane was onboard, we discovered we were at the tunnel and had no recourse. We had to enter the tunnel. Approaching the tollbooth, having cleared the tunnel, the woman attendant asked if we had propane onboard. I responded yes. She said, "You're through, I guess you can go." Before we could breathe a sigh of relief, a uniformed officer came around the corner of the booth. He said, "I'm not sure you are free to go." He then informed us of the thousand-dollar fine driving through the tunnel with propane in the vehicle. I told him we were on our way to Disney World, and the fine, when imposed, would bring our trip to an end. What did he say to our plight? He said, "Get the hell out of here." A thank-you to him and away we flew without another word. If fined, our trip would have been cancelled since that expense certainly was not in our plans.

We had bought sufficient insurance to cover the unforeseen. The RV was proving to be comfortable and fairly good on gas compared to our anticipation. We were able to spread out, giving us room for eating, stretching out to rest, and sleeping. Our excitement grew as we left one state and entered the next one, especially with the sunrise in the East. We arrived south of the border, leaving North Carolina and on into South Carolina. We had breakfast and serviced the RV. Jeannie took over the driving for a stretch. Down the road after a food stop and checking the RV, Cindy took her turn at driving. While the two of them drove, I crawled up in the bunk over the driver and passenger seats for a nap. We had made reservations to stay in the Yogi Bear Campground between Orlando and Disney World. We arrived at 9 P.M., discovering the campground in the middle of an orange grove. When we were to leave, we were invited to help ourselves to oranges. The location was good for us, being out of the mainstream of traffic, enjoying the quietness at night for our sleeping.

A long day of sightseeing, food, and rides found all of us needing rest. We returned to our RV tuckered out from the day's activities. Before sleep came upon us, there was some clowning around with me talking in Donald Duck lingo until Rita announced, "I thought we came back to the RV to sleep." All got quiet, going to sleep in preparation for the next day's activities. We were disappointed in Cindy having to rest due to her leg injury. She didn't want to slow us down and insisted we meet at a designated site.

At dinner in the Crystal Restaurant, having finished our meal, we left the tip on the table, preparing to leave. The next thing, Melanie came running to us with the tip in her hand, saying we had left the money on the table. We explained it was the waitress's tip for her serving us. She said, "Oh, I didn't know; I thought you forgot it." Melanie was five years old at the time. At this present age, she prompts the given amount in tip.

We tried everything we came to, including the animated bear show. We were unable to see the full show due to a breakdown. On two occasions, we returned, never able to see the entire show. Magic Mountain was a mammoth visit, especially the mountain ride with Melanie seated on my lap. Melanie and I only went once because she ended up sliding down between my feet. I was caring for her safety. At one point in the ride, we did a turn of 90 degrees. I wrenched my neck, giving good reason for only riding once. We spent five very active days. One of the highpoints for me was a five-piece band playing Herb Alpert's, Tijuana brass music. I still like his music today, hopeful of getting a CD of Tijuana brass.

Departing from our wonderful visit to Disney World, we decided to drive to the East Coast to Melbourne. We enjoyed the surf since we were on the coast. We passed the Space Center and, viewing the number of visitors waiting, we decided to continue north. Rita was teaching in Florence, SC. The plan was to drop her off on our way north. Jeannie was teaching in the Baltimore area. We dropped her off in route to our return to the farm. We have relived the trip often when together. Cindy returned to her horses in New Jersey, hopefully realizing it was true, that we miss her at home.

As life unfolds, things change and so they did for Cindy. Her position with the stable in New Jersey changed when the girl Cindy left home to work with in New Jersey left and did not include Cindy. Cindy continued with her job until she learned the couple had filed for divorce. Cindy liked working with horses, and she found employment with the Kohr family's horse farm in New Jersey. They owned the Lauxmont Farm in York County, located not far from our farm south of Wrightsville. Cindy was found to be responsible and was given the care of the broodmares as their time came to drop their foal. She spoke of how she enjoyed the horses, and learning such detail of their appearance, she was able to draw likenesses of them in her evenings. Unfortunately, the drawings got wet and she destroyed them. This position lasted until the day Cindy was working with one of the horses. When she had hold of the halter, suddenly the horse reared up, caused by the owner's wife striking the horse on the flank. The purpose was to break the horse of reacting violently when made aware of unexpected noises and movements. This was not unusual, though Cindy was not aware of the action. Fortunately, Cindy's shoulder was not dislocated. Her notice was given, ending her career with horses. When Cindy left the horses, she took residence in the Neshanic Station Inn and found work in a canning company. In my concern for her happiness, I felt her free time spent in that setting, she would be less apt to meet a "Mr. Right." Apparently she took exception to my letter, causing ill feelings toward me. Her coolness led me to believe I was accusing her of an immoral life. My intent was for her greater happiness with the man of her life, having greater ambitions. Lynn, who was living with Cindy at the time, informed me later she felt my letter applied to her as well. Further assurances of my intent were felt to fall on deaf ears. Parenting does at times create difficult and hurtful experiences, bringing learning. Yes, our Lord is present in each and every new unfolding of our lives, mine in particular. My prayers contain the request God be with me to keep the learning fresh in my mind.

Melanie was taken along with the rest of us with the Olympics. She decided to try her hand in the exercises on the swing set in the yard. Her screams brought us running to find her on the ground with her right arm out flat from her shoulder. Mom and I tried to console her as best as we could, aware of the pain she had to be feeling. We reinforced her in praying with her with the presence of the Lord being with her. We quieted her, supporting her arm outstretched, gently bending her elbow, placing her arm across her tummy. We gathered her up and drove her to the Columbia Hospital. An x-ray showed the bone just above her elbow was fractured. She proved to be a trooper, weathering the storm and pain, healing over time.

Since the Lenten message before the men's group, God and Christ have directed my faith and my thoughts to an earlier call upon their presence in my circumstances. My words and my actions, when immediate, are recognized as selected and directed by a presence of God not yet recognized. Question: Was this the indwelt Spirit so unfamiliar in my life? Please know these revealing acknowledgments are of the Spirit, learned in and through the living of the humanness of life. All witnesses to the confession of life where I live today are credited to the surrender of much of the humanness we have born in us. Scripture in the words of our Lord admonish us to rely upon the wisdom and knowledge of the Word of God. The sobering thought when realized God handles our matters differently than we when are left to our self-reasoning and thoughts. God has a better way. Thank you, God, for second chances. Jesus spoke to His disciples in specific words they did not understand. For centuries, man, woman, and child have had to learn individually the blessings of living in obedience to God. History reveals the failures of the multitudes not believing in God's prophets or writings. Today we have the call to come to God by the invitation of Jesus. May there be time addressing these writings in more depth as I write?

Receiving the trust from Uncle Harvey's estate, Cindy requested the funds used to improve her transportation, deciding not to further her education. She purchased a new El Camino Chevy. We purchased the 1963 Dodge Dart she had bought from Uncle Roy's estate for $250. Prior to Lynn moving to New Jersey, she was employed by Mailman's department store. Lynn used the Dodge to drive to work. On a very cold Friday night in January, Lynn had gone to supper, taking time to fill up the Dodge with gas. At nine o'clock, she went to come home and could not find her car. She called in tears from the store, informing us of the problem. The management called, reporting the car was missing to the police. When they arrived, the information was taken and a bulletin was transmitted with no results. We had little hope of it being found. A period of time convinced me it would not be returned. In May a phone call for me informed us a 1963 Dodge Dart was found in an apartment complex parking lot in Fairfax, Virginia. We could claim it by identifying ourselves and recover it without any cost. Upon arriving on Saturday afternoon, we realized the car registration had expired, requiring the need to tow it home. No business was open due to the hour, requiring us to return Monday to tow it home. I at once replaced the spark-plugs and cleaned it up. Getting the car running, we placed an ad in the paper and priced it at $250. A young lady called, drove the car, and bought the car for transportation to work locally. We gave thanks to the Lord.

On the Fourth of July, 1978, Romitos invited the Krsek and Keesey families for a picnic, preceded by golf at the Host Golf Course in Lancaster. The Coopers family moved to Troy, New York, so they were not with us. We missed them. Bob brought up the prospects of our playing golf once a week. His friend, a business partner, Dick Ackerly, would be his partner, and I chose Charlie Adams to be my partner. We played every Thursday, trying a different course each week, giving us a challenge. We played for ten cents a hole.

In the fall of 1978, Dr. Paul Stambach introduced the Bethel Bible Study to members of the church and friends. After discussion, Juanita and I enrolled, interested in furthering our knowledge of the Bible. We studied the Old Testament the first year. We studied the New Testament the second year. Harley Swiggum, who was the writer of the study, lived in Madison, Wisconsin. The class had twelve faithful enrolled students, some other than Asbury U. M. Church members, all making their contribution from the life experiences and previous studies, which we all brought to the study. Pastor Paul, a learned student of the Bible, informed us when we completed the two-year study our learning would be equal to the credits of a seminary study. The learning of Pastor Paul's previous study assured us this would be our accomplishment completed.

Lynn's high school graduation in 1979 differed from Cindy's, being conducted indoors. It was attended by Mother and Dad Hildebrand, Aunt Pearl, and the Keesey family. With Lynn's experience having worked in the photography department at Mailman's Store, she made plans to attend Harcum College in the suburb of Philadelphia, studying commercial art, photography, and design.

In the fall of 1979, Aunt Edna became ill. She was hospitalized a short time, suffering with heart complications, and died on November 27. Uncle Don is the last of his family, Bob and I his closest living family members. I assumed a personal responsibility for Uncle Don living closest in distance. It was meaningful for me to provide his daily transportation for appointments and shopping trips, as well as settling the selling of his house, furniture, and his car. We explored the available retirement homes in the Lancaster area. He took up residence in a personal care home. After trying it, Uncle Don felt it too expensive. We searched for another home at a lower cost. The folks where he was residing agreed if it did not work out, he was welcome to return. We presented Uncle Don at the chosen home late Saturday morning. Satisfied he was settled, I left for home. About five o'clock that evening, he called me at home to say his residence was unacceptable. When asked why, he said he was uncomfortable with his roommate, who was blind, that it was unnerving him. I called the previous home when told he was unpleased, and they agreed to have him return the same evening of the day he left. I gathered his effects, returning him amid his apologies of causing me so much trouble. I reassured him my greatest concern was his comfort and satisfaction. Having gotten him settled, I bid him goodnight.

The doctor appointments and shopping needs were in addition to the selling of the house and the car. Successfully accomplished, with the approval of prices these produced a settling of some of my time. During one of the appointments, Uncle Don confided he was uncomfortable with the amount of time I was giving in serving his needs. He related once more his commitment to Aunt Edna that their estate was to go to her niece. I assured him it was no problem. He felt he had to do something in repayment. With this situation, I suggested he speak with his attorney, giving me power of attorney and making me executor of his estate. I would be provided for according to the law. He followed my suggestion, setting up an appointment with his attorney. The attorney's name was Reese. He had no relationship to Uncle Don or my mother's mother's maiden name. Her name was Dora Reese, my grandmother. Met by appointment, I was introduced to Mr. Reese, and after the get-acquainted conversation Mr. Reese invited me to leave the room to discuss the matter with Uncle Don. A short time later, invited into the room, I was informed I was to be appointed as Uncle Don's power of attorney and executor. Mr. Reese informed me of the duties I would be called upon to perform. He further stated I would receive a percentage of the final estate, satisfying Uncle Don's wishes to defray some of my time away from family and my daily work.

Our Bethel Bible Study was concluded in the spring of 1980. Unfortunately, Uncle Don was hospitalized after experiencing shortness of breath for a short period of time until he was released. This delayed our trip to Wisconsin to complete our study. Once again, Uncle Don was disappointed his care was interfering with our lives and plans. Uncle Don being settled into his routine, we felt comfortable to proceed with our planned trip. On Saturday in the last week of June, we packed our bags, destination Madison, Wisconsin. We drove to Gary, Indiana, had an evening meal, and settled in a motel for the night. Arising at 6 A.M., we had breakfast and prepared to drive to Madison headquarters for Bethel Bible Study. Impressed with the facility, we were introduced to the staff and were comfortable with the greeting.

On Monday morning, our sessions began of meeting with the originator of the study, Harley Swiggum. The week was highlighted by July 4th programs. The week brought the study to a meaningful conclusion. Scriptures were becoming more and more personal as to my belief and faith in relationship to the Trinity in my life. In free time, I ventured to use a canoe to exercise, enjoying the stream close by the campus. Floating along and looking into the sky, to my great surprise a hundred or so hot air balloons filled the sky, an array of every color of the rainbow. Can you believe God placed me in that location to enjoy such a sight? I do!

After Sunday morning worship service and breakfast, we drove to Blue Island, Illinois. While there, we visited Juanita's family members, Aunt Mattie and cousins Dorothy, Howard, and Robert. We stayed overnight with Aunt Mattie, heading for home Monday morning. Looking forward to our return to family, we drove straight home without an overnight stay. We arrived home to learn all was under control and were informed how much we were missed. Isn't that nice, being missed? On our return, I called on Uncle Don to determine his needs since we were gone. He was fine.

I related my previous interest in the game of baseball. Dad took Bob and me to Connie Mack Stadium to see the game between the Philadelphia Athletics and the New York Yankees, a good experience for two boys thirteen and ten. Our Athletics lost to the Yankees. I was prompted to write about this for the reason Dad and I, down through the years, had been avid fans of the Philadelphia Phillies. Through the late seventies, the Phillies became very competitive, winning the games in the late innings. It made it interesting listening, taking Lynn to Harcum, and bringing her home when needed. I thought of Dad and the hours we had spent listening to them lose time after time. I hope Dad knows about today's games.

The summer visits to Uncle Don were on a regular basis. Our family, as far as we knew, were the only visitors he had. A routine in looking after his investments gave me much satisfaction, convincing me of the love and care I had for this man, my mother's brother. His health was good until October, when he had heavy breathing and congestion. Hospitalized, he died on November 2, 1980. Juanita and I discussed the funeral for Uncle Don. He never spoke of his faith. We knew he and Aunt Edna were members of a church until the visiting pastor insulted them about their lack of attendance. I am once more led in thought to this generation's privacy in expressing their witness to their faith in God, Christ, and the Holy Spirit. Their presence in church gave evidence of believing. To my ears, never was discussion or witness of Christ in their lives as previously spoken in my relationship with my dad. Being as open with my witness raises questions to mind as to how I am regarded not only by family and friends but by others.

We requested Pastor Paul Stambach to perform the service, providing information about Uncle Don's life. Pastor Paul performed a service for a small gathering of family and few friends at the same mortuary he had for Aunt Edna. Uncle Don was laid to rest beside his Edna after a full life at age eighty-three. Mr. Reese finalized the closing of the estate and called me into his office for our final duties as power of attorney and executor of Don and Edna Newswanger's estate. I was presented with a check for over $5,000 for my services, accompanied by a warm handshake and thanks for the fine care he knew Uncle Don received. Mr. Reese told me Aunt Edna's niece was to receive over $86,000. In a later letter to me, he stated there had never been any estate he processed given greater attention than Uncle Don's. You must know the happiness and satisfaction I felt knowing Aunt Edna's and Uncle Don's wishes were carried out to the fullest. There was never any contact from Aunt Edna's niece. David Sylvester's and Dora Reese Newswanger's family had been laid to rest. I was struck again of the generation of Newswangers and Keeseys absence of their Christian witness.

Money available, Juanita and I addressed the possibility of moving the workshop out of the house. A likely location was right as the lane turned left down a grade to the house. Question: What size was needed? Nestor Bowen's name came to mind; he was a member of our church. Nestor was known to be in building supply. Nestor considered our need and recommended the Shenango Steel Building Company. We needed size 24x40 to provide 24x16 for the shop area and 24x24 for a two-bay vehicle garage space with overhead doors. Surprisingly, it was delivered to the site $6,859 complete. We purchased the package with a two-week delivery. At this point in time, Mark Stambach, Pastor Paul's son, was working for us, doing various jobs. He needed funds toward his college education; his services were put to good use. One of our projects was installing a bathroom on the second floor we could have used when Dad was living. Also, he cut wood for our stoves in cold weather. A onetime henhouse joined to the corncrib was in need of being removed. We tore it down. Our Shenango building was the challenge of a lifetime, laying out the squaring of the foundation, pouring the bases for the upright support beams, and spacing the bolts to secure the upright beams in place. The operations are routine for experienced construction workers; however, a college student and electrical, electronics-qualified engineer left much room for error. Concrete-poured support beams in place, the masterminds devised the method for joining the crossbeams to mount the roof. The two crossbeams bolted together, one end was lifted to place a bolt in the low hole of the upright beam, then the other end the same action, joined both ends to respective upright beams. The van was driven under the center of the joined crossbeams rotated by hand, placed the bolt in the hole, positioning the other bolt holes to be inserted and bolted tightly. Eight uprights were needed for the length of forty feet, requiring four cross-sections for the roof. That done, we installed roof ribs in place to secure the sheets of roofing with self-drilling fasteners. We put the building on hold to earn a living. Success was the name of the game with the building thus far. What interest has this for you, the reader? It's a miracle, Mark and I able to do this without the Lord? Nothing is done without the Lord.

After playing golf on a Thursday, I invited the four families to join us at our log home. We came together, enjoying the fellowship and good food. Bob asked when I expected the building to be under roof. We expected to work on it as the business free time permitted. Bob responded with wanting to help, to expect him on Monday morning. We had no idea the plan he had, but knowing Bob to be one to get things done, we weren't sure what he had in mind. Monday morning at 8:30 A.M., a caravan entered the lane, three vehicles. Bob told us they missed the exit at Wrightsville. If they hadn't done that, they would have been here at 7 A.M. They saw the material and told me to go ahead with my plan for the day. With building plans in hand, they went to work. It was Dick Ackerly and four Amish men employed by Bob. It was no surprise to me, for I knew Bob to employ them. When I had returned, the building was completed, including the concrete floor poured. I asked Bob for the bill, thanking him most of all for our friendship we have had through the years. He had great satisfaction contributing to our need. He handed a bill to me for the concrete only with the caution of not placing anything upon it for two days. Our togetherness over the years learned an insisting would have accomplished little; once Bob made up his mind, there was no time for argument.

Coming together for golf on the next Thursday, Bob asked if we were pleased with the building. Once more I insisted we pay for their time spent. Once again he related his faith, his prosperity was provided by God to be put to use helping folks where he found needs. I have long time treasured my friend.

Lynn announced she had met a young man in New Jersey while she was with Cindy. She would like us to meet him. He drove a truck and would be coming to visit on his trip through our area. Lynn directed Barry to park at the Canodochly Elementary School parking lot and she would pick him up. I remember first meeting him seated on the sofa in the living room. He was working on the log trip. He was introduced as Barry Totten. I met him with much interest as to who this young man might be. From my experience in the manner Juanita came into my life, let us wait and see until we get to know Barry and his life.

Lynn and Barry continued the friendship of dating while in her studies at Harcum. Driving to and from Harcum in Bryn Mawr, the radio was tuned to Phillies baseball. They had been playing good competitive ball the last several years. Nineteen-eighty was interesting. They were winning a number of games in the late innings, including the playoffs and the winning of the World Series. They did it, Dad!

The spring of 1980, we applied for the visit of a Fresh-Air Child to visit with us for two weeks during the month of August. Her name was Maria, from New York City. Maria was two years older than Melanie. She became our family, attending Sunday School and church with us. The three years we vacationed in Delaware camping, she joined in the activities of the day. In the third year, contact was made from her family. She was forbidden to take place in the program, ending Maria's visits. We learned to relate to a child not our own, loving, respecting, and disciplining her the same as our own. We missed her.

Lynn completed her study at Harcum. Graduation was attended by Grandmother Ethel, the Keesey family, and Barry Totten. We had a picnic at the Valley Forge Park after the program. We recognized Lynn and Barry were very fond of one another. Lynn moved to New Jersey after graduating, living with Cindy. She was employed traveling as a representative for the Atari game company. She was employed after Atari by a travel agency. While employed by the travel agency and joined by her girlfriend, Lynn was afforded a trip to Europe. We learned the most about Switzerland having great interest for me having been there.

Kathryn's graduation from high school was in 1980. She chose to attend Penn State as her college. On a Sunday afternoon, Lynn and Barry arrived from a weekend in Williamsburg, Virginia. Lynn was sporting an engagement ring. As a parent, I had some coolness considering they might have had their honeymoon before marriage. Reconciled to today's lifestyle, my mindset, it was none of my business. I needed time with my Lord. How different were Lynn's and Barry's beliefs from mine? This is another aspect of parenting; it never ends, only getting more involved. What was I learning? I had held my tongue, giving time for thought. I considered the love of my life, Juanita, asking, what are her thoughts? My next question being, could I have done this without the teachings and learning of God's Holy Word? The patience, the consideration, and the right of others to make their decisions? It was their life.

Lynn and Barry had made their commitment to each other; it is that commitment that binds them. My mind immediately relived the days Juanita and I had found one another. How could we possibly deny one meaning so much to Juanita and me to impose my beliefs other than offering our blessing? The date of their wedding would be October 22, 1983, with announcements and preparations. We rejoiced learning Lynn was to be married in her home church in York, Asbury United Methodist Church.

At this time in my life, the Eastern York School District became a focus of interest and concern, owing to a new growth planning of expansion. A building contractor was hired to draw up plans for a new high school to be built in Hallem Township on a very large area of farming land. A group of concerned residents met, exploring the need and the politics behind the plan. The group establishing themselves as being in opposition to the need for such an expansion was Bob Flanagan, Louisa Hake, Norma Huyett, and me. Several community meetings were held in the communities of Hallam Borough, Wrightsville Borough, and Lower Windsor Township. All three were well attended, producing many questions for the committee. The committee was prepared and was able to answer, in a very informative manner, questions put to us. During this course of action, tempers flared on the part of both sides of the issue. A lawyer, Allen Smith, a resident of the district, became involved, representing the committee and residents of opposition. The committee learned the projected growth of our district presented to the Pennsylvania Department of Education was inflated. A friend employed in the Department of Education invited members of the committee to meet with representatives of the Department. The committee, under the advisement of Attorney Smith, sued the school board to delay the plans. In this interim of time, the Department of Education investigated the projected figures of growth, refusing to honor the board's request to build, owing to discrepancies of figures. This action followed the court's decision to dismiss our suit. Why is it important including this experience in my life? Prayers offered daily to the rightness of the position, we were led to take imposed responsibility of costs and sacrifice on those we represented, including ourselves and our families. Prayers daily offered, led by faith and confidence, we were right and gave evidence we were led to pursue the course we followed. The next election for school board members numbered three. I placed my hat in the ring. The outcome gave a majority for me in the Lower Windsor Township, losing both Hallam and Wrightsville Boroughs. I was not too disappointed, considering my time needed to fulfill the responsibilities of the office.

The year of 1983, Fred Krsek and I agreed our teaching of the fifth and sixth grades of Sunday School was coming to an end. I began teaching the end of the summer of 1958, and Fred joined shortly thereafter. Twenty-five years we taught Fred and Hope's two boys and our four daughters. Where had the time gone? I believe God has had his hand on me from the very beginning of my life. True, many times I have ventured forth on my own prior to and after giving my life to Christ. I have been brought up short in review of the results of experiences, now recognizing the presence of the Holy Spirit.

The planned October wedding was coming fast upon us. Cindy is our first child. Lynn was our first child to be wed. Pastor Paul Stambach of Asbury U.M. Church would be performing the service counseled with them. Barry, a cowboy boot-wearing western music lover, brought to Lynn's mind a teacher at Eastern High, Kerry White, a leader of a western band. We learned Kerry and the band were playing in West York at a bar. We went to give a listen. Lynn and Barry liked what they heard. On a break, we sat down at a table to negotiate a deal and arrived at a price. The reception was to be held in the Yorktowne Hotel Ballroom. Lynn and Barry asked me to read scripture in the service, which warmed my heart. The years of Christian living in our family give evidence to our faith. The day had arrived. The Keesey and Totten families and friends gathered together, witnessing the uniting of two young ones in love, looking forward to their oneness as husband and wife. Wedding members were in place while daughter Lynn and father walked down the aisle to the chancel. Pastor Paul asked, "Who gives this woman in marriage?" Her father responded, "Her mother and I do." Lynn's hand placed in Barry's, her father was invited to read the requested scripture. Father took place next to Pastor Paul, Bible in hand, and reached for his glasses, discovering an empty pocket. The search was on, one pocket after another. A look at Pastor Paul, he made a move to offer his glasses to Father. At this point, the glasses were found in the right coat pocket, a pocket never used to carry Father's glasses. Collecting himself with emotion, he read the planned scripture. The scripture selected Wives and Husbands: Ephesians 5:21-33. "Submit yourselves to one another because of your reverence for Christ. Lynn, submit yourself to Barry as to the Lord, for Barry has authority over you, Lynn, as Christ has authority over the Church; and as Christ is himself the Savior of the Church, His Body. And so, Lynn, you must submit yourself completely to Barry just as the Church submits itself to Christ. Barry, love Lynn just as Christ loved the Church and gave his life for it. He did this to dedicate the Church to God by his word, after making it clean by washing it in water, in order to present the Church to himself in all its beauty, pure and faultless, without spot or wrinkle or any other imperfection. Barry, you ought to love Lynn just as you love your own body. Barry, you love Lynn as you love yourself. Barry, you don't hate your own body. Instead, Barry you feed it and take care of it, just as Christ does the Church, for you are both members of his Body. As the scripture says, 'For this reason [Barry], you will leave your father and mother and unite with Lynn, and the two will become one.' There is a deep secret truth revealed in this scripture, which we understand as applying to Christ and the Church. But it also applies to you, Barry. You must love Lynn as you love yourself, and Lynn, you must respect Barry."

A later moment after the service, Father was open season over the glasses issue. Lynn and Barry, in the presence of God, submitted vows to one another before families and friends, focused lovingly upon each other. I remember Barry's mother repeatedly expressing her losing her son, not one word expressing her gaining a daughter she had never had. The receiving line of Tottens, Hildebrands, and Keeseys gave evidence of the support this couple had. The period of time for pictures was accompanied by greetings among families and friends prior to the party moving to the Yorktowne Hotel. Pictures at the setting of the church were taken for future reference for this wonderful day for us all.

All assembled in the ballroom, the MC of the reception, Bandleader Kerry White, took his place with mic in hand and announced the arrival of the wedding party with an exuberant outpouring of the party. Each of the bride's attendants and their escorts were introduced, the maid of honor and her escort, then last but not least the bride and groom. A beautiful bride and groom party it was. This was all met with the accompaniment of the band's fanfare, recognition of the families, and the toast to the couple. A fine meal was served, with the cutting of the cake, accompanied by the usual antics of the bride and groom, bringing much to the festivities. Strike up the band: They commenced with the dancing of the bride and groom, followed by family members and guests. From most everyone's comments, it was a happy and joyous wedding. Caught up in the excitement of the occasion, I, unbeknown to Mother Juanita, invited the party to a post-wedding breakfast at the old log farmhouse the following morning. Needless to say, during the ride home the question came up as to how this could be carried off. Upon arrival at home, things began by purchasing the food, drinks, and breakfast pastries for an estimated number of folks who might arrive. The big question after things were purchased was: What if we don't have enough for everybody? The girls were very involved and went in their different directions in the purchase of supplies for the following morning. We got eggs, bacon, sausage, milk for drinking and cereals, flour for pancakes and waffles, V8, orange and cranberry juices, donuts and breakfast pastries, tea and coffee, regular and decaffeinated, plates, cups and eating utensils, and napkins. Question: What had we overlooked?

On Sunday morning, we were up bright and early in preparation for the arrival of…we had no idea how many, maybe twenty or perhaps twenty-five. At eight A.M., they started arriving. To our delight, they had taken the invitation seriously. Amazingly things began happening in a well-ordered manner due to the number of hands chipping in to help. Everyone was served. We estimated about forty or more attended the breakfast. Bob and Jeannie Romito were among the first to arrive and chipped in to help. Everyone joined in the festivities, providing lasting memories added to the wedding. When all was said and done, it was quite an endeavor. Satisfying! Lynn and Barry's wedding was one to be remembered. Never to be forgotten.

We learned the Romitos were leaving for Florida after the breakfast. The thirty-some years our families had bonded were lasting, even though they had moved from the York area to Lancaster. Bob had a fine mind for business, establishing the ACM Business Equipment Company, surplus furniture, and business supplies. Bob was elected Treasurer of Lancaster City, a partner in the Rose Bowl Restaurant. In addition, Bob was owner of a Ford Agency Dealership. I acknowledged his work in helping folks needing assistance such as the work he and his people provided in finishing our building. Our friendship was the personal relationship based on our Christian witness and fellowship love for each of our families. When we played bridge in our early friendship, we usually took issue with one another on most issues much to our mutual friends' amusement as we were playing bridge. Lynn and Barry set up a home where Barry was raised all his life. Juanita and I were extremely happy and pleased with our first SON-IN-LAW, SON! After four daughters, I had male support, not that I needed it, for our daughters have always been everything a father could hope or want, loving each one of them with all my heart. Of course, you already know of my love, respect, and admiration for my Juanita.

Thanksgiving, Christmas, and the New Year brought families together, sharing fellowship and the many experiences of stories of previous years with jokes and laughter. Early in January, we received a phone call from Dick Ackerly, informing us our friend Bob Romito was diagnosed with lung cancer and given just days to live. I was deeply saddened and was moved to go see him. I called Jeannie and was told he was seeing no one. The depth of his despair was more grievous to me knowing of his future days he had planned with his family, in particular their new grandchild. I suffered with this pain for Bob and my relationship more than any member of my own family, save my mother's death in 1935 from this dreaded illness called cancer. I was prepared to drive to Florida, had Jeannie not been so firm in Bob's insisting he would see no one. Immediately I wrote a letter expressing my love for Bob, Jeannie, Gale, and Chuck. Christian faith filled with the love of God moved me to offer my life for his were it possible. I truly felt the sacrificial love Christ gave to us in His suffering for us.

At Bob's funeral, Jeannie thanked me for the letter expressing Bob's response for the love I had offered. His funeral gave evidence of the loving life Bob had given many. As my relationship has continued with my mother spiritually, my life with Bob has never known a separation. Thinking of Romans 8:35-39, may I, at this time, relate the presence of the Spirit, God's Spirit, grown and growing ever greater in my being. My relationship and life with those dearest and closest show little evidence of the indwelling, nearness, and power of the Holy Spirit. To this day in the leading of Bible Study, much controversy is stirred in the souls of individuals when led to believe in the Holy Spirit, the power enabling us to overcome sin in our lives. The Word of God by faith is able to overcome all things. Our life in the human body hinders the faith from accepting the newness of life in the Spirit. As one of the conveners, I must be surrendered to resist being arbitrary and insistent of being strong in faith to be sin free. The term "perfect" is introduced, quoting: "Jesus is the only perfect one of the world." How are we to be empowered to receive and know the power of the Holy Spirit refusing to act in receiving the indwelling? I continue praying to God. Lord, am I more holy than I am permitted to think of myself given by Your Holy Love and Grace? May I embrace the subject more intimately as my story continues.

Cindy, home for a visit, introduced Rick Robinson, a friend from New Jersey. Rick had asked Cindy for her hand in marriage, but Cindy responded that she was not prepared at that point. I was surprised to learn at a later time my sister Jeannie was not happy that Cindy hadn't been the first daughter married.

Dad Hildebrand had developed Alzheimer's disease, steadily regressing and becoming a threat to Ethel. For a period of time, he was in need of bathing care. I was more than willing to help him. Dad was a modest man, accepting me, knowing me, and trusting me. Mother finally took the action to have him entered into the Lebanon VA Hospital. He lived a year, dying on June 15, 1983. It is a very difficult experience seeing a loved one fade away, but I was so pleased to have spoken at his service. If I may, my life was enhanced, knowing and loving him.

The heavy work in erecting towers and lifting TVs, furniture, and appliances had caused a strain, developing hernias in both of my groins. A veteran of the Korean War period, I made an appointment to be examined by a doctor in the Lebanon VA Hospital. I set up a time to be examined. I understood a mesh procedure was performed by some surgeons. The doctor examining me did not practice that procedure. He required a week stay in the hospital for recovery, which I agreed to undergo. My first surgery was scheduled for March 1984. My faith was strong, venturing with the memories of the previous surgeries performed upon body. I was released on Thursday, one week after surgery. On Sunday I stayed in pajamas, watching TV after Juanita and the girls still living at home had gone to church. I felt moisture in the area of my incision, discovering the incision had opened. Juanita returned home, learning of the problem, and asked, "What are you going to do?" We called the VA hospital, relating the situation. We were told an ambulance would be sent to take me back to the hospital. I said that wouldn't be necessary; I had applied a towel compress. After dinner my wife would drive us over, arriving around 3 P.M. There was a bit of discussion until it was made clear this was the plan. We arrived at the hospital about 3 P.M. and found they were ready to receive me. I was placed in the same room and bed previously occupied. The next week, my meals were more than I could have ever expected. The doctor noticed a growth on my back shoulder high left of my spine. He asked if I wished to have it removed. I agreed. It was a minor surgery requiring local anesthesia to cover any discomfort, which I learned was needed since I was experiencing much pain. Healed, I arrived home, anxious to get to work. The previous surgery for my hernia was in March 1984. In August I had healed well, and the doctor agreed to perform surgery on my second hernia. I entered the hospital in late September and remember watching the World Series, won by the Detroit Tigers, managed by Sparky Anderson. A friendship I made with a colored patient became a sad lesson for me after his surgery. Entering his room, I asked his wife and daughter, "How is our boy?" It was as though I had slapped his wife in the face. My apologies meant nothing to his wife. I saw a softening of the daughter's eyes, recognizing my sincerity.

My surgery was successful. During recovery, the doctor informed me the growth on my back had returned. The doctor scheduled to remove it again. I was prepared, discovering a team of two younger doctors were to perform the surgery. The anesthesia injected, they began the surgery. The period of time and pain experienced in the previous surgery had no comparison to these doctors determination to get the root. Pressure was extreme, and the pain was unbearable. I was encouraged to hold on, as they were near finished. I gritted my teeth, holding on until completion. It was a success. Recovery complete, I was released from the hospital. I was moved to write to President Ronald Reagan, detailing the wonderful care I received at the Lebanon VA Hospital. My return in a follow-up appointment, I was met in the hall by the attending nurse who cared for me. She took me by hand to the bulletin board, where my letter written to President Reagan was displayed. You must know the honor and respect grown for the president. I held a high regard that prompted my writing initially. The presence of God surely was with me in and through this experience.

We learned Cindy had a great fondness for Barry when he fell in love with Lynn and they married. Neither Cindy nor Lynn gave evidence of differences between the two of them. Cindy and Rick announced their engagement after Rick's third proposal. Juanita and David, in our lives together, understood the others' thoughts on subjects as they came to be addressed. On important issues with the girls, we listened and gave our input without criticism, the final decisions being theirs. After Dad Hildebrand's death, our time spent with Mother had not changed. Our attentiveness was needed in the sale of her house and her move to the Powder Mill Apartment, where all of her needs were met but for doctor appointments and shopping. Our occasional visits with Ruth, Rita, and Jeannie, when Rita was home from Africa, were enjoyed, bringing us to date on our activities, coupled with the growth and changes. Our families are blessed in the continued love grown in our togetherness.

Thanksgiving and Christmas continued to be in the old log farmhouse, which had been home these past thirteen years. Two of our girls had flown the nest. Kathryn's first two years she attended the Penn State York satellite in York. Kathryn had taken up residence in a dormitory at State College. In addition to her studies, she met a young man, John Fisher, and it became a warm relationship. Upon the completion of Kathryn's studies in therapy, both Kathryn and John enrolled in Boston University, furthering their therapy studies. The study required two years. Ah, yes, then there was Melanie, our youngest, who had grown to her thirteenth year. At this time in life, Melanie entered seventh grade, enabling Juanita to apply for substitute teaching. In the coming years, Juanita taught in as many as five school districts. My admiration and greater respect had grown more when, at the ring of the phone at six in the morning, she would be called to teach children she never had seen before. Thirteen years Juanita taught, in all a year full time and sub-teaching.

We all looked forward to our visit with Aunt Pearl. She was now bedfast. We inquired at the station of the attendants, without exception smiles, one of them telling how they each took hold of a corner of the sheet, rolling her around, hearing her laugh, the need being to prevent bed sores. That was our Aunt Pearl, true to everything she had brought into my life. We were informed by Ann, her daughter, that Aunt Pearl had passed away, having lived into her ninetieth year, born on August 9, 1895. Her service was held at the Brethren Home, with the eulogy given by her nephew, Pastor Robert Garber. I knew him in his youth as Bobby. Cousin Ann asked me to do graveside. I had never seen a faith in God witnessed in Ann. My point of interest was my understanding as to how Ann felt I was spiritually prepared to fulfill her request. May I make further witness to the fact one's faith is visual to others in your language and the manner in which one carries oneself?

Conscious of family and friends at graveside, my mind turned to Bob, my brother, older with a greater education, and considered where his mind would be at this moment. I believe this was probably my afterthought rather than my presence of mind at the time. "May we pray, Heavenly Father, we gather in your love experienced from the life we come to celebrate laying to rest one whose childhood, adulthood, motherhood, and aunt-hood have touched us with your presence. Pearl was the mother's love I knew and know the place in my life taken after my mother's death at my young age. We pray in our lives you will give us the peace and comfort as we live out our lives, filled with loving memories of her motherhood and friendship. May we close with the Lord's Prayer!" It was brief, welcomed, and appreciated by those present who expressed themselves, especially Ann. Brother Bob made no comment.

The subject came up relating to Juanita's and my part in the cost of Cindy and Rick's wedding. We had announced before these happenings began our amount would be $1500. Cindy informed us weddings in New Jersey cost as much as several thousands of dollars. We responded we were from Pennsylvania, and our figure was $1500. It wasn't received too well. Cindy and Rick's date for marriage was May 31, 1986. The wedding was held in the Clover Hill Reform Church, where Lynn, Barry, and family were members. A beautiful bride Cindy was, with her handsome husband, Rick. Meeting Rick's family was an enlightening experience. When asked where they lived in Florida, Rick's dad responded, "Let us know when you are coming. We won't be home." That ended that conversation.

I rode along with Lynn when she drove Cindy and Rick to the motel, where they stayed for the night, catching their flight the next morning to Cancun. Upon their return, they set up housekeeping in High Bridge New Jersey.

Golf playing had come to an end since the death of my good friend Bob Romito. Several visits to the Keeseys' in New Hampshire provided Brother Bob, Kevin, and me the opportunity to play a round or two. Their family had grown up; additional weddings included Kathy to the associate pastor of their church, Chuck Gross, and Kevin's marriage to Kathleen Toner. They met at the University of Connecticut. The family of Kathleen lived in New Jersey. Kim married a New Hampshire native, Jim Norton.

August 6, 1987, was a great day for the Tottens and the Keeseys. Our first grandchild saw the light of day, one Nathaniel Kip Totten. Granny Juanita was delivered to the Totten home on Otto Road to assist the new mother and father in their family rearing. Gramps David and Mel were on their own for a while.

The Birth of Grandchild #1
August 6, 1987, Nathaniel Kip Totten.
We grandparents live for these days,

Anticipating the gift, the outcome to play,
Knowing it has to be a boy or a girl,
Maintaining all of us in somewhat of a whirl,
Lynn and Barry expecting this child to be
The combination of them both, they agree.
With trust in the Lord, the child is a boy.
In all of his life, he has never shown to be coy.
Nathaniel Kip is his given name,
Kip he is called, has led him to his fame.
A family began trusting in Almighty God,
Has us all giving thanks, praising the Lord.

The year was 1989. My dedication to business had lessened, influenced by the income from my inheritance from Uncle Harvey. The business had changed. The failure of a TV no longer repaired was owed to the lower cost to replace. The antenna business had lessened with the coming of the cable. I had reached an age realizing my sight and my patience had lessened, and the new electronic advancements called for the decision to give up the business. After three weeks, the family said I was a different person.

Juanita saw an ad for Royer's Flower Shop to deliver flowers on special occasions. I answered the ad, and I learned I needed to use my own vehicle and went to work for them. I worked for Woody, the manager, for the better part of the year. I approached Woody about fulltime work, and he said he would keep me in mind. A week later, Juanita saw an ad for a fulltime worker at Royer's at Eastern Boulevard. I took the ad and walked into the garage, where I met Julie, the assistant manager, to ask her about the ad. She got an application to be filled out. Woody came out into the shipping room and asked what I was doing. When he learned I was filling out an application, he said he had forgotten about our conversation. Looking at the application, he questioned my age. He couldn't believe I was sixty-two. He tore up the application and told me I had the job.

Mother Ethel had lived in Powder Mill Home, Lutheran Home, and now moved to the Normandie Ridge Methodist Home for her care. She was losing her strength since a fall. The year of 1990 began with the birth of our second grandchild, one Courtney Alyssa Garber Totten, born on January 30, 1990, missing my birthday again. Once more, Granny made the visit to be with the new mother and baby. Wow, what a baby she had turned out to be! Lynn was very fond of Aunt Pearl, the reason for Courtney having

Garber as a part of her name. Courtney and Gramps didn't get acquainted until she was over two years old because Kip and Gramps were always wrestling with one another. Kip was usually riding on Gramps' back, Gramps' down on hands and knees.

The birth of grandchild #2
January 30, 1990,
Courtney Alyssa Garber Totten
A boy, a beautiful girl blessings galore,
Interesting to see the future in store;
For this family now the number is four,
Time elapse, Courtney showed the score;
The talent she is blessed with and more.
Granny, Courtney took to at once,
Gramps, didn't count til' she got to his hair.
Courtney took all our hearts that is fair.

In May of 1990, in addition to Courtney's birth, Mel was graduating from high school. Kathryn and John, who had enrolled in Boston University as graduate students of physical therapy for their master's degrees, graduated in Boston on May 14, 1990. A week later, on the twenty-first, they were married in the Lutheran church in State College, Pennsylvania. State College was where John was raised in his childhood. Ruth, Rita, and Jeannie were with us, completing our family gathering. They were always comfortable, warm, and good conversational members. They stayed in a motel. Our lodging was in a bed-and-breakfast on the property of a vineyard and winery. An exciting tour was a bonus for us, also the sampling of the wine. Oh, I shouldn't have told you about that.

Kathryn and John's wedding was typical of our family ceremonies and functions, always including every member. This wedding had the fiddler on the porch roof of the Fishers' family farmhouse, playing as the bride and groom, arriving in the horse-drawn carriage. This was John's mother's idea. She wasn't kidding! Kathryn asked me to offer the blessing before eating. Apparently when I finished, from the looks of some I must have overdone it. A young couple responded with raised eyebrows. There was dancing and families and friends visiting. A string quartet, followed by a brass quartet, supplied music. A large tent provided the protection from the weather, which was needed at one point, for the skies opened up, causing relocation of some due to water pouring in. The food was delicious. Off they went, honeymoon bound. Kathryn and John went to Greece and other countries on their honeymoon. They told several interesting stories, most unique, about their lodgings. It must have been quite exciting. They both found employment as therapists with different companies. They agreed working together they would kill each other. They lived in the Mountain Top area, living in a farmhouse we enjoyed on our visits. Mel, as we call her most of the time, decided to pursue her voice training and music at Mansfield University. Her mind was not really into it, for she had eyes for one Ryan McWilliams, a grade behind her through high school. After a term at college, Mel informed us she was dropping her education at Mansfield. She spoke of the impression the life of a musician had made upon her not to her liking. Mel decided to attend York Colligate Institute to pick up business credits. Having worked at Finley's Restaurant prior to going to Mansfield, she was again employed by them. Mel spent late hours with Ryan at his home, coming home well after we were in bed. After Ryan had graduated from school, Mel informed us she was moving out to live with Ryan in an apartment they had rented. Juanita looked at me and I looked at her. Ryan didn't enter into this discussion with Melanie. Notice the change in how she was now being addressed. "Melanie, you are sure this is what you want?" Her answer was, "Yes." End of discussion. To this time in our lives, Melanie had always included Mother and Dad together. Our discussion was, how do we handle this? Juanita and I, in agreement, told her the door was always open to her. She gathered the furnishings and effects belonging to her and left. Our relationship with her and Ryan was cool with few contacts for a period of time. In time Melanie and Ryan realized their decision had made little if any difference in the relationship we had toward them, and things warmed up. Juanita looked at me with the expression of thankfulness with the direction our Lord led us.

Now working for Royer's, my hours became 7 A.M. until deliveries were completed. My fulltime employment with Royer's had changed our lives considerably. Business was begun in November 1960 and closed in November 1989, twenty-nine years serving the public. Opportunities of ministry many times at the kitchen table, when a job was completed, became a time of listening to a need for conversation, leading to a time of prayer at parting. We have thought often had we charged as much as we were entitled, we financially would have been better for retirement. I have rationalized we wouldn't have operated any differently. I most always slept well at night as a man of prayer in business by faith in God's love for people.

Sidon Ritz approached me on one of my visits to his store, requesting I bring the message in his church, Zion United Methodist, in East Prospect, on August 19, 1990. I learned I was available at that time, willing to satisfy the request. August 19, 1990, had arrived, producing the following message: "He That Is in You!"

"Good morning. I greet you in the name of our risen Lord and Savior, Jesus Christ. I welcome this opportunity to share God's Word with you. Pastor Derr informed me that you are presently in a weekly Bible Reading Program. From those scriptures this week is selected the verses you have heard, the basis of the message this morning. Before we begin, let us join together in prayer: Our gracious and all-knowing God and Father of us all, we give you thanks for providing this time, this place, and your Word. We offer our praise and adoration to you, our creator. In thankfulness for your Son, our Lord and Savior, we humble ourselves knowing of the salvation that is ours through His life, death, and resurrection. Comfort comes to us knowing of the indwelling of the Holy Spirit, your presence with us always. Holy Spirit of God, help us in this time to receive the blessings of this hour together. May the words, thoughts, and expressions bring Glory to your Name and purpose for our lives. We pray in Jesus' Name. Amen. To begin, keep in mind the words of the hymn we just sang, 'This Is My Father's World.' Yours and my Father's World. I John 4:1 begins in the Good News Bible: Dear Friends, that is what we are. We are dear friends in God's love. We confess Christ as Savior, and we have accepted and received God's Holy Spirit. Yes, you are my friends in the love of God. John tells we Christians, followers of Christ, do not believe all who claim to have the spirit. But test them to find out if the spirit they have comes from God. Many false prophets have gone out everywhere. We today are to beware of false prophets. Every Spirit confessing that Jesus Christ has come in the flesh is of God. Every spirit that does not confess Jesus is not of God is the spirit of the anti-Christ. The Bible refers to that spirit as the enemy of Christ, the devil. How about you young folks this morning? Peter, the Apostle, in his Epistle to the Christians in Northern Asia Minor, says, 'Be sober, be watchful. Your adversary, the Devil, prowls around like a roaring lion, seeking someone to devour.' The Devil devourers us in separating us from God, Christ, and the Holy Spirit. Sin is the thought, word, or deed that is contrary to the Word and Will of God. Today we are continually told we are creatures born to sin as though the coming of Christ has no purpose or power to overcome sin. Friends, God's Will in giving us Christ purposefully, forgiving our sins, as Paul states, 'Running the race toward perfection in Christ Jesus, our Savior.' We have not been brought into God's world to be sin dwellers but the likeness of Christ, our Savior. Today, we Christians are continually called upon by our God and Savior in the power of the Holy Spirit to stand against the onslaught of none believers to destroy the world God has intended for all He has created, fueling the hopes of the Devil, who is already defeated by Christ by we believers in God's Word. Our greatest power and strength is in our will to surrender to the Will of God, taking up our crosses in following Jesus the Christ. God says shameful acts are wrong and an abomination; let no false prophet tell you otherwise. My brothers and sisters, my friends, there is no coexistence in this world for Christ Jesus and the evilness of the Devil. Neither can we have coexistence in our hearts with God. We are God's in Christ Jesus whole and completely, or we are not at all. Christ has said, 'Not all those saying Lord, Lord, will enter the Kingdom of Heaven.' Sisters and brothers, have you given, do you know Christ Jesus, and have you given him first place in your hearts? He that is in you is greater than he that is in the world. In closing, may we pray: Our Lord and our God, speak to that heart in this moment that wants and needs to come closer to you. Move in the power of your spirit in love and your grace. In Jesus' name, we pray. Amen."

In 1993 Juanita discovered a lump in her left breast. Our appointment with an oncologist and biopsy determined it was precancerous. Doctor Rothrock gave an option, one: surgery, the removal of the breast, no need for chemo or radiation or chemo and radiation. He recommended we meet with the radiologist. We opted for a second opinion at the Hershey Medical Center. Records in hand, we met with oncologist doctors and came away confused. We returned to Dr. Rothrock and reported our findings resulted from the second opinion. Again, he recommended we meet with the radiologist. We agreed. Our meeting with the radiologist began by reinforcing the procedure Dr. Rothrock recommended of surgery of the breast, no chemo or radiation. The radiologist spoke of being pleased to take our money, again supporting Dr. Rothrock. The surgery was performed successfully. I assured Juanita of my love and undying support, that nothing had changed. There was never any indication of any doubt on her part as to my sincerity. I need not go into other experiences where differences were made in marriages in light of like situations. God has and is leading our path.

In November we were anticipating a call from Kathryn and John about the arrival of a bundle of joy. Given time, November 14, 1993, the bundle arrived in the name of Benjamin Reese Fisher, Kathryn and John's first, and a fine young man he is. At this writing, he is now in his second year of college.

The Birth of Grandchild #3

November 14, 1993, Benjamin Reese Fisher
Reese, as we call him in the start.
Was strong willed, bright, and smart.
Knew his wants, wanting them now.
Learned of others, need to bow.
His Granny and Gramps see in him
A wonderful life, for future did begin.
Put his energies into kicking a ball
Accomplished in giving it his all.

Granny and Gramps were filled with thankful hearts with the blessings from the Lord coming to our families. One has to believe the Bible is surely correct; hearing and obedience brings blessings untold.

At this point in our lives, we were involved in dismantling the properties of the business. The steel building was cleaned out and advertised for sale for $4,000 in the newspaper. A phone call from the Hanover area brought an interested party. Saturday arrived. He examined the building and offered $2,000, stating he would completely remove to slab. We countered at $2,500, upon which it was agreed. He arrived the following Saturday at 7 A.M. with men and tools. They had the building down on the flatbed lashed down by 10:30 A.M. They paid the bill and were gone. God provides in the evidence of answered prayers. We had previously sold off five acres of the fifteen we owned. The steel building was on that plot of ground, requiring us to have it removed, the reason for the sale. Efforts continued in preparing to sell the farm. A real estate agent was contracted to represent the farm at over $100,000, considerably more than our original purchase price. The agent advised the price to be fair in that day's market. Surprisingly, a week after it was put on the market, we had an interested party look at the property, making an offer $20,000 less than our asking price. We were advised by our agent to seriously consider the offer. Yes, the greed comes into your life, believing you can have more. We took it to the Lord, considering our needs more than our wants. Our agent advised us to accept the good offer. The buyer wanted the property; it met the need for his plans. Are you getting the picture? We expect our life to continue in this manner, as it has.

Next question: Where do we establish our new home near to our work? Juanita was working for Matthew Card and Gift Shop in the Galleria Mall. I was at Royer's on Eastern Boulevard. Our agent suggested we look at Avalong

Condos, located east of Mt Zion Road, to begin. It must have been God's preference for us. Out of the first three on Jean-Lo-Way shown, we agreed on the same condo. The Lord is good. This land prior to the condos being built was where Cindy was employed by Avalong Riding Stable after her graduation from Eastern High School. Our life has had direction beyond our natural comprehension. Our faith and trust in God has seen us through our almost forty years of marriage. This brings to mind the words of Christ when He says, "Take up your cross and follow me." In our walk with Christ, it has been continually brought to my mind the words of pastors and religious leaders when inviting those to accept Jesus into their lives. It is said, "All you have to do is invite Jesus into your life." We are taught the indwelling of the Holy Spirit will make us into a new creature, a new creation. Is the Holy Spirit winning our battle within us? Once again, believe in the promises fulfilled in the obedience of God's Holy Word. God's book, the Bible, teaches from cover to cover the fruits of disobedience. The Old Testament is evidence of the results of man seeking his own way, ignoring prophets decreeing the way to go. In New Testament scripture, God calls us to live the life of Christ Jesus our Lord. "I'm trying" is the response continually falling back on previous words. We are sinners. Jesus is the answer, more later.

Melanie and Ryan's decision to marry prompted them to ask us for financial help for the down payment to purchase a home in York. Ryan's dad offered help. After discussing the request, Juanita and I agreed to help. The home was located on Wellington Street in East York, about a two-mile drive from our home on Jean-Lo-Way. Melanie, with Ryan's agreement, desired to be married in the church where she had been baptized, confirmed, and educated in her Christian belief and faith, now to be wed. Seasonally she chose December, requiring the church adorned with poinsettias. December 9 was the date for an evening wedding with the poinsettias and laurel gracing the sanctuary. The reception was held at the Billy Bud Holiday Inn, located off Route 30 in North York. A beautiful wedding it was, families and friends joyously celebrating the festive occasion. A joy is Juanita's and my having been led by our Lord in Melanie leaving home to live with Ryan. Had we followed our disappointment and vocalized it to them with argument, it may have brought a misunderstanding and lack of trust they were led to believe we had in them. How long does one live never to become cognizant to the presence of our God in His guidance and direction when submitted to His Spirit and His Will? We give thanks to God for the understanding hearts given to Melanie and Ryan. We are here for them. God's leading in Melanie's life has been good for Ryan. Yes, we know of those and we hear them speak of life being the case of coincidence and by chance until God's presence is acknowledged in their lives, and they say, "Ah-ha!" I discovered changes taking place in my spiritual life, owing to my surrender to the Holy Spirit.

More storage, plus the ridding of more items was necessary. Time came and the move went well. This was taking place in the year of 1994. We moved to the farm in 1971, rearing our girls. We were now preparing our lives to be lived alone as husband and wife. I was not sure of the thought Juanita might have had arriving at this point in our lives. Some friends we have heard lament over the children raised coming to an end faced with living alone, just the two of us. Our children have never been far from us, for we have always been close.

Life in the nineties was filled with many personal and family members' experiences. Courtney Alyssa Totten was born on January 30 in New Jersey. Kathryn and John graduated from the college of physical therapy in Massachusetts, and they were married in State College on May 26, 1990, honeymooning in Europe. Melanie graduated from Eastern High School in June. On November 14, 1993, our third grandchild arrived, born to Kathryn and John Fisher. His name was Benjamin Reese Fisher.

I was found to have a bleeding ulcer upon reporting to work at Royer's on Valentine's Day morning in 1995, which led to several days in the York Hospital. A memory in that experience is being gently nudged by the nurse at 2 A.M., checking as to whether I was all right, for my pulse was down to forty. I assured the nurse it was customary when sleeping or inactive that my pulse dropped. My stay was of short term, and I learned I was cleared to return to work.

In September 1995, Juanita and David celebrated their fortieth wedding anniversary with a dinner party in the Yorktowne Hotel, where Lynn and Barry had their wedding reception. Brother Bob, Ruth, Rita, and Jeannie, the four girls, and their families made up the wonderful time we had. This was evidence of God's blessings. There is mystery associated in the lives Juanita and I have lived with the Lord. The mystery is found in God's presence owing to study, preparing them to be led by the Spirit in tune with the learning of God's Word. It is impossible to account the hours of Biblical study, teaching, preaching, prayer, and meditation, leading once more to the direction of Jesus, telling us to "Take up your cross and follow me." The following of Jesus requires the new believer to hunger and thirst after every Word, leading us to become the likeness of Christ himself. Few ever come to the full realization the possibility of us human beings ever witnessing the accomplishment of one's self assuming the likeness of Christ in us. The accomplishment is not for one's self laying claim to Christ. The witness of Christ in one's life is acknowledged by the beholder, others sighting vision and actions by the presence of the Spirit.

The summer of 1995, our friends the Ritters invited us to join them for a few days in their mobile home at West Bay Park in Delaware. We agree to three days early in the week so we would be available at our respective places of work. It was very nice. Larry had a boat, providing fishing, crabbing, and clamming. On November 7, 1995, a call from the Fishers informed us of our becoming grandparents for the fourth time. We knew of the coming of this blessed event, anticipating the news of the arrival of another young man given the name of Nolan Christopher Fisher. Granny and Gramps arrived, congratulating Kathryn and John, taking opportunities of holding our latest grandson welcomed into the family being held in our arms.

The Birth of grandchild #4

Nolan Christopher Fischer
Nolan, a Fisher and a Keesey we all agree,
Is it John or Kathryn, it is a mix, a pedigree.
We all are of one opinion to us all he belongs,
At first sight he is healthy his features strong.
The family has received him with loving open arms,
To keep his brother company saving Nolan from harm.

Our third summer we visited the Ritters again, looking at the available homes for sale. We had done this each year we visited them. Never had Juanita and I considered before arrival this year any serious thought of a move to the shore. This year was different. After having looked at three homes, we liked one. The asking price was $25,000. Serious, Juanita and I agreed to make an offer. To my surprise, Juanita offered the figure of $20,000. Fred was unable to reach the party selling the mobile home. We returned home on Wednesday. On Thursday, to my surprise Juanita asked, "Is this the right time for this decision?" I assured her she was to be happy and satisfied. If she had her doubts, we would withdraw our offer. I left for work, turning this over again and again in my thoughts, coming to the realization I might have talked Juanita into this change. I had been sensitive in our married life about doing this very thing to Juanita. I beat myself up all day. Upon my arriving home, there was little conversation that evening. During our breakfast, we had more talk without anything definitely agreed upon. A few minutes after we had finished discussing the matter, the phone rang. It was Fred, the manager of West Bay, informing us we could have the home for $22,500. Juanita was in favor of accepting the counteroffer. I told Fred we needed a little time before we could give him our answer. Juanita felt it was the right thing for us to do, but she needed more time to be sure. We called Fred and said we could not accept the counteroffer. He would call back if further discussion was fruitful. Juanita questioned why we hadn't accepted the counteroffer. It was ten minutes when the phone rang again. It was Fred, the manager, telling us the seller agreed to our offer. Fred asked if we were prepared to go ahead with the sale. I turned to Juanita, asking if we should accept the price of $20,000 we had offered. She said yes. I informed Fred of the time we needed to get financing. Financing was provided, and the closing date was September 8, 1997, in Fred's office, at 1:00 P.M. Juanita and I then established our last day of work, she with Matthew Card and Gift Store and I with Royer's Flowers, on December 24, 1997. Our next need was the sale of our condo. Contact was made with the previously used realtor's office setting the sale price and condition time needed to finalize the sale. Our decision made, we were obligated to give an account of the removal from our attendance in Asbury United Methodist Church and her members, our dearest friends in the Lord. Juanita and I, standing before the congregation, spoke of the fifty-plus years our friendships had grown in our ministry for the Lord and His Church. We expressed the reality of their presence in our lives filled with memories never to be forgotten, reminding all we are never separated from the Lord nor from one another in His Spirit. Their spirits would continue with us in our future ministries. May those blessings we had shared remain with all of them as they traveled with us in the years ahead. Blessings all, praise our Lord in our togetherness in His love.

Here we go again: another downsizing, determining our needs to keep and those to discard. Much was to transpire in this interim of time before our move. As written before, the 1990 years were filled with many experiences, producing much in Juanita's and my maturity for life. Juanita was now at the age of sixty-five, and I age seventy. Juanita had surgery on her left breast in 1993.. I had a bleeding ulcer and also carpal tunnel surgery on my right hand.

The sale of the condo was made in good time. My weekends were spent in Delaware, installing a drop ceiling in the add-on porch. New carpet was installed in that area as well. We had no idea the furniture and items we wanted to take with us. We were moving into a fully furnished mobile home. The family all chipped in to get us moved in a U-Haul truck. Upon our arrival, the Ritters were on hand. Larry, in particular, was telling Kathryn we would have to have a golf cart to get around the park. Everyone had one. Juanita and I had made up our minds there would be no golf cart.

On the weekends we were there before we moved, we attended the Long Neck United Methodist Church. The woman pastor, Karen Booth, was very friendly and greeted us warmly. This was after she had asked if we were first-time visitors. My wife will tell you I would have to tell everyone who we were and where we were from. After the service, a woman approached with her hand extended to Juanita, telling us she was from York, giving evidence we were at home in this church. At this time, we had no evidence of God's plan among these new Christian brothers and sisters.

Our furnishings had been moved to Delaware. We were working on Christmas Eve. Out on delivery, I developed chest pain. I went to the hospital for examination and was released later in the day. We looked for a meal only to find every restaurant closed. No beds, so we spent the night sleeping on the floor. We felt we had moved the majority of our furniture and smaller items. Wrong: The Contour and the Jeep both loaded, we headed to our new home. Juanita, driving the Contour, was a bit nervous about the trip. She did very well without any incidents. Closing for the condo was the thirtieth of December, requiring us to return to York that day. Completed, we had an appointment at York Bank to invest the proceeds. Returning to Delaware, Lynn, Barry, Kip, and Courtney joined us for our evening at the Crab Barn Restaurant on Long Neck Road. Meals were all-you-could-eat for $19.95. Kip was now ten years old. Granny felt she would help him select his meal. Out of Kip's mouth came, "I want a T-bone steak, French fries, and applesauce." This was a memorable meal featuring the menu to partake in raw oysters and mahi-mahi fish. We were able to select from the whole fish, served in the center of the serving table, eyes completely whole. It was our first meal we had in Delaware with the family. Our eleven years lived in West Bay Park, we anticipated from the beginning fishing, crabbing, and clamming. The next need was reducing furnishings and furniture, enabling us to settle in to enjoy our new home and surroundings. We found a used furniture dealer. We entered the store and were informed this to be the last week in business. Juanita was standing next to a cabinet and pointed out the picture of a boat for sale. We wrote the phone number down and called it later at home. We called and liked the boat, and we believed the price to be reasonable. It was equipped with safety vests and utility items. We asked for an operation of the boat. Pleased, we arrived at an agreeable price. We bought it and towed it home on the spot. This proved to be only the beginning. We disposed of the extras one way or another. A church friend, Ralph Allen, was very active in the Christian Storehouse. This was a major recipient of excess furnishings and odds and ends of all shapes, sizes, and descriptions. They welcomed everything and anything we had to remove. Friendships were made on first contacts, leading to the renewal of our earlier life relationships with people. What is it to find the warm reception of people at first meetings? First acknowledgements go to Almighty God, based upon our faith, belief, and trusting in God's being. All my life has been moving from one location to another, being received and accepted in mostly every new area. Greater witness to our lives, Juanita's and mine, was in the many new friends coming into our lives. We had belief and faith based upon trust, knowing the Lord goes before us, relinquishing the fear of the unknown taking any suspicion out of the next introduction to a new face with a new name. How does one get there other than the trusting in God? I have no other reason than to believe it is our close walk with our God.

The management in West Bay Park was most accommodating in helping us get settled in our new surroundings. A woodstove in the home gave need for wood. We learned the fall of trees in the park provided the supply when a request was made. We made the request, which produced three trips of their front loader of five logs twenty-four inches in diameter and six feet long. We had our trusty chainsaw rebuilt, making short work of cutting them to size for splitting. While sitting on one of the cut logs splitting the others, a neighbor, Wilson Green, came by and asked why I didn't use a wood splitter. I replied, "I have a wood splitter; I'm it." It probably didn't help our first meeting, though we became fast friends with him and his wife, Helen. Our experience continues as friendships develop as in every residence we have lived. On a tour walking in the park, we met a couple walking. We stopped to say hello and learned their names to be George Pintarch and Sarah, not married at the time. Weekenders or vacationers living across the street, we became fast and lasting friends with our entire time, continuing to this day. Once more our attraction in learning and showing personal interest in folks make us family, interested in placing the others before ourselves.

We had a new setting with access to the Rehoboth Bay and the ocean's shore. This was the inviting area of activities that prompted our move to the shore. A boat slip was rented and available on the north waterway of the marina. Our boat was twenty feet, limiting our maneuverable space to get in and out of the slip. This was a challenge for an inexperienced boatman; the most difficult condition was due to wind. Moments of uneasiness were experienced for a period of time. Our home was a 14x70 mobile home, green and white in color. Two bedrooms provided sleeping arrangements for ten with our two single adjustable beds in the back room, our wedding gift, a double bed in the center room with the bunk beds, plus two sofa beds, one in the living area and one in the add-on porch. During our years in the mobile home, we had floor sleepers as well. Our heat was propane hot air with floor vents. Remember, we were living in a mobile home. Fishing in 1998 was limited to flounder, a most sought-after catch to seventeen inches in size. Quite a far cry from our experiences forty years ago when camping at Zach's. Crabbing was good, sizes being five inches point to point. Clamming was good when we found the good locations. You have the reason behind our move to the shore believing our families would take advantage of weekends and vacations. Surprise, we learned in the eleven years at the shore the privilege was not certainly abused. As a matter of fact, in the later years they took to renting multiple-space homes on the Outer Banks in North Carolina, enabling more than one of the families at one time. No problem.

We entered Long Neck United Methodist Church and were received, as we were the church family, adopted with open arms. Pastor Karen Booth put our Bible knowledge to work in study and in services. An experience during the first Lenten season upon entering Maundy Thursday service, one of the participants was ailing. Ralph Allen approached me as I entered and asked me to take that individual's place serving as Thomas, one of Christ's disciples, at the Last Supper enactment. I was willing and pleased to be asked. To this day, Hal Deubert recalls the evening noting the friendships lasting from the evening. John Schutt, along with seven of the members prior to Juanita's and my arrival, had attended the Rally of Promise Keepers in Washington, D.C., in the fall of 1997. John had started a weekly gathering of those men and several more from the church and community. I had become a part of the group, learning much from input and living experiences of those present. John was our convener. Member Fred Brown, as we would discuss issues repeatedly from one session after another, told John, "You should become a minister." John witnessed to his lifestyle before Bridget and his joining Long Neck Church. He witnessed to trips to the bar on occasions. He did not have the call. It was exciting to witness as God laid His hand on John later to accept the call, taking those actions needed to begin his journey. We learned the summer of 2013, John completed his study, eight years of school, two weeks in August each year, studying weekly to complete the reading of basic Christian study and application of the Word, becoming a Certified Lay Preacher.

As the years passed, we recognized God's purpose for our location to Delaware. There was work to be accomplished for our Lord in the Long Neck area. Bible studies gave Juanita the name Jay and me opportunity for leading the study of the Bible at times. Several studies led by Pastor Karen brought intimacy of sharing life's personal experiences, bringing us ever closer in our relationships in our Christian faith. The water experiences were daily. While I was checking crab pots one morning, the motor began to miss, creating much smoke. The purchase of the boat included the manual for the Evinrude motor. I spoke with Juanita considering our next move. She remarked the possibility of buying another motor. Taking into account the mechanical mind I have been gifted with, I decided to tear down the motor. I selected containers placing parts individually in the respective part names according to the manual. The inspection found two of the four pistons covered with slag. I took the cylinder block to a machine shop for information and guidance. I was informed the block did not require re-bored. What was needed to put the motor in service? The parts list consisted of four pistons, rings, and fittings. The price totaled to $895. I asked the machinist if he thought I was capable to get the motor to run again. Speaking with me, he was convinced I was capable. I ordered the parts and went to work, assembled the motor, set the timing with the assistance of a friend I had made, and put the boat in service, surprising me once more. "David, did you know?"

In the middle of the first summer in Delaware, Juanita and I had a phone call announcing one David Alexander Fisher had made his presence known to the world, born to Kathryn and John Fisher; our fifth grandchild, blessings of healthy young children brought into the Fisher-Keesey families.

Birth of Grandchild #5

David Alexander Fisher
July 27, 1998
Granny and Gramps asked, for Gramps he was named?
David, fourth David in four generations to his fame.
His great, great Granddad, his great Uncle and his Gramps
With heritage such as this he is bound to be a champ.
Alexander to be learned was a great Uncle on the Keesey side,
A Fisher, many family ties of professional history bring pride.
Likeness of his brothers is some, without doubt he is his own,
The mark David makes in life, is how he will be known.

Our families, we are known to be of God, continuing to praise Him for these many blessings received. We share the joy in celebrating the accomplishments made in the children's and grandchildren's lives.

Sometime later, on Labor Day weekends with sons-in-law Barry and Ryan, we were fishing in the crowded Indian River Bay, and the motor went to reduced power and started smoking. We were able to limp back to our slip. Having done it before, I tore it down, discovering two of the pistons were full of slag. I called upon the machinist (by this time a friend) and purchased two pistons with the advice to have a professional mechanic set the timing. My church friend and brother, Gregg Biener, came to the rescue. Gregg, a top boat motor specialist for Short's Marine, set the timing on the water under power. Reading the accounts of these experiences, we must realize God's presence with us daily prayed through it all. Where you are in your relationship with your God, believe He is always present. Call on Him.

The summer of 2002, we learned Brother Bob and Eileen were invited to an oceanfront mansion by one of their close college friends for a visit. Close by, they would like to visit us while in the area. Of course, it was anticipated. To my great surprise, Bob had slowed down considerably. He showed little interest in the boat, even to taking a ride in it. Their visit was a short but enjoyable one.

In the Advent season of 2002, I received a call from Ike Holtzinger. She informed me the church planned to enact the Christmas story "Scrooge." Was I interested? The ham that I recognized myself to be, I said I would. Believing myself to be funny, I asked if the part I was to portray was Scrooge. To my surprise, Ike asked how I knew that was the part they wanted me to play. I cheerfully replied, "I was kidding." I agreed and set about procuring the articles needed: one top hat, tails, tie, and I had the trousers. Lodge 266 in York came to mind to secure the top hat and tails, which filled the bill, but I was still in need of a flannel nightgown and cap. Juanita set about making those items. Other members of church filled the roles, including Ralph Allen, Keith Rogers, Wayne Eisenhart, Dick Wood, and Drew Biener was Tiny Tim. One of the high points was Scrooge coming upon the scene at bedtime, dressed in his nightshirt and cap, and entering, causing laughter. Scrooge then turned, telling the audience, "It is not funny." I brought down the house. Scrooge's hard heart melted in the conclusion, giving his employee, Bob Kratchet, a hug to the applause of the church members.

One suggestion of ministry in church was to begin an early-morning session for prayer. The time was established at 6:00 A.M. on Thursday mornings. Seven of us gathered in front of the chancel rail on folding chairs. The seven were Elaine Wood, Mary Jo Wood and Dick Wood, Karen Booth, John Schutt, me, and Sprig Hudson. After a few sessions, Elaine and I were the remaining faithful prayer partners. Our prayers were most inclusive of daily life needs. We continued to be faithful for the better part of two years. We learned much of our faith as the two of us matured in the love and focused on God's intentions for two believers. Were there fruits as a result of our faithfulness? We knew God heard in His presences with us the needs lifted and the results. Elaine was a caregiver for her invalid husband, John.

In January 2003, in search of work to supplement our income, I placed my name with the Boulevard Lincoln-Mercury-Ford Agency. They gave me a call for one trip to the Mannheim auction to pick up a car. It wasn't until September that I began receiving calls followed up for work the following day when finished. The job consisted of picking up and delivering vehicles in the Middle Atlantic states to other dealerships. Early in 2003, Bob Apfl, a good church friend of Juanita's and mine, suggested we look at the Pot Net Mobile Home Parks for employment as security people to serve at the entrance to their parks beginning on Memorial Day. Following his lead, we applied and were hired for the summer to begin work on Memorial Day weekend. Both Juanita and I worked for five years. We learned Pastor Karen and her husband, Pastor Randy, were being transferred to service in Minnesota. Karen was dedicated to bringing enlightenment of the sinfulness of the lifestyle of same-sex living, to bring enlightenment in the subject to those either ignorant of the Word or putting body before a Spiritual life. With hugs and kisses in a sendoff for Pastors Karen and Randy, we bid love and Godspeed. Pastor Chris Lee was assigned to the charge at Long Neck Church.

In August 2003, we made a surprise visit to Eileen and Bob in New Hampshire. It was for the occasion of Bob's eightieth birthday. The family learned in our coming together that all was not well with their mother and father. It was known Eileen had spoiled Bob most of their married life. It isn't to say Bob didn't help or do needed things on his own. We never witnessed Bob involved in the kitchen. Juanita and I, in our recent visits, observed the pressure Eileen was living under catering to Bob. Gathered for the family meal, it was witnessed that Eileen was confused. Her absence from conversations pointed out the concern we had for both of them. Our visit was enjoyed, having time short as it was.

The family was moved to look into care for Brother Bob and provide the relief Eileen needed. They visited a rest home with Bob for a meal, hoping to learn of his acceptance to such a move. Surprisingly, a family member heard him say, as he walked down the hall of his home, "I have to get out of here." Shortly thereafter, the change was made. About a year later, Eileen made arrangements to move to the same home. Eileen lived in independent quarters at first. A year later, Eileen resided in the same living area with Bob.

The fall of 2003, I learned of blockage in my arteries, the result of a stress test. I was given the option to have the catherization performed at Beebe Hospital in Lewis, Delaware, or Christiana Hospital, north in the Newark area. Options revealed Christiana doctors qualified to implant stents during catherization; Beebe was not prepared to perform that procedure, so the decision was to have Christiana take care of me. A Dr. Ritter was scheduled to perform the procedure. This name was familiar to us, knowing the Ritter family, Larry and Doris. We learned upon arrival, Dr. Ritter had the flu and were informed Dr. Stilbauer would perform the procedure. We learned he was the department head. It was found one artery had 90 percent blockage and another artery 70 percent blockage. The procedure was begun. I was conscious and informed the doctor I had pressure in the upper center of my chest. The doctor told me to keep him informed of changes. I reported at once after he had said it the pressure had lessened to half. Shortly after that, it ended. The doctor touched my shoulder, telling me it was fine. The stents had eliminated the need at the time for surgery, providing a better life. Thanksgiving to our Lord for the wonderful care he continues to provide in our lives.

Juanita was lovingly faithful, supportive in every way. Calls from Boulevard Ford Rehoboth and Georgetown became more often much to my liking, learning work was still available to me at the age of seventy-six. Thank you, Jesus.

Daily, when time permitted, woodcutting and splitting was a wonderful time spent with my Lord, keeping my body in tune. Time spent in God's presence, I received greater experience in the company of the Holy Spirit, knowing thoughts of love and concerns for others and supportive prayers for conditions in His world used my attention. How do I express this to one seeking to find this closeness, this bond with the Trinity? One day, would or could God's presence be so relevant in everyday life? At this time in our married life, we alternated Thanksgiving and Christmas celebrations between our daughters' family homes. There is every reason to believe God's presence in the child rearing by His Word and His leading are the foundation as to who we all have become. We give God our praise, honor, and glory for His guidance and direction.

Many faiths of men and women have portrayed the Masonic Institution in an unfavorable light. I became a Mason the evening in April 1954. I was initiated in the mystery of the 1st Degree, revealing the teachings of the enlightenment of history, the nature of the fellowship of men coming together for the purpose of love and fraternal brotherhood. I served Masonry most especially as Master of my York Lodge 266 Free and Accept Masons the year of 1965, governed by the time and determination, following primarily in the shadow of one Harvey C. Newswanger. He, the brother of my mother, Kathryn Elizabeth Newswanger Keesey, served as Master of York Lodge in 1927, the year I was born. During the time from 1955, the year Juanita and I were married, until the year of 1965, the year I was installed as Master of my Lodge, the woman I married was always supportive, encouraging me to realize that goal. I served as Chaplain for seven years and Chairman of the Charity Committee. Larry G. Ritter, a pharmacist, and Dr. Howard McDougal served on the committee in those seven years. The year of marriage, 1955, Juanita became a member of her Eastern Star Chapter of White Rose. Committed in service to become Worthy Matron the years of 1971 and'72, she served each station, supported and encouraged to achieve her goal by her family. You may ask what significance this has in *David, Did You Know?*

The unfolding of the story has brought us to the year of 2004, the year David Edward Keesey was presented with the recognition of fifty years in membership of York Lodge #266, an accomplishment of life many in life don't achieve. The morning of Friday, February 13, 2004, on my way to work for Boulevard Ford in Georgetown, a patch of black ice was destined to change my life. The road was wet with no evidence of ice until the road shadowed by trees had a colder surface, creating ice. Approaching the area, the car in front did a bit of a fishtail. Unable to explain, my Jeep backend and began moving left, and I responded by turning the wheel to the left in an effort to right the slide. We call this overreacting. Apparently my actions caused the vehicle to rotate in the opposite direction, in this case a full 180 degrees, which ended with the rear of the Jeep backed into a shallow gutter. I discovered the spare tire mounted on the outside rear had sprung loose on the ground under and between the rear wheels. I pulled the frame with the tire mounted on it and placed it in the back deck. Unable to close the hatch, I drove across the road, believing I was well off the road and clear of passing traffic. As I finished placing the wheel in the bed, closing the hatch, I lost consciousness. I had no consciousness of time or presence of physical happenings. A bright round light came into my being. Gazing into the light, I experienced a complete peace, which enveloped my being. Continuing to gaze into the light, I knew I was in my Lord's presence. Free of decision, I was at ease to remain in my present being. Focused upon the light, I had a willingness to remain in the presence of my Lord at peace to submit to His leading. A smile came into my being, determining my future. The decision by the power of Spirit, I realized my life in God's plan. God has a purpose for me in my present life I am living. Once more, how does one explain the decision made by the Power beyond oneself? Present of being, at this point spiritually aware of work Juanita would be hard pressed to face alone, I learned I was to remain in the body. Understand in all this time, my physical being knew of nothing. The story to be told is related to by those closest to the experience. Juanita received a phone call from Beebe Hospital, asking if she was family of one David Keesey. Identifying herself as my wife, she was told I was involved in an accident and was in the Beebe Hospital. She drove to Beebe. Upon arrival, the social worker and a nurse took her into the chapel, giving her cause to believe the worst. She was told the decision was made to transport me to Christiana Hospital for more extensive care needed. When she saw me, my eyes were open and moving in a disturbed manner as they secured me in the helicopter. A state policeman informed Juanita that transportation had been arranged for her trip to Christiana. She was told she was in no state of mind to drive. She was introduced to a woman transporting her to a rest stop in Smyrna. Juanita was then introduced to the woman volunteer to drive her the remaining distance to the hospital at Christiana. Knowing Juanita as I do, how did she feel comfortable in only saying, "Thank you"? It was the only acceptable response. Cindy, the eldest of our four daughters, spread the word of the accident. At this period of time, Melanie, our youngest, was employed in Towson, Maryland. Her employer would not permit her to drive on her own and drove her to the hospital, arriving just before Juanita. As they were approaching the steps to the ICU, they met Pastor Chris Lee. She had had prayer with me preparing to leave Christiana. Entering the unit, they viewed the doctor sewing up my tongue; eight stitches were needed to complete the closure. It was learned later the EMT unit responded inside of ten minutes from time of the call. I was found face down in the gutter. The Jeep was driven twenty feet from impact from where I was lying. A tracheotomy was needed for breathing due to bleeding from the lacerated tongue. The neck brace in place for protection, I was placed on the transport board, which was a normal procedure. I was transported to Beebe Hospital. Beebe's decision having diagnosed injuries was to send me to Christiana, for the care needed was more than Beebe was prepared to provide. I was then transported by helicopter to Christiana Hospital. Juanita and Melanie were surprised at the amount of visitors coming and going permitted in the ICU to offer their support and prayers for my recovery, which was hardly if ever allowed. They learned of the openness of Christiana in the care and regard for family and friends of the patient. The family kept arriving in support of my care and recovery. The most serious injuries were the fractured of the fifth and sixth vertebrae, a broken neck, the lacerated tongue, and trauma blows to the head. The only recollection of this next week on the part of me was seeing my grandchildren, Kip and Courtney, at a distance in the hall. Nothing more. A fall backward into the waste container inflicted an abrasion on my back. It is believed I had gotten out of bed to straighten the bed covers. My injury to the back abrasion required some time until it would be completely healed. I was told the stay in ICU resembled an open house with the coming and going of relatives and friends. Juanita was ever present. That first day, Juanita met Bob and Barbara Scott, members of Long Neck Church living in the Christiana area, enjoying their mobile home on weekends and vacation in Long Neck. They learned I was admitted and made a visit. Bob had been the first member we had conversation with on our first Sunday as residents in Long Neck Church after our move. Living in the area, they insisted Juanita stay with them until I was moved closer to home. God's presence is with each and every one, coming together as family and friends in prayer and thanksgiving for His guidance and direction. Believers everyone. I learned I had no knowledge from February 13 to 21.

During this time, communication was made by me writing my questions and answers on paper since I was unable to speak due to the tongue injury, none of which I had memory of even when shown the papers upon my return home. How could this be? Saturday the twenty-first of February, I vaguely remember the removal from my room for transfer by ambulance to Milford Rehab Center. The following three days and nights, I was not in charge of myself. I was monitored for my safety. Perhaps the move was a bit premature. During the night I was restrained, I would not use the call button. Bob, the night person, informed me I was to use the call button. Kind and gentle, Bob, a big man, very firmly explained to me my need to cooperate or suffer the consequences. Fortunately for me, I never learned what the consequences might have been. For two days meals, my meals were served in my bed. When it was deemed I was able to go for meals, I refused. Unsound in my present state until the urging encouragement of Juanita, I finally agreed. Wheeled to the dining area in a wheelchair, I began my recovery. Occupational therapy began the fourth day after my arrival. Progress was made rapidly. I left on my own, doing the repetition of exercises. The therapist returned, asking why I wasn't continuing with the assignment. I replied, "I have already done twice and more." A session with the psychologist and speech therapist proved me to be of my right mind, rattling off my daughters' names, ages, and dates of births. Juanita admitted she could not do it as quickly. End of session.

Juanita had asked the doctor the result of taking the neck brace off. His response was my chin would be resting on my chest. The cleansing care was accomplished with great support given. During the entire period of time, each daughter, son-in-law, and grandchild was very present. Grandmother Ruth, my stepmother, and my sisters, Rita and Jeanne, visited as often as possible. An early visit from Lynn produced a CD player with a selection of CDs. One in particular became my favorite, titled "Gaither's Vocal Band." The Gaither organization, established by Bill and Gloria Gaither, gained great success with their gift of songwriting, coupled with the attraction of Christian talented musicians. The battery-operated player permitted me to enjoy the healing process, knowing and feeling the presence of my Lord three to four times a day. This is a lasting practice to this day for a time or two during the week. Pastor Chris visited and many church friends kept close watch on my recovery. Blessings taking away the concentration of the mind on the pain from the accident befell me. Juanita informed me the inspection was due on the Contour car. This responsibility had always been mine. The car had been checked for the check engine light coming on. When told by the dealership the cost would be several hundred dollars, they suggested we use the car. The experience they had found that the sensors often gave the wrong indications of trouble. Juanita was troubled that the car would not pass inspection should the light be lit. A prayer on her lips on approaching the inspection station, the light went out. The light remained out until the inspection was completed, coming on shortly after she left the inspection station. You can read into that what you will, but we call it the providence of God.

I was released from Milford Rehab having met the requirements for release. The requirements were extensive, getting in and out of the bathtub, exactly how it was to be done. I had to learn how to walk but never crossing one foot over the other and also the procedure of getting in and out of a car. Any doubt as to understanding or following directions to the T, the therapy would continue. I caught on quickly. On March 8, I was discharged from Milford Rehab, enabling me to keep the schedule to meet with Dr. Kenneth Eppley, given the responsibility of putting me back together again. An x-ray was taken on that day, and surgery to restore the fifth and sixth vertebrae was scheduled for the twenty-seventh of March. It is remembered Dr. Eppley saying he would be going skiing, which was the reason for the lapse of time before the surgery would be performed. It is also remembered Juanita telling him to please be careful. It was during the time pre-surgery arrangements were made and the meal in the cafeteria I had experienced great pain, causing me to lie down on a bench in the large entrance to the hospital in Christiana. Kathryn and grandson David were present. Therapy continued at Beebe in a Rehoboth facility, wearing of the collar day and night. There was a knock at the door one morning, and there stood Dick Wood, one of our Promise Keepers from church. Do you have any idea of his remark upon his leaving? "David, you need a haircut. I will return." Sure enough, he did.

The morning of surgery arrived, March 27, 2004. Upon arrival, we were met by three of our four daughters, Lynn, Kathryn, and Melanie. Preparation for surgery was an enlightenment to behold. Full-length white skintight hoses were put on from ankle to above the knee. Sensor probes were put in place from the top of the head to the soles of the feet. Prepared for surgery, it was begun. Surgery completed, I was constantly prompted coming out of sedation to continue to keep breathing deeply. When it was time to remove those beautiful white hoses, I learned the tragedy that had happened to them. The probes caused runners and holes all over. The specialist placing the probes explained they served as guides in response as to the delicate degree of expertise performed in the incision made and the plate screwed in place to the two separated vertebrae and cadaver bone put into place. Learned during my writing, when asked, Juanita spoke of Dr. Eppley showing the four of us what he had done. This was news to me. The instruction to me from Dr. Eppley was, "Don't look down." I was disappointed I was not given that showing. Therapy continued. I was returning to have an assessment as to my recovery for an x-ray overseen by Dr. Eppley. We were given instructions for the use of the soft collar when we learned healing had taken place. The ridged collar was no longer needed. I asked if I could work the security job in late May. We were given an okay. Dr. Eppley was disappointed the three daughters were not present. With an x-ray in August, Dr. Eppley extended his hand, proclaiming the injury healed.

Now is ten years since the accident. The conscious aftermath proved the words of Dr. Eppley, "You are healed." I am free of any pain or restriction of movement. Belief, faith, and trust have seen the Keesey family and friends to the results achieved with thankful prayers to our Lord for the miracle of healing. Services received from numerous doctors, nurses, therapists, caregivers, and food servers were blessings offered by everyone. Most folks have found it hard to believe. God is good as I can attest ever believing his presence in every way. I have spoken in numerous churches as to the experience, including our former church in York, speaking in four services, receiving words of appreciation, recognizing miracle after miracle how God provided the right people in the right place at the right time. Juanita never gave evidence of lack of faith, persevered being by my side, convinced we were being provided in every need. Spirit and uplifting with encouragement offered help in meeting our needs. Recalling our wedding vows repeated brought tears to my eyes and warmth to my heart. Our children, our family, and many friends living and fulfilling Biblical love are witness to the fact God is not dead as some minds would have us believe. It is impossible to recognize the many people, believers, and perhaps nonbelievers who had a vital healing hand in who I am and who the family is today. The person driving the car that lost control hitting me was not seriously hurt. We were to learn he had a laceration of his forehead. Maximum insurance coverage was $50,000 from his insurance company. We learned up front the helicopter transport was performed by an independent service, requiring a payment of $10,300. Had the State Police helicopter been available, the cost would have been zero. Beebe Hospital services that morning was another $9,000. Cindy, who was in the insurance business, recommended a lawyer be on the case. Our insurance, no-fault and comprehensive coverage, paid $150,000. The lawyer's fee up front was one-third, requiring $50,000. When all services were finalized, Medicare issued a bill for $27,000. Yes, all said and done, the balance was ours to meet the other expenses not covered by our insurance. There was payment received, $1500.00, for the demolished Jeep. The point to be made is our thankfulness to our Lord, His presence with us each and every day.

In August of 2004, the Keesey family had gotten on with a semblance of normal living. The use of the boat came to a standstill, owing to the unknown being on the water. We returned to worshiping on Sundays and were active in daily activities in the church program. Ah, yes, the healing process of continued therapy and the lingering instruction of Dr. Eppley, "Don't look down."

In conversations with many friends and new acquaintances, Juanita speaks openly of our ordeal. I find a natural response to the care I received from Juanita and her hand in caring for the function of the home. When spoken of the blessing she is, a humble and embarrassed self, seldom recognizing the giving on her part. Blessings continue. We learn during the recovery from the accident the family was about to take on a new member. One Colin Zane McWilliams was to come upon the scene on December 7, 2004. Nine years since their marriage, Melanie and Ryan are parents of this our sixth grandchild. Colin is a chosen name Melanie and Ryan liked. Zane Baker, a close friend of Ryan's playing in their band, lost his life in an auto accident.

Colin Zane McWilliams
December 7, 2004
Colin Zane McWilliams has been given this name,
Endeared by the memory of Ryan's close friend, Zane.
From day one God's plan is in every new beginning,
The members of this family together are winning;
The blessings as they come we've received from God,
Fishers, Keeseys, McWilliams, Robinsons, Tottens, the nod.
Contributors, each and every one, are none to be forgot.
This new arrival, Colin, we all know him by his name.
The life he lives, loved by all will one day reach his fame.

From the first grandchild to the sixth, as a family we have grown, our joys and our trials. God's been with us through them all, providing His presence, and with faith in Him we have joined together. As parents and grandparents, we celebrate this day, the wonders of the blessings, recognizing the fruits of living obedient to our Lord's Word. Our lives are spent in the service of our Lord at Long Neck Church and the community of West Bay Park as leader of Neighborhood Watch. I had been involved since moving into the park. Work continued with Boulevard Ford and Security with Pot Net Parks. God's plan was our move to Delaware. In 2005 I was recouped from the accident with the desire to visit Bob in the home with the secure facilities. His dementia had increased. Told he had weakened moved me to visit while he knew I was there. Juanita had let it be known she was not up to making such a trip. Maybe it was the memory of Dad Hildebrand. Lynn, learning of my plan, volunteered to accompany me on the trip. Our time together was enjoyed by covering the family in our relationships of our life experiences together over the years. We arrived, were shown our room, and headed to seek Bob's location. We were given entrance into the area and greeted by one of the staff, who said, "You have to be Bob's brother." Bob was coming from the restroom. He looked up and saw me. The first word he spoke was "MAGIC." He could hardly believe it was Brother David standing in front of him. Our visit was good. He was able to pick up on his memory recollection, such as his saying, "Smokey." It came to mind the comic in the newspaper, Smokey Stover. His eyes brightened, saying, "That's right."

Many other memories of our childhood were enjoyed. The highlight of the trip was Kathy and Kim arranging to take Bob to dinner at Newick's, his favorite seafood restaurant. We arrived and were seated when daughter Kim entered with Eileen; she was still living in their home. He looked at her with wide eyes and a big smile. Memories of previous years flooded into my mind and my heart. The meal, the time shared, was more than riches could have provided. My favorite meal when visiting Bob and Eileen and family was always lobster. Why not? I had one.

On our drive back to Lynn's home, she related to me her Uncle Bob made no recognition of her. Lynn had a soft spot for Uncle Bob when quite young. I should have introduced Bob to Lynn.

Since the accident, I no longer use the boat. It has come to a standstill. Larry had been calling upon me to operate his boat as he tended his traps, taking two of our traps, giving us crabs as well as some of Larry's catch; he has always been generous with us that way.

In the spring of 2006, Juanita discovered a lump in her right breast. There was great concern, having been told at the time of her previous breast surgery this would not take place. After consulting with an oncologist, mastectomy surgery was recommended. It was difficult to be confronted, having been told of the little possibility of this happening. Our faith led us to the source of our strength, knowing repeatedly God has always been there for us. The family, in every and all circumstances, has been present for one another. The surgery was successfully performed, and the process of healing followed. This is my wonderful wife I will forever love and cherish.

At this time of our lives, we took inventory of life ahead. Considering conversations we had of making applications to the Masonic Home in Elizabethtown, Pennsylvania, we did just that. Upon inquiry, we learned even when approved we would be placed on a waiting list and at present could possibly be as long as a year. Our history of knowing of the wonderful facility and care for life, the application was submitted. Pastor Chris Lee has been pastor since July of 2003. You recall the prayer and presence she had rendered to me and my family at the time of the accident. This makes evidence of her ministry difficult to speak about. Facts show new people filling pews for a short time then no longer are with us. Some regular members of a period of time are also absent. It has continued to be believed Pastor Chris's lack of spiritual presence is the reason for the results of attracting new worshipers, then losing them. A plan was presented to build a new sanctuary. Many of us found little need and moved ahead, having established an earlier contemporary service, maintaining the conventional service at the usual time. Many pros-cons were addressed, underlined with the fact the church was not growing. Getting back to Pastor

Chris. A great behind-the-scenes was witnessed among active longtime members. The Pastor Parish Relations Committee's annual report failed to give an accurate evaluation of the church leadership under Chris. My good friend and brother, Sprig Hudson, in his concern with the support of two faithful active members of like mind on Council brought up the issue. Sprig stood alone, the two failed to speak in support of the issues Sprig presented. Consequently, this killed Sprig's and Chris's relationship. I wrote to the District Superintendent, offering my insight as to John Schutt's presence and Spirit indwelling would bring the church alive were he the pastor of the church. I received no response. Okay, you can say it is none of my business. I agree, perhaps you are right. Many members of Long Neck Church will attest to the same belief the ministry led by John would bring the church alive. It has been learned the superintendent told John to his face he would never have Long Neck Church as pastor. Speaking to this issue is a ministry in faith stepping out with God's leading by prayer and meditation, directed by the Holy Spirit. I believe it to be the truth.

The Keesey-Ritter oyster feeds had continued. On occasion, oysters were provided by a trip to Chincoteague, Virginia, for the Outer Bay salty oysters. Larry had become quite good in his shucking, a bit more innovative in his trying to find a better technique. Our party included the Aldingers, Shirley and Carl. We continued with raw, fried, stew, and Juanita's oyster pie with the addition of roasted oysters done in the oven to satisfy Shirley so all appetites could be satisfied.

In the summer of 2006, Lynn informed us she and family were going to Maine to visit a former neighbor from New Jersey who had moved to Maine. The offer provided me a ride to New Hampshire to visit Brother Bob and Eileen. They continued on to Maine. I jumped at the opportunity knowing of Bob's mind. I drove to Tottens' in preparation for the trip to New Hampshire and Maine. I arrived in Durham and the home where Bob and Eileen live. Settled, Lynn and family drove to Maine to return in five days. Eileen and Bob's conditions have changed in the year since I last visited brought disappointment. Eileen is now in residence in the same secure area as Bob. Sleeping areas are separated by a wall, neither closed as a room. The two areas were closed from the areas of other residents, affording each with individual baths. Bob was communicative with responses from him in normal conversation. Eileen was removed from conversation, acknowledging you only with a smile. At meals Bob and I spoke to one another. Eileen sat and ate a bit and would rise, walking through the secure area. She would return, sit down, eat a bit more, then move through the area again until the attendants determined she had finished. When she sat across from me, I would speak to her, receiving a smile and an occasional nod. Never a word. In all of the years we visited with Eileen and Bob, I was without a personal conversation with Eileen. Bob or others were in conversation without my being one on one with Eileen. There were differences owing to political and views on some faith matters. I respected the views she had expressed. Kim, daughter, and Matthew, grandson, visited. They had stopped at Dunkin' Donuts and brought smiles on the part of both Eileen and Bob. This changed the entire mood of the morning. It was amazing to see them enjoying the donuts as though they had no breakfast. During the visit on two occasions, Bob, tired, arose and went to his bed without a word. Fine, I sat and enjoyed the residents watching TV until Bob would return. At that point, our visit continued. Upon Lynn and families' return for me, I was facing the reality knowing this would be my last visit with Eileen and Bob. Lynn had no mention of wanting to meet with them in their present state of mind. On my return home, I informed Juanita of the state of the health of both Eileen and Bob, knowing of the opportunity it afforded me for the last visit.

The fall of 2006, we learn our application for admission to the Masonic Village was approved. Contact would be made as space was available for us to make our selection from available quarters. Our previous Bible Studies, teaching and preaching by Lay Speakers, had been curtailed owing to Pastor Chris assuming that a lack of knowledge existed among layman and laywoman. She felt that she and John were more qualified, excluding the Lay Speakers, of which there were six in Long Neck U. M. Church. Since Juanita had become a Lay Speaker, we were rarely called upon or given the opportunity. The year 2007 had arrived, learning of Juanita's discomfort in her left hip. X-ray results revealed her pain was caused by bone on bone of the hip. Surgery was to be the only effective relief performed by Dr. Wiegman. It proved with successful results. Rehab was an extensive period of time with much pain. During this time, my mind went repeatedly to the care Juanita had provided for me during my injury and recovery. She was a trooper, providing all of my needs, leading me to pray that I could provide for her needs. In September, walking through the home, I caught the toe of my left shoe on the floor heat vent. This threw me to the wall, wrenching my left hip, leading me to believe the hip might be broken. This had no more than happened and the phone rang, informing us that Brother Bob had died. I told Kathy of my condition, doubtful I could make a trip that distance even learning my hip was not broken. She was sorry but understood. I turned to Juanita, expressing my desire to be with the family. She, knowing of my pain, not knowing the condition I was in, sensibly stated, "David, you are unable to do the impossible." This was Friday, and I knew I was unable to see Dr. Wiegman until Monday. It was settled; there would be no trip to New Hampshire. Bob died on September 14, 2007. I remember Bob in the nineties, expressing his desire to live to the year of 2000. He had made it plus seven. I am unable to feel any sorrow of Bob's passing. A likeness to the passing of Dad Keesey, it was related to his funeral, speaking of the memory of lighter times rather than sadness. My desire of searching for the substance of peace and comfort with the family passing has found purpose in my relationship with God. An integral fact lies in the response both reacted to any witness given to their faith in the name Jesus Christ. Reasoning, the question was and still is, what was their unwillingness to speak the name of Jesus Christ? I will never know, thus they are in the arms of the Lord. My point of caring is beyond further concern for their salvation. As stated, they are in the hands of our Lord.

Kathy was sensitive to her Uncle David's absence at the funeral and provided a recorded account of the entire service. This is evidence of my relationship with my wonderful niece. Kathy has drawn closer to her Uncle David in the passing of her father. My fatherly love for Kathy is just as stated.

Birthdays were flying. Juanita was now seventy-five on September 17, 2007, and I was eighty years young. We had fifty-two years of wonderful married life, enjoying our four daughters and six bright, happy grandchildren. All believers will give witness to the presence of our belief, faith, and trust in our Lord, having walked in His presence these years of our married life.

The year of 2008 brought the need for Juanita's right knee to be x-rayed due to severe pain. Dr. Wiegman was called upon to supply relief needed for Juanita. We arrived at the doctor's for the x-ray to determine the seriousness of the condition. Dr. Wiegman explained surgery was needed to achieve relief. He offered a shot for immediate relief if effective. Juanita did not look favorably upon the shot, consenting to it for the relief of the pain. We witnessed the shot being given much to the dread of Juanita. When Juanita stood on her feet, the pain was gone. The expression on her face was unbelievable. She was told the relief would be only effective for a short period of time. Her decision was the knee replacement. During the spring of 2008, a call was received from Erin of the Masonic Home in Elizabethtown. She asked if we were prepared to make the move. After we explained the scheduled surgery, Erin said she would call in July after the recovery of the knee. Recovery in therapy for a complete movement of the joint was interrupted due to our move. Juanita never accomplished the full movement worked toward. Kathryn and the Fisher family were visiting us at the end of July. Having just left, we received a call from Erin on the thirty-first of July. Healing of the knee was in progress, so we were ready to make the change. A date was made to look at three of the available facilities for our selection in August. The date met with Cindy and Lynn's plans to assist in our decision. Upon arrival at the admissions office, Erin directed the tour of the facilities. The first comprised of two rooms on the first floor of the Kuhlemeier Building. Rooms were torn up at present, being prepared for the next occupancy. The second room available was in the Levis Building on the second floor. It was one large room with a bathroom and closets. Erin had kind of set me up as to this being the nicer of the three. The third was in the Daman Building, third floor. It was a quite large broken-up single room with ceilings sloping due to the contour of the roof, reducing the overall use of the complete floor space. All three were equipped with hand-icapped facilities, affording safety in and around the bathrooms. These were all well planned and thought out being in use some years. Mom and the two gals felt we would be happier with the first-floor two rooms. I toyed with the thought of the Levis, one room Erin had leaned toward. Having completed the various plus and minuses, the Kuhlemeier was selected. How could you come to any other decision, three against one? After all these years, with three of the five, it was a right decision. Cindy raised very good questions, finding it difficult as to how we could afford to live in these beautiful facilities costing some forty thousand dollars a year. Try as we did, the fact that we would be provided when our funds were exhausted provided for by Fraternal Care. Our income was received into the finance department in our name to meet expenses providing sixty dollars a month each to Juanita and me. Granted, it was hard to understand in this day such a living was available. Cindy was questioning how this could be. It worked, for we have been living in Kuhlemeier over five and a half years, just as explained to Cindy. The Village, the size, and facilities at one's use requires some adjustment to adopt to the life for living each and every day, three meals a day, three hundred sixty-five days out of the year. We had health-care, doctors and nurses, personal care, and skill care. Providing pharmacy sup-plies were covered by Medicare and now Freedom Blue supplemental insurance. The history Juanita and I have known of existing since first being introduced in the sixties has little to compare with the living residency full time.

Kathy Gross called on September 4, 2008, informing us Eileen, her mother, had died. It was ten days short of a full year since her husband, my Brother Bob, had died. I wanted to be with the family, but it was impossible under the demands of cleaning up things in Delaware in preparation for our move to the Masonic Village. Once more Kathy was understanding, presenting to us the accounting of the services in the church where Eileen had served as organist for over thirty years, in addition to many services for her Lord and His people. Our move was possible, having sold our Dakota Dodge truck the week we prepared to leave on the twenty-sixth of September. The boat was given to Jim, one of the maintenance men of the park. The chest freezer was given to the men in the maintenance shed. This was not a loss, giving us relief, having them disposed of for a good cause. These people were always good to us in so many ways. A U-Haul was rented with the assistance of Jerri Gaudioso and her son, Ernie. Our Kathryn was down from State College. David drove the truck, Jerri drove the Taurus for Juanita. The trip was uneventful. Upon arrival, we were met by Melanie and Ryan, making our move easy particularly with the good help. We left the U-Haul and headed to admissions for keys to gain entrance. Family and friends took charge of the unloading of the U-Haul while we met with the social worker, Jill Luzier, and the finance officer, Sharon Schreiber. That completed, we arrived at our rooms to learn our belongings placed better than expected. We all went to the 3 Loaves Restaurant on campus for some renewal of strength. Food, that is! Our thanks all around, we shared in the love we have for one another, and we found ourselves alone in the new surroundings, happy with the decision we had made.

The following morning, we were to be met by a resident to introduce us to the dining room and breakfast. No one appeared, which left us standing in the hall entrance to the dining room to be directed to the table designated as the table for newcomers. We were introduced to the host, Bill Russell, enlightening us in his words we now lived in his description, "An introduction to heaven." A more fitting term could not be found. We learned our guide didn't eat breakfast and explained the individual she had asked to meet us apparently didn't do breakfast, either, especially that morning. Our family fell in love with our living arrangements and the Village. They were witnessing the healthcare, food, opportunities for volunteer services, activities, and entertainment would be difficult to be found elsewhere. Our grandchildren were of no exception, taken with the tunnel facilities providing our access to our dining room and all of the areas of our living while remaining in doors out of the weather. Names were coming at us from every direction with over two hundred residents in our Village Green area housed in nine buildings. As we settled in, we were given advice to take our time until the areas became familiar to us. Our funds were sufficient the first year, giving us the comfort and travel to the family gatherings and provisions we needed. Family had continued to appreciate the wonderful meals we were served three times a day every day. The servers providing our needs at the table with smiles of cordiality were ready and willing to please us. The living arrangements and house care every other week on Thursday included the vacuuming of floors, bathroom, and general cleaning. Breakfast was always a treat introduction to the day. Bill Russell was host, and Miriam was the hostess giving us good information. Bill asked of interest I had in the Bible and the faith I had for the Lord. He mentioned the Bible Study, suggesting I not attend it, for he spoke of his getting very little in attending. For the time being, I took Bill's word, not attending. We learned our stay at the welcoming table was much longer than was the custom. Assigned to our seating, we were at table 33 with the Hartmans and the Barnharts. These arrangements lasted for the better part of our first year in the Village, when changes were made permitting us to sit with those we chose to sit at tables that were available.

Juanita and I were more than happy with the change we had made, though we had the concern of the sale of our mobile home in Delaware. The first three months were involved in learning the location of facilities, enjoyable, in addition to putting names to faces, which I found by surprise names coming easy when related to faces. On the morning of Christmas Eve, Juanita took her shower, finding her heart beating irregularly. She was sitting in her lounger, calming herself after the shower. Her expression revealed a concern, my wanting to know the reason. I felt her pulse, which was irregular. I asked if we should we call the nurse, the procedure to follow when circumstances such as Juanita's situation developed, so I decided it was. I called the operator as instructed. I gave her symptoms and was directed to hang up; she would call the nurse. I apparently didn't hang up fast enough, for she repeated, "HANG UP." The nurse arrived, making the decision to call CMT for further examination. Their decision was the need for transport to the hospital. When asked what hospital, we chose Lancaster General. Informed of icy roads, we were told Hershey Medical was closer, suggesting Hershey to be the destination, to which we agreed. I was directed to stay off the road until the roads were made less dangerous. I obeyed the information they had given. Our first Christmas was Juanita going to the hospital. Prayers had been offered from the outset. I restlessly spent the day until three in the afternoon before venturing out. I had called Juanita, seeking information on her condition and learning her heart had settled to a normal pace. She was to be released when later results were read. Upon arrival, I found Juanita very uncomfortable on a litter, where she lay on all day. She had no food all day, anticipating her release. She was critical of her care. Ignored, she had no food all day. On our way home, she spoke of getting something to eat. I drove as safely as I could with one thing in mind: the oyster stew the dining room served once a year on Christmas Eve. Little did Juanita know of my effort to get back in time for the stew. We arrived. I drove to the dining room, left Juanita in the car, and dashed inside. I approached the entrance and asked Lee, a supervisor, if they had food for two poor wayfarers. To my pleasure, she had just placed two meals in the refrigerator. With meals in hand, home we went to enjoy our oyster stew meal served ONCE A YEAR, Christmas Eve. It must be said, prayers were answered in the Keesey family once more. God is good all the time!

It is a time in my life prayers for full service to the Lord were offered. Now realized, I am given such an opportunity. Several issues, one the absence of the Name of Jesus used in prayers offered in the dining room. The second, the information about the existing Bible Study. A letter was written concerning the prayer practice in the dining room. When completed it was presented to Kathi, head of the volunteer office. When received, having read it spoke of the strength of the letter, knowing the person it needed to be presented. Saturday, a week later, I received a phone call from our director of retirement services. After a cordial greeting, it was made known the Committee of the Masonic Grand Lodge of Pennsylvania ruled that was to be the procedure. Thanks for considering my thoughts, having him know as the letter addressed the fact that "No one comes to the Father only by Christ Jesus." I closed, saying this is the way of the world. "God loves you, and I love you, too!"

The issue of prayer put to rest for the moment, I attended the Bible Study. After the third session, I was convinced Bill Russell was correct. Each session was conducted by the same individual in the same manner. G. Vernon Magee's commentary was the only acceptable word. The participation and attendance had dropped from forty folks enrolled to four or five people. After the third session, I inquired how Jean felt about starting a new Bible Study. She was agreeable were I to lead it. I asked Jean why she felt I should take the lead. She spoke of my apparent knowledge of the Bible. I spoke with both Jill Luzier and Kathi Natsaka, and they felt it was appropriate, using the conference room to begin. My faith led me to believe our Lord had brought us together in this wonderful Village community for this very purpose. We were given good reason to believe Bible Study would be well attended, dependent upon the Word. All the Bible Study, teaching, and preaching of the Word has brought greater purpose for my life. I have read recently, *The Sermon on the Mount*, written by Emmet Fox. The power of the scriptures fundamentally is not dependent on the interpretation, theological, doxological, archaeological findings. They do not change the power of the Spirit speaking in the wisdom and knowledge God has for us in the following of His Son, our Savior in the Word. The copy was presented to several folks whose opinions are valued highly. Those voicing a position upon the reading came to an entirely different enlightenment related to the positive teaching of Christ's New Testament. The advocacy of positive thinking led to the faith and organized religion of Christian Science Monitor. Emmet Fox, this reader received the unadulterated Word of God expressing the truth. More positive life will never be preached than Christ's. I read Emmet's *Sermon on the Mount* several times and was challenged to continue searching the Word against the learning of experiences of life lived in reference to the Spiritual responses to the presence of God receiving in my life, growing closer in my friendship with God in Jesus Word's in John 15:12-17: "My command is this: Love each other as I have loved you. Greater love has no one than this, that he lay down his life for his friends. You are my friends if you do what I command. I no longer call you servants, because a servant does not know his master's business. Instead I have called you friends, for everything that I learned from my Father I have made known to you. You did not choose me, but I chose you and appointed you to go and bear fruit—fruit that will last. Then the Father will give you whatever you ask in my name. This is my command: Love one another." My life has grown to this proportion in my dependence, trusting in my relationship with God, prayers in the Name of Jesus, fully filling the presence and directions of the Holy Spirit. The majority of believers who heard witness from me look with suspicious eyes of the soundness of my mind. "David, did you know?" Yes, David knows with every confidence God has drawn him into His Kingdom. God has provided an unquestionable presence in all of my life. How often in teaching the Word speaking of newness of life, becoming a new creation is rarely accepted, understanding, surrendering oneself to the power of the Holy Spirit. It is true, the absence of the experience prevents any and all learning of the true nearness of God.

A week later, we announced the study would begin on the first floor of the Grand Lodge Hall in the Conference Room at 1:00 P.M. The room had accommodations for eighteen. The time arrived, there were folks standing outside, unable to find seating. The date was March 8, 2009. Five years later, we had seventy names on the list with an attendance of twenty-five to thirty-eight every Monday morning at 9:30 A.M. Each eager for the study, we were studying Matthew, Chapter 19. I heard from many the study has brought learning for their life and greater understanding. God has shown purpose for our lives living here at the Masonic Village. The individual leading the other Bible Study wanted an explanation as to why there was need for another study. The explanation had to do with attendance and the representing of God's Word. At a later time, the individual joined the new Bible Study.

In August of 2009, Juanita experienced similar heart irregularity, prompting a call for the nurse. The EMT was called for service, recommending a trip to the hospital, informing us it was our call. Looking at Juanita, it was evident she didn't want to go. They said it was a possibility we would need to call them back had we decided not to go at this time. Convinced, Juanita went this time to the Lancaster General Hospital, which was a right decision. She was then given several tests, concluding she was in need of a pacemaker. August had been the family time to gather near the twenty-second owing to the date of Brother Bob's birthday. We joined together in the absence of Juanita, she being in the hospital. Calls were made to speak with her. Later our niece Kathy, from Massachusetts, and I spent time with Juanita on Saturday evening in the hospital. She surely was missed in the midst of it all. Juanita's stay was a considerable time, owing to the placement of a pacemaker to regulate the pulse of her heart, creating the need to thin her blood, requiring the proper dosage. It was critical the thinning be monitored periodically. Juanita's stay in the hospital was ten days. Her experience in the Hershey Hospital brought forth complement as to the care she received in Lancaster General.

In October, Cindy and Mike paid us a visit for Mike to update our computer to Windows XP. They learned of the need for a new printer and went to Kmart to purchase a Lexmark and installed it. They refused to accept payment for it. Thanksgiving was one happy family togetherness enjoyed by all. Our number had grown to sixteen, including four daughters, three sons-in-law, Mike, Cindy's companion, and six grandchildren. It was a wonderful family. A wonderful meal was held at Melanie and Ryan's, served in the garage, providing sit-down space for us all. We are blessed for the three husbands to our daughters who know their way around the kitchen. We learned in December that Mike was not well and was in the hospital. Talking with Cindy on the phone, we discovered her voice was very hoarse, and she seemed to be short of breath. Cindy was visiting Mike in the hospital. When an attendant heard Cindy's condition, he sent her to the emergency room. It was discovered she needed to be admitted herself to the hospital. Mike's condition had improved and he was released. He would be at home alone, prompting Cindy to release herself to take care of Mike. Kathryn, being informed, went to be with them that Saturday. We were very concerned and phoned to inquire if we could be of some help. We talked with Cindy in an effort to convince her she needed to be in the hospital. She spoke no more and turned the phone over to Kathryn. I asked her if Cindy would like us to come over. I heard Cindy say, very emphatically, no. That was the end of the conversation. A visiting nurse had checked on both of them on the same Saturday, knowing of their conditions. She informed them a nurse would call on Monday. Initially Mike had been in a local hospital in the Poconos region close to their home. On Monday the nurse checked Cindy and called for an ambulance to take her to the hospital in Bethlehem. Cindy had been in the hospital for several days when I received a call from her, expressing she was sorry and that she was scared. I remember saying we were scared as well. I spoke of her labored effort in speaking and told her I loved her, ending our conversation. I have relived that conversation with Cindy time and time again, praying for an understanding of Cindy being sorry. Responding in an empty meaningless manner, I was scared for her as well. I asked God, reliving the conversation, was she seeking Spiritual support? Numerous conversations with Cindy related to our faith in God was responded to informing me she knew her God, end of subject. I have appeased my afterthoughts in ending the conversation based upon her becoming more upset than she was. Was she seeking reassurance knowing of God's love for her? Was I cowardly, refusing to venture the subject? I will never rest, failing to have offered in a loving manner God's presence in her life. I will have her know we all will approach the day, questioning, "Are we ready to enter our place in heaven God has provided for us?" I spend a time every day communicating with Cindy in the Spirit.

I have spent my life in spiritual communication with my mother, Kathryn, Cindy I related before. Melanie provided transportation to visit Cindy as Melanie's time permitted. On our first visit, as I walked into the room, I approached the foot of the bed and was unable to understand the look in her eyes or the expression on her face. I reached out to touch Cindy's hand resting on the bed to have her draw it away. I heard a chorus of voices reminding me of the needles she had been experiencing. I was silent. It was then the Monday after Cindy's fifty-second birthday of Friday, January 22, that we were summoned to the hospital for the purpose of meeting with the hospice doctor. We were assembled in the visiting room, affording some privacy. The doctor, whose name escapes me at this time, proceeded with his laptop, revealing the stark information that her recovery was impossible. Prayers had been offered by many, knowing of the faith we all have believing our God is a miracle achiever. Cindy had been placed on an aerator instrument to assist her breathing. Cindy's attending Dr. Silver entered the room and introduced to us in attendance, assuring us in revealing all of the known procedures were administered to give Cindy continued life. We recognized the personal relationship Cindy and he had grown in the time he had treated Cindy. His words of disappointment, absence of hope with the information he had for us, brought tears to our hearts and to our eyes. I offered my expression of deep thanks and appreciation for his love and wisdom. It was a day I have always known of the possibility of occurring in our family and our members. In and during this time, I felt and saw Mike with tears in his eyes, watching me. I pray strength was present with him, knowing we were all one in our love for Cindy and for him. Hugs were embraced, leaving out no one. A prayer was offered. The information given to us gave reason by our family to remove the respirator, making her as comfortable as possible. As I stood by her side, knowing there would be no response, in tears I told Cindy once more how much I love her. I recalled the day she had visited us in West Bay upon her leaving. Standing in front of her, I rested my hands upon her shoulders, looking directly into her eyes. I spoke of always loving her: "I love you now and I always will love you, Cindy." Her response, again, she assured me she knew her God. I then said goodbye, knowing Spiritually we would never be separated. True, each day I have spent time with my Lord with Cindy's Spirit present.

On Tuesday, Kathryn arose in need of being with Cindy; she had not been with us the day before. An opportunity talking with John's dad, her father-in-law, he urged Kathryn to be with Cindy were it be the fulfillment to satisfy Kathryn's need. The conversation moved Kathryn to be at Cindy's side. She was with her when Cindy breathed her last. Much can be said about their relationship. The emotional inner presence of love in the midst of each member of this family in our oneness grown to maturity in the years of faith, knowing God has always been with us. Father, without hesitation, has gone seeking, asking, and knocking with blessed assurance our God has been there all the time. All of Cindy's friends and her family and her family's friends offered their love and prayers. George Pintarch drove from Delaware and was present at her viewing to offer love and prayers with hugs, asking, "Is there anything you need of which we may be a part?" Our response witnessed to God's love and presence evidenced in the outpouring of love everyone witnessed to their being with us in our time of need. Cindy's friend and boss was present, sharing his loss, witnessing Cindy's importance to him in their work together. Cindy's service was conducted in the Clover Hill Church in New Jersey, where she had been wed. The service was conducted by Jack Cherry, and Cindy's sister Lynn was his secretary. Words from Rick, her divorced husband, were asked if he would be welcomed to pay his respects. He was welcomed in love for his respects. A great surprise was Scott Wampler, a longtime friend from church in York, arrived. Scott had attended the Sunday School classes Fred Krsek and I had conducted, continued in friendship these many years. His wife, Yuki, a music major professor in college and director of choral groups, one of whom sister Jeanne faithfully had joined. Our family joined together in the parlor of our Kuhlemeier home on a Saturday, the custom of celebrating the birthdays of me, Cindy, and Courtney. Dates respectively are the nineteenth, twenty-second, and thirtieth of January.

A weekend after the services for Cindy, we were gathered together. Lynn received a cell phone call from a friend of Cindy and Mike's. He wanted to stay in touch with Mike. He was at the home, where he found the doors locked and had no response to the bell or his knock. In order to gain entrance, he called the State Police. Upon entrance, Mike was found on the bathroom floor. He had died. Our being together brought a comfort for us, speaking of Cindy and Mike's relationship, especially the happiness they found in each other. Cindy and Mike had no marriage, and our family had no relations with Mike's family. Cindy's affairs were private as had been with the four of the girls concerning their mother and father. Lynn was most informed in her close relationship with Cindy, owing to the daily conversations with each other. Much needs to be said relevant to the coming together of our three daughters. Lynn took hold of the leadership with Kathryn and Melanie together in every step of the business and procedures needed to bring a close to Cindy's effects only so far as it related to her family. Lynn hired an attorney required for legal advice as to requirements of our relationship. Mom and Dad were innocent "bystanders" in the manner they worked together with those effects of Cindy's. The girls were assisted by their husbands. Cindy was cremated. The ashes Lynn had until she asked if we would like the care of them. We agreed. Lynn walked in the door and was met with the question as to her traveling alone. She responded, "I wasn't alone; Cindy was with me." We agreed, Cindy surely got a chuckle out of that one. Cindy would be put to rest with her grandmother, grandfather, mother, and father in the Quarryville Cemetery. We thank God for His loving comfort, guidance, and perseverance with us all.

This life of mine has been totally dependent upon God, Christ, and the Holy Spirit. The lessons learned and those to be learned as they come to light will lead me as my life has been a mystery. Our family continues to be closer than ever. Since Bob and Eileen's deaths, their daughter Kathy and her Uncle David have grown more intimate in our communicating with each other. Kevin and Kim, Kathy's brother and sister, have taken on a closer family relationship with one another. Those family celebrations are inclusive, especially in August. It was June when our families were informed a new member would be introduced. A child had been conceived by Melanie, predicted to arrive in December. Colin's birthday is on the seventh of December. The child we learned would be known as Chloe Ruth in that month. They were not sure where "Chloe" came from. Liking the name "Ruth," they would name her for Grandmother Ruth Keesey. Ruth was all smiles learning the child's name. The day had arrived, December 29, 2010. Chloe Ruth was born. Grandchild #7, Chloe Ruth McWilliams, December 29, 2010.

Grand Child #7

Chloe Ruth McWilliams
December 29, 2010

Grandchild number seven, like the others, a gift from heaven,
As grandparents we learn to receive the number is at seven.
Of course at our ages of today the title the next would be great,
Number seven, known as Chloe Ruth with all a welcomed date.
Her Great Grandmother, Ruth was overjoyed to tell the truth,
When the two are together Chloe brightens Grandmother Ruth.
To see her cousins using Chloe fill our time, she is their amusement,
Chloe's passed about from one to another as we watch her movements.
Oft times in a serving as a ball not to gently hearing her glee,
brings a joy to us all followed by, we're glad it is not me.

As life continues to unfold, God's presence is constant during day and night. During the day as faces come in view, names are spoken, identifying each. The question continues: "How are you able to remember the names of all of the folks you call by name?" The answer remains: "By speaking the name whenever and wherever the opportunity presents the meeting." A friendly acknowledgement of a name with a smile brings a smile. Work on behalf of our Lord continues to fill days and evenings with calls to serve. The primary services continue with Jean Botts and the Bible Study. I have been called upon to introduce programs, introduce musicians, and general knowledge presentations. I served four years on Masonic Village Council as building representative of Kuhlemeier Building, our resident building. I am called upon to open council meetings with prayer. Ministry has taken place when sitting publicly, an individual will ask to sit. Before long a subject in need of airing with someone is revealed for the purpose of one hearing themselves verbalize where they are coming from without response, only when asked, "What do you think about that?" Never sure if a response is called for. An hour may pass when to the point, the individual speaks of the enjoyment, the support, and thanks me for time spent. Cindy's death has brought me ever nearer to my Lord. I continue to have the quiet time with God in the presence of mother Kathryn's and Cindy's spirits. It is my most peaceful and fulfilling time of my day. In recent weeks, my day is closed in the stillness of the night on my knees by my bed. In prayer of the days, experiences, names, and faces bringing to mind the needs of others and giving thanks for our loved ones.

We had known of this young lady that had come into the life of our grandson Kip, one Alissa Ann Wheeler watching a love grow for the other when came the announcement of a wedding we were to be a part of on June 23, 2012. The wedding was held in a beautiful park with the presence of a large lake in the area of Meyerstown. Delicious food and drink. Family and friends accompanied with music and dancing. A beautiful couple and attendants brought happiness to all.

Juanita and I attended church in the chapel each Sunday, receiving spiritual nourishment preached by the four pastors serving the Masonic Village. Our pastoral care is led by Pastor Preston Van Deursen, assisted by Pastors Kenneth Krietz, Gary George, and Margaret Rohnacher. The four of them preach, alternating services Sundays and during the week services. Pastor Preston preaching on June 3, 2012, touched me on the subject of the Holy Spirit. It had such impact, I returned home and wrote the following:

"THE HOLY SPIRIT"
David Edward Keesey
June 3, 2012

A message this morning we did hear,
Of Galaxies of Stars made very clear;
The Majesty of God, everything He made,
The things upon His Earth to us He gave.
The Wonders of His World we know are true,
Their presence all around us for both me and you;

God, Son and Holy Spirit their presence are local,
With this World around us our minds are rarely focal.
Could it be as Nicodemus, Jesus, he could not understand,
The Holy Spirit in us through Jesus just as God planned;
How long will we live confessing our belief and faith,
Everything is possible Jesus spoke, "Asking in His Name."
God's power in us the Holy Spirit, God's Will in command,
Gives us truth and direction when His Will we disband;
Surrendering our humanness to be spiritually fed and led,
Jesus leads saying, "Follow Me" you'll never be misled.
Many, in response with question in mind reply, "I'm trying."
There is new birth a new way of life in our faith applying;
The Holy Spirit we received the day Jesus was invited,
Come into my life make me like new in God be united.
Why do we hope when asked, "Are you born again?"
Jesus tells us in John 15, "You are my friend."
You need not hope, so speak, by faith you can be certain,
Bring others to the truth for in Christ's life is Eternal.

Juanita and I decided to transfer membership from Long Neck Church in Delaware to the chapel. Our pastors, both George and Krietz, are visitation pastors as well as preaching ministry. Pastor Ronacher supplies music and primarily Health Care Ministries. Pastor Krietz, in early 2013, submitted his resignation in search of the change in his future. The search was on to replace Pastor Ken. We were informed many applicants had submitted their credentials and desired to fill the position. Inquiring minds interested as to who would be selected were informed with the announcement of Pastor Deborah Valiton-Carnish. Deborah's primary ministry would be visitation to our residence in the Health Care Center, caring for more than three hundred residents and a time of preaching.

I experienced several days of tiredness and breathing and met with Dr. Baer, discovering fluid and increase in weight and irregular heart, which brought forth an EKG. Dr. Baer read the EKG and immediately told me I was going by ambulance to Lancaster General Hospital. This was February, Friday 15, 2013. I spent the weekend with reduced activities, anticipating tests and procedures on Monday to address my problem. My evening meal Sunday was the last meal, fasting for the procedures necessary Monday morning. I was told of two oral examinations. One exploring the passage to the heart, making sure passage was free of obstructions. The second, to see if there were any blood clots around the heart. That done, there was an effort to have the heart return to proper rhythm by inducing shock treatment. Noontime came on Monday, creating an uneasiness on my part. I'd had no food since Sunday night's meal, and as it was approaching 2:00 P.M., I was getting antsy. I was about to give up when the voice within me said, "Simmer down. You are not running this show." What could I do? With that two burly men entered the room, spun the bed around, and out the door we went. The two men were Frank and Chuck, who presented me into a small room, revealing eight individuals to administer the procedures. They were having a high old time, back and forth. It was thought to be a three-penny opera. Was that for my benefit? Sedated, I was out of the picture. Upon awaking, I was told everything went well, only the shock treatment had not restored the rhythm of my heart. Wheeled back to the room, I was told medication was the next procedure. Hooray! I was given food to eat at 4:30 P.M. on Monday night. I had to fast for the MRI on Tuesday. Tuesday at noon had arrived, experiencing no activity with me. One o'-clock and then two, I went wheeling down the hall to only the people nowhere. I was placed in the room with three other littered patients while I waited. Other MRIs were completed. My MRI completed, I was told it had to be done again because it was not conclusive. I was wheeled back into the waiting room, awaiting another try. Time passes slowly when there is nothing to do left to one's own thoughts. After a period of time, I was wheeled in for the second attempt of a successful MRI. That proving successful, I was wheeled back into the waiting room. I was now waiting to be prepared for a nuclear injection for a third MRI. Placed in the waiting room alone, everyone else having been taken care of, I waited. I was thoughtfully wheeled over close to the TV for entertainment. Wonderful, *General Hospital* was on, to which I would make no account of what I witnessed. I was simmering once more, witnessing the inner voice calling me to account. I asked for pardon once more in twenty-four hours, giving thanks I was being cared for in my wellbeing. An injection made directed me to move my feet back and forth with vigor. Wheeled in for the third MRI, this was completed satisfactorily. This diet had become routine. Hooray, another meal!

On Wednesday morning, I was informed the medication Tikosyn had brought my heart into rhythm. Praise the Lord. An eight-day stay had the heart in proper rhythm when I was not responsive to the shock treatment. Surprised, I learned the medication Tikosyn, taken twice a day for seven days a week, thus far had done the job. Upon release, Dr. Bernabie related a need for a pacemaker implant might be needed in a year or two. Kathryn was present that Friday the twenty-second. She had presented me with a donut cushion to relieve the pressure points experienced on my bottom earlier. She was always thoughtful, caring for her mother's and father's needs. She drove us home after the unexpected stay in the hospital.

In June, Grandmother Ruth was celebrating her ninety-fifth birthday. We inquired about her being able to have a family visit. Twelve family members arrived. In the midst the smiles and conversation among us all, Ruth enjoyed our visit. The main attraction was seeing Ruth speaking to Chloe Ruth, her namesake, and Chloe's answers. Colin was the man handled by the older grandchildren. Our great concern was of tiring Ruth; it did not appear to happen. The joy of watching Ruth observing and talking with Chloe Ruth brought smiles to us all.

Juanita and I had gone to the Diecke Auditorium to a movie. I parked my walker up front and upon returning to the seats I caught my left toe on the carpet, throwing me down on my right knee. I got up without any apparent injury. I sat through the movie for two hours and thirty-nine minutes. I had discomfort but not enough to prevent walking home with the walker.

The following morning, I discovered swelling and much pain, so much walking was impossible. The need for transportation in a wheelchair to Dr. Baer was provided by our good neighbors, Marti Chard and Parke Toner. Dr. Baer made an appointment for the next day with Dr. Becker, an orthopedic doctor. The call was made to the family. Lynn volunteered to come to transport me to Dr. Becker. A number of critical stories were heard about Dr. Becker. In my mind, I was prepared for a surgery. Three of us met Dr. Becker in the examining room. He entered, extending his hand in greeting, including the three of us. Examining the knee, he immediately probed the fluid-swollen knee, putting surgery to rest. He spoke of the removal of the fluid, then injecting medicine to settle down the arthritis that had been activated. Both Juanita and Lynn showed more displeasure with the injection of the syringe than I did. All was cared for with the one needle. Dr. Becker informed us the knee should not give any more problems. I was to place an ice pack on and off every half-hour. He spoke of his being available the second Tuesday of each month at the Village HCC. We met with Dr. Becker at that time and were given news that all was well with the knee and were told to call him if he was needed. We found Dr. Becker to be a fine, caring doctor. Our evaluation, listening to him, don't tell him. A monitor was placed for twenty-four hours in September prior to the appointment with Dr. Bernabie on October 9, resulted in receiving a phone call, alerting me to go to an emergency room should I experience dizziness or possibly passing out. The appointment kept on October 9 with Dr. Bernabie immediately revealed great concern for my continued good health. Dr. Bernabie relaxed in his chair against the wall. It was evident he was preparing me to understand my need for the pacemaker. I was prepared, knowing in my mind it was necessary due to the condition I experienced. Told the need of the pacemaker, without delay I returned home to find the message on the answering service that I was to be in the Lancaster General Hospital at 6 A.M. on October 10. The implant was successful. Since the implant, my improved condition is evidence of the need.

Family and friends speak of the improved color in the face and mental reaction in conversation. It was at this time Jeanne called to inform us Ruth had gotten up during the early hours of the morning and was in the kitchen cooking something. Jeanne had gone to the bathroom and heard Ruth downstairs but did not go to check on her. Soon Jeanne heard Ruth calling out to her. She found Ruth in a pool of blood. Ruth had fallen, resulting in a compound fracture of her left arm. Amazingly Ruth endured the period of time to heal accompanied by therapy, and she was able to return home. From this time on, she continued to be in a weakened condition. We called, continuing to pray following reports of her progress.

Thanksgiving 2013 was celebrated at the Tottens' in New Jersey. The McWilliamses provided Granny and Gramps transportation, enjoying family time on the ride. I asked Ryan if he had ever heard of the band by the name of Sauder/Finnegan. He said no. In the next instant, he had the information on his iPad. That was amazing to me, for people when asked had never heard of the band. That ended the conversation the rest of our trip.

Colin and Chloe always livened up the time together. Thanksgiving was a special time as family. Blessings on these occasions to sing praises to our Lord. All believers! On Christmas, Melanie picked us up near ten in the morning, anticipating Ryan's preparation of prime rib, never a disappointment. I was seated in the living room and suddenly heard the tune "Doodle Town Fifers." Ryan had gone online and purchased the Sauder/Finnegan CD. He had made a copy for me. A real present for me. We were finished eating by three when the McWilliams' mother, Peggy and Ryan's brothers, and families descended upon all for the exchange of gifts. One cannot describe the actions if you didn't witness the unwrapping of gifts. The meal eaten did not call for more food for Juanita and me.

Christmas Day celebrations of families Keeseys, Tottens, Fischers, and McWilliams have come together on the twenty-eighth of December in the

Kuhlemeier Building of the Masonic Village, home of Juanita and me, known as Mom and Dad and Granny and Gramps. Eighteen in all were munching and drinking the provisions provided by the families present. It was a glorious time, thanking God for the blessings represented by each and every one. Grandmother Ruth and Jeanne were not with us due to Ruth's failing health. Lynn left with the announcement she would pay us a visit on the eighteenth of January to wish me a happy birthday on my eighty-seventh year.

The New Year's Eve party began at 9:00 P.M. in our Brossman Ballroom with music for our enjoyment. We had food and drinks until the magic hour of midnight. Juanita and I enjoyed the night with my friend Walter DePrefontaine, his son Kevin, and his daughter Michele. It was a grand night enjoying conversations with friends passing by our table. New Year's Day was celebrated eating our wonderful meal of numerous selections, most especially the partaking of Saurkraut, mashed potatoes, and pork in order to get the New Year started right.

On January 18, a phone call at 8:20 A.M. from Lynn informed us the party was on. Kathryn and Melanie, learning of Lynn's plan, joined the group with the presence of Courtney and her friend Casey. The total was the group of ten. They started arriving to celebrate this eighty-seventh birthday, requesting a restaurant. The decision was Simplee-Seafood in Mt Joy. Reservations made, they began arriving at Kuhlemeier at 10:40 A.M. for dinner at noon. What a meal filled with much visiting, sharing in love and memories, and the singing of "Happy Birthday to the Birthday Boy," eighty-seven. I remember those not present with blessings in our coming together.

We returned to Kuhlemeier for more family time. My birthday was a Sunday, to church followed by dinner with Marti Chard and Parke Toner. Would you believe the menu included prime rib? It was a birthday to be long remembered.

Reading has taken new value related to Bible meditations in addition to morning time with my Lord. Recently a daily meditation was placed in my hands by a woman, a friend of our music leader of our Bible Study, George Lutz. George had told his friend Ruth of my faith and love for God. George presented me with the book *Jesus Calling*, written by Sarah Young, to read first thing every morning in addition to the *Upper Room*.

Five days a week, Bob Benson, an acquaintance made in our active Promise Keepers meetings in Delaware, sends scripture readings bringing to light the Power of the Light of the Holy Spirit. For years in my ministry, the Holy Spirit has been given little relationship with the unity in the Trinity. Our Bible Study continues to witness little knowledge among the study of the Power of the Spirit. Repeatedly we are told our members have learned more in this present study than any they have attended. In addition to daily morning meditations, the mind is instilled by the presence of God. A most realistic challenge motivating one to live the life God has called us to live.

In early February, we received a letter from the Village office, informing me my presence was requested on February 8, 2014, in the Brossman Ballroom to receive my sixty-year service emblem to be presented by the Right Worshipful Grand Master of Free and Accepted Masonry of Pennsylvania. I discovered the living compliment produces thirty-one members to receive fifty-year, sixty-year, and one seventy-year presentations. Word from Jeanne on the sixteenth of February mentioned Ruth was now bedfast; she had hospice and was no longer speaking or communicating. Prior to this time, Jeanne told us of Ruth's waiting for her Lord's call to come home.

On Monday morning, upon Juanita's entrance to Bible Study, she told me that Jeanne had called to say Ruth had died. The service was scheduled for March 1. Jeanne informed us it was Ruth's dad's birthday. Melanie and her family picked us up at 7:30 A.M. on Saturday morning. Visitation with family and friends was at 9:30 A.M., and the service was at 10:30 A.M. It was a Catholic Mass attended by visitation of an untold number of family members, Sisters of Notre Dame, and members of Ruth and Jeanne's church, where Jeanne serves assisting the Father. In all that time, Mass was delayed twenty minutes in its beginning due to the wonderful relatives and friends paying respect.

A great chapter in my life has been my love of country. The history, creating a wonderment as to me having been blessed by God, being born in these United States of America, to have served two years in the defense of this God-established country of people governed by the Constitution, Declaration of Independence, Bill of Rights, and Amendments we find under attack in these days. In this day and time, we learn every day of rights ruled unconstitutional by our courts, infiltrated by persons of political persuasions guided by liberal doctrines against the right to life, liberty, and the pursuit of happiness. In this land of ours overseen by Supreme Court Justices split down the middle on the sides of conservatism and liberalism. Issues brought before them for judgment, the outcome can be determined before the vote is taken. The populace governed by the minority rather than the Constitutional rule of being governed by the majority is also a foregone conclusion. Established majorities long instituted based on the Christian principles of Freedom of Religion of the Constitution and the Bill of Rights now trampled underfoot by the recognized rule of the minority. The common sense of decency of life for the common man no longer exists. The letters written to people of government complimenting the actions taken in support of our people, all people, are never acknowledged. This finding is based upon thirteen letters written to the office of the Speaker of the House of Representatives of these great United States of America never acknowledged. A corps of members of the House of Representatives openly speak out against the oath they have taken upon taking their office, the oath to support the Constitution of the United States of America. I have taken the use of our remaining right to write to four of our presidents after their terms in office, thanking them for the service to their country and her people. In return I have received pictures from each of the four presidents with their wives in response to those letters. A pride is maintained for the love of country. Juanita, our family, and I are blessed to be the citizens of our great country. The wonderful God-fearing family and friends have brought blessings in fulfillment of my eighty-seven years of life. The presence of God, Christ, and the Holy Spirit have given reason to express by faith the constant walk I had learning of those by their words and actions to be impossible. Believe it, it has happened.

What have I learned in these seventy-five years since I first met Jesus in the little Brethren Church at age twelve when told, "David, take up your Cross and Follow Me"? Matt 24:16. Much later I learned the words when Jesus said, "I am the light of the world. Whoever follows me will never walk in darkness, but will have the light of life" (John 8:12). In all of scripture, the Old Testament, Genesis to the Book of Revelation in its entirety, life's downfall can be attributed to disobedience, "Through him and in his name sake, we received grace and apostleship to call people from among all the Gentiles to the obedience that comes from faith" (Romans 1:5). I walked with Jesus for much of my faith in having accepted Him, having little understanding of the power of the Holy Spirit. The teaching of John learning of the scripture titled "The Work of the Holy Spirit" (John 16: 5-16). I learned and recognized the presence of the Spirit's actions in my life.

How do we conclude the life's story of one walking with the Lord? Giving God, the Father of the Universe, His Son, reason for looking to Him, knowing of the Eternal Life for the believer offering the Way, the Truth, and the Life to my Father, God. The indwelling of the Holy Spirit gathering maturity for the believer as Scriptural learning, the Words of God, are evidence of recognized actions in conduct of the presence of the Spirit. Credits are acknowledged to the thousands of lives and experiences too numerous and widespread in this lifetime, I feel this would bring discontent in overlooking them. "David, did you know?" I had no idea where my Lord's leading would reveal His presence and direction in my life through the writing and the conclusion of life lived to this present time. My family, young and old, have filled my contributing to the provisions of God. Families and individuals known in the beginning of writings and those in the course of time have given great purpose, driving the means for and to a conclusion. An individual to be recognized is one Rosemary M. Merwin, who stepped forward when asked to offer her expertise and time to bring guidance to proper English and punctuation. I know and thank the Lord for bringing her to the fore. Thank you, Rosemary. My personal acknowledgment and recognition of Raymond and Ruthann Dahlheimer for their love and encouragement providing the furthering of the publishing of *David, Did You Know?* my life's story. Thank you both; "God loves you and I love you, too! Thank you, Father, Son, and Holy Spirit!

"David, Did You Know?"

by

David Edward Keesey

DORRANCE PUBLISHING CO
EST. 1920
PITTSBURGH, PENNSYLVANIA 15238

Dorrance Publishing Co
585 Alpha Drive
Suite 103
Pittsburgh, PA 15238
Visit our website at *www.dorrancebookstore.com*

ISBN: 978-1-4809-2033-0
eISBN: 978-1-4809-2148-1